A Promise Kept

A PROMISE KEPT

Memoirs of a Metropolitan Councilman

James Bruce Stanley

Hillsboro Press
PROVIDENCE PUBLISHING CORPORATION
FRANKLIN, TENNESSEE

Printed in the United States of America

09 08 07 06 05 1 2 3 4 5

Library of Congress Control Number: 2005928784

ISBN: 1-57736-349-3

Cover photo by Gary Layda/Metropolitan Government of Nashville and Davidson County

Cover design by Joey McNair

Unless otherwise indicated, photos are from the author's collection.

HILLSBORO PRESS
an imprint of
Providence Publishing Corporation
238 Seaboard Lane • Franklin, Tennessee 37067
www.providence-publishing.com
800-321-5692

To

My mother Rosemary, my late father James, and siblings
Robin, John, and Tom, and their children
Derrick, Daniel, Rachel, Matt, Elizabeth, and Savannah

and to

the resident citizens of District 14
who gave me the opportunity to represent them
on the Metropolitan Council

Contents

PREFACE

The adoption of the Metropolitan Charter in 1962 and the implementation of the metropolitan government in 1963 combined the governments of Davidson County and the city of Nashville. It represented a unique form of local government in the state of Tennessee. What was unique about the metropolitan government was its desire to make local government services uniform throughout the county. Such uniformity was unheard of in the ninety-five Tennessee counties. The uniformity would present the resident citizens of Metropolitan Nashville and Davidson County with public services considered unparalleled. In addition, the initiation of the metropolitan government unveiled a forty-member council that was to be truly representative of the citizens of Metropolitan Nashville. The Metropolitan Council was the legislative body responsible for representing the citizens in municipal issues and alleviating the adverse impacts associated with those issues.

During the first twenty-four years following the birth of Metropolitan Nashville, growth controversies were limited. However, in 1987 urban sprawl emerged and began to intrude into numerous suburban communities. Rapid growth and a failure to provide appropriate upgrades to the community infrastructure to accommodate this growth represented a key component of sprawl. This failure adversely impacted substantial portions of the established community and resulted in residents becoming more active in the political arena.

Active involvement in local politics educated these citizens on the local political procedures followed by elected representatives. Citizens of Metropolitan Nashville became aware that many councilmembers subscribed to old-school politics. That political school of thought promoted the use of closed-door politics to obtain approval for proposed projects. In addition, councilmembers that subscribed to closed-door politics were referred to as good-ole-boys. They made themselves inaccessible to the citizens they were elected to represent and made decisions without input from the community. To citizens facing extreme adversity associated with urban sprawl, this was an unacceptable way to govern.

The citizens of Metropolitan Nashville rejected old-school politics in general beginning in 1987. A new type of politician was elected to represent the citizens of Metropolitan Nashville. These new politicians subscribed to an open-door policy that promoted open communication between all parties to be affected by growth. In addition, the open-door policy embraced citizen activism in local affairs and gave credence to the variety of input presented by the affected community. Finally, the open-door policy had a positive effect on regulating the growth ushered in with urban sprawl as Metropolitan Nashville continued to grow.

My involvement in the local political arena was motivated by urban sprawl and certain proposals that could be detrimental to the community in which I had lived my entire life. The political policy I was to follow was the open-door policy. My initial eight years involved my serving on numerous community organizations designed to stabilize growth in our community. This service educated me on the various positions taken by citizens of our community on growth. The citizens were not against regulated or progressive growth. However, they did voice reservations about being subjected to growth that was unregulated. Such unregulated growth exemplified regressive development that would adversely impact the existing infrastructure and the established community in general. The open communication promoted by an open-door policy allowed public opinions to be voiced and given considerable weight when a councilmember was determining a position to take.

When elected to the Metropolitan Council in 1995, I made the citizens of District 14 aware of my belief in this open-door governance. In subscribing to this school of political thought, I promised that input from impacted citizens would be given priority consideration when debating controversial issues or determining municipal policy. The variety of opinions voiced from resident citizens was the prime element I used in determining policy and guaranteed true representation of the people.

My experiences during the eight years that I served on the Metropolitan Council are catalogued in these memoirs, including issues that were to affect a wide range of resident citizens, from municipal programs to specific land-use proposals. They illustrate the positive effects that open-door politics had when addressing such issues. I was able to keep my promise of including all citizens in determining policy for Metropolitan Nashville, and the promise of an open-door policy to meet my responsibilities as an elected municipal legislator for our city and its citizens.

James Bruce Stanley

Acknowledgments

I have always had a great love for the Donelson-Hermitage community in which I was raised and have called home since birth. The adoption of metropolitan government included the integration of the Donelson-Hermitage suburban community into Metropolitan Nashville. Following the integration, our community's slow pace of growth limited controversy concerning citizens.

However, the successful installation of various urban services over the years caused the emergence of urban sprawl into our community. Urban sprawl was characterized by "the rapid demographic and developmental growth of a community and the failure to provide the appropriate infrastructure improvements to support the growing community."[1]

By the mid-1980s, controversy aligned with sprawl was rampant and was a primary factor in citizens taking an active role in questioning the positions taken by councilmembers. This political activism educated citizens on metropolitan procedures and how to best regulate potential growth. Firm regulations would minimize controversies associated with growth. In addition, citizens embraced open-door over closed-door politics. Open-door politics allowed open communication with the parties that were to be immediately impacted by proposed growth. This policy effectively regulated growth and ushered in the election of a much more inclusive Metropolitan Council.

The emergence of urban sprawl promoted my active involvement in local politics, which, in turn, prompted my interaction with numerous resident citizens when addressing growth issues. This interaction enlightened me on the various views taken by citizens. I wish to thank the innumerable citizens of our community whose positions were instrumental in curbing controversial growth and further developing my political philosophy.

In addition, my interaction with community leaders and councilmembers was invaluable in directing our community toward positive growth. These leaders instructed me on the importance of using open-door politics when addressing community controversies. Among the leaders to whom I am grateful are Larry McWhirter, Randy Kennedy, Ben West Jr., John Stern, and the late Edward Nave. The lessons learned from these leaders paved the way for my election to the Metropolitan Council.

During my eight-year tenure on the Metropolitan Council, it was my promise to govern in the most effective and equitable manner possible. This necessitated obtaining valuable input from impacted citizens. To obtain this needed input, I sponsored community meetings that allowed citizens to voice their concerns on proposed development. In addition, I worked with citizen organizations that sponsored positive additions to our community. The variety of opinions expressed by citizens during these open meetings enabled me to determine the position to take on certain issues. Finally, such meetings allowed our community to achieve specific goals.

Furthermore, the cooperation extended to me by certain metropolitan departments provided relief to resident citizens facing different issues. In addition, these departments played a vital role in assisting my legislative endeavors. I gratefully acknowledge the assistance provided by the following municipal departments: the Department of Planning (Jeff Browning and Richard Bernhardt); the Codes Administration (Terry Cobb and Lon "Sonny" West); the Department of Public Works (Marlin Keel and Randall Dunn); the Department of Water and Sewerage Services (Buddy Williams and Scott Potter); the Stormwater Division (Tom Palko); the Metropolitan Police Department (Chief Emmett Turner); the Metropolitan Fire Department (Chief Buck Dozier); the Metropolitan Development and Housing Authority (Gerald Nicely); the Department of Parks and Recreation (Jim Fyke); the Greenways Division (Shain Dennison); the Photographic Services (Gary Layda); the Metropolitan Nashville Airport Authority (Gen. William G. Moore Jr.); the Metropolitan Nashville Public Schools (Dr. Richard Benjamin, Dr. Bill M. Wise, and Dr. Pedro Garcia); the Metropolitan Library (Donna Nicely); and the Metropolitan Historical Commission (Ann Reynolds).

Additionally, notable private organizations provided vital input and cooperation in developing legislation. The input such organizations submitted in the legislative process illustrated how they protected their interests within reason. I was extremely grateful for their input and the guidance they offered. Their involvement educated me on the role such private interests play in our society. These groups included the Nashville Neighborhood Alliance, the Tennessee Environmental Council (TEC), the Cumberland River Compact, the Leadership Nashville Alumni Association, and the Homebuilders of America.

I wish to thank the resident citizens of District 14 for giving me the opportunity to represent them on the Metropolitan Council. In the role of municipal legislator, I was given the responsibility of providing each citizen with true representation. The fellow councilmembers that I served with ensured that such representation was achieved. I am thankful to all fellow councilmembers for openly debating issues impacting our citizens. Although we were not always in agreement, the various positions taken by councilmembers on specific issues educated me on differences existing in our community. Such differences represent the strength of our society.

I am grateful for the cooperation given by Governor Phil Bredesen, Mayor Bill Purcell, Executive Director Richard Bernhardt of the Department of Planning, and Dr. Bill M. Wise and his wife, Peggy, when developing this book. In addition, the input and cooperation given by them during my tenure on the Metropolitan Council was valuable in addressing the needs of our community.

Finally, this text and my election to the Metropolitan Council could never have been achieved without the strong support of my family. I wish to thank my parents, Jim and Rosemary Stanley, and the rest of my family for the stable and loving home they provided me over the years. The examples you provided to me through your professionalism and volunteer work were invaluable in developing my political philosophy of open-door politics as the manner most appropriate to govern our community.

CHAPTER ONE

INTRODUCTION

The Charter of the Metropolitan Government of Nashville and Davidson County, Tennessee, was adopted by referendum in June 1962. The adoption of a metropolitan form of government unified the local population of the city of Nashville and the suburban communities of Davidson County. Similar to the federal and state constitutions, the charter of the metropolitan government acted as the governing instrument for the newly created city of Metropolitan Nashville and Davidson County. As dictated by the Metropolitan Charter:

> the governmental and corporate functions now vested in the City of Nashville, a municipal corporation created by Chapter 246, Private Acts of 1947, and amendments thereto, are hereby consolidated with the governmental and corporate functions of the County of Davidson, such consolidation being pursuant to constitutional power granted by Article XI, section 9 of the Constitution of Tennessee, as amended, and in conformity with section 7-1-101 et seq. of Tennessee Code Annotated, as amended. Said consolidation shall result in the creation and establishment of a new metropolitan government to perform all, or substantially all, of the governmental and corporate functions previously performed by the county and by the city . . .[1]

There were numerous benefits projected for the citizens of Nashville and Davidson County associated with the metropolitan government. One of the most prevalent of the benefits was the unifying of separate city and county government bodies that were responsible for specific public services. The merging of separate city and county departments created uniformity in government services that the citizens of the city of Nashville and Davidson County had never witnessed. Such merging laid the foundation for a uniform municipal infrastructure to better serve the expanding urban area of Metropolitan Nashville and Davidson County.

The creation of a uniform public school system represented an example of such a merger. The adoption of the metropolitan government meant that public schools located throughout the city of Nashville and Davidson County should be unified as a single system and administered by one board of education and director of schools. In 1964, public schools that had been administered by either the Nashville City Board of Education or the Davidson County Board of Education were all placed under the sole jurisdiction of the newly formed Metropolitan Nashville and Davidson County Board of Education. This created one of the largest public school systems located in the southeastern United States. Funding for local public schools was to be distributed equally among the facilities in the system. This public school system used adequate funding to implement a uniform curriculum and supplemented various educational programs that provided excellent benefits to the students enrolled in the public schools of Metropolitan Nashville.

Another benefit to be received by the metropolitan government was the coordination and creation of a uniform infrastructure supporting the expansive growth of the city. Infrastructure projects that received priority consideration were municipal roadways, the extension of water and sewer service, and property maintenance. The metropolitan departments that were responsible for these projects included the Department of Public Works, the Department of Water and Sewerage Services, and the Codes Administration. The employees of these departments were to be accessible to the councilmembers and cooperate with these elected officials and the general citizenry to address infrastructure issues brought to their attention.

The state-ordered takeover of both the privately owned Harpeth Valley Utility District and the Cumberland Utility District of Davidson County by the Metropolitan Department of Water and Sewerage Services illustrated the desire to have a uniform water and sewer service throughout Metropolitan Nashville. Specifically targeted to receive improved service by these takeovers were two of the fastest-growing suburban communities of Metropolitan Nashville: Bellevue and Hermitage. By ordering these takeovers, state officials argued that uniform water and sewer service was to be received by the existing resident citizens and would be able to accommodate the numerous developmental proposals of those communities.

However, such governmental merging and takeovers had a Jekyll-and-Hyde effect on the existing community, in that it promoted adversity. One example of this adversity was the federal judiciary acknowledging that a uniform public school system served the entire Davidson County area. This acknowledgment paved the way for the schools of Metropolitan Nashville to be included in the federal busing mandate in 1971. The busing concept, as clearly defined in the federal case of *Swan v. Charlotte Mecklenburg Board of Education* (1971), was viewed by federal authorities as the quickest way to desegregate public schools. It involved the busing of inner-city students to suburban schools and suburban students to inner-city schools. One of the setbacks associated with the busing mandate was a substantial removal of administrative authority from local elected school board members. Overwhelmingly, federal judges were responsible for administering the local public school system serving Metropolitan Nashville.

Certain sections of society did not accept this administrative setup and removed their children from the public schools. Their children were then enrolled in private schools or home schooled. From 1971, the year busing was ordered on the Metropolitan Nashville Public School System, there was a steady increase in the number of private schools established in Davidson County.

There were three categories of private education used as an alternative to the public school system. Roman Catholic schools represented the largest and oldest form of private education in the nation. Established in 1784, Roman Catholic schools reflected Roman Catholic beliefs and practices. The Christian school movement was founded in the 1970s, and represented the second-largest category of alternative education in the United States. Home schooling represented the least restrictive of the educational alternatives in that it was neither associated with the public school system nor individual private schools.

The citizens' position against forced busing was illustrated in the continual reduction in the number of students attending Metropolitan Nashville public schools. When busing was initiated in Metropolitan Nashville, the number of students attending public schools totaled 90,242. In 1998, the number of students in the public schools was 70,517. As my coauthor and I noted in our book *Donelson & Hermitage, Tennessee: A Suburban History*, "This reduction occurred despite the continual growth in population of Metropolitan Nashville during the same period."[2]

In another example, the takeover of private utility districts by the municipality adversely impacted the resident customers of a specific utility district. One result was a sizeable increase in monthly charges for resident citizens for sewer service in Hermitage. Previously, the Cumberland Utility District had not raised monthly rates for consumers in several years.

The failure to adequately fund needed water/sewer upgrades by Cumberland promoted an unhealthy and unsafe communal environment. Ultimately, the amount of revenue required to fund the needed capital improvements on the water/sewer infrastructure serving the Hermitage and Old Hickory communities of Metropolitan Nashville was substantial. The overwhelming amount of money needed for such capital upgrades was to be obtained through the monthly payments made by resident citizens. The takeover, and the required water/sewer upgrades, forced the citizens to pay a monthly sewer bill to Metropolitan Water and Sewerage that was approximately three times what they had been paying to Cumberland. Additional required upgrades to the water/sewer infrastructure projected further increases in both water and sewer bills. Although such upgrades were sorely needed and were required to promote a healthier environment, as well as accommodate additional development in the community, these increased utility charges were viewed by many as adversely impacting their income.

The initiation of the metropolitan government promoted the installation of a uniform infrastructure to serve the entire area of Davidson County. The early infrastructure projects were viewed as necessary to accommodate the ever-growing Metropolitan Nashville. It is important to realize that federal, state, municipal, and private infrastructure served Metropolitan Nashville and Davidson County. Previously, the variety in ownership prevented a uniform upgrading system. Although infrastructure upgrades were welcomed by resident citizens as providing essential relief to an outdated system, such projects also laid the foundation for increased development. In the initial years following the adoption of the Metropolitan Charter, proposed developments were extremely isolated. However, the intrusion of urban sprawl into the suburban communities situated throughout Davidson County caught the attention of resident citizens.

In addition, developments associated with sprawl overwhelmingly included commercial or extremely dense residential projects. The initial infrastructure upgrades made by the metropolitan or state governments were unable to accommodate the increased activity associated with these sprawling developments. Resident citizens became more politically active in order to have their concerns about new development appropriately addressed.

The vast majority of the elected metropolitan officials holding office at the time urban sprawl began to intrude throughout Metropolitan Nashville and Davidson County subscribed to the old school of political thought. Officials believed their election gave them authority to make decisions without input from the citizens they were elected to represent. The adverse effects of urban sprawl quickly exposed the inappropriateness of this type of old-school politics. The resident political activity ushered in with urban sprawl resulted in many good-ole-boys associated with old-school politics losing their jobs representing Metropolitan Nashville. It was this mandated political activity that promoted my involvement in the local political system. I was able to use my past political experiences as a guide to address the issues forced on our community by sprawl.

Personal Political Experiences

There are several parallels between my life and the metropolitan government, a few of which have encouraged my involvement in local politics. One key parallel is that the metropolitan government and I were born the same year. The metropolitan government was officially put into effect on April 1, 1963. My birth date is March 1, 1963. Because of this similarity in age, I have personally witnessed numerous changes resulting from being part of the larger metropolitan government. The strong nuclear family that I was born into allowed me to learn and personally experience the political changes as our community became a part of the greater Metropolitan Nashville urban area.

My parents, James B. Stanley and Rosemary Stanley, were professional individuals. My father was a senior engineer at the DuPont plant in Old Hickory. Throughout the years, I was impressed with his mathematical dissemination of issues or projects affecting our family or the local community. For example, he used his math skills in designing the finished basement for our home in 1971, and designating every available inch of space for living area. As another example, he cared for history and expressed that there were invaluable lessons available through our learning of history. I inherited the same caring for history from my father, and understood the importance that historical events had in providing a proper direction for current times. (In addition, historical research would play a vital role in supplementing legislation that I brought before the Metropolitan Council. Such information proved invaluable in that it illustrated the potential benefits that both present and future citizens of our city would receive from the proposed legislation.)

My mother was a certified educator, and used her expertise for the benefit of the community. Exemplifying this was her cooperation with the Emmanuel Lutheran Church officials of Hermitage to create a daily kindergarten program at their church in 1964. This program was established prior to kindergarten becoming a mandated program in the Metropolitan Nashville Davidson County School System. She was director of the Emmanuel Lutheran kindergarten from 1964 to 1968, then she was hired as a first grade teacher by the Board of Education. From her hiring, she taught first grade and kindergarten at Hermitage Elementary School for thirty-five years until her retirement in 2003.

McGavock Raider fullback James Bruce Stanley in October 1980

Her active involvement in the community through the years also included serving on the board for the Donelson-Hermitage Neighborhood Association, Inc. This residential interest group was organized and incorporated in 1987 to battle urban sprawl and protect resident investment. She served as president of the association in 1994–95. In 1989, my mother was a member of the Citizens Advisory Committee for the Subarea 14 Plan, which addressed specific land-use issues in the newly adopted subarea planning process. Her participation in the community and care for its citizens were crucial in influencing the development of my political philosophy.

Both of my parents presented a professional demeanor and knowledgeable understanding of issues that they faced. They addressed each issue with integrity and were, therefore, pivotal in educating me on the value of integrity when addressing issues in our community. Witnessing my parents and close neighbors take action to protect their investments, and my active involvement in public school were instrumental in defining the open-door political philosophy to which I subscribed prior to the intrusion of urban sprawl into Donelson-Hermitage.

My extracurricular activities in public schools was very enriching. The team concept was truly emphasized while playing football at McGavock Comprehensive High School. The 1979 season saw the transfer of Coach Wes Elrod from Maplewood High to McGavock High. When he took over as head coach of the McGavock Raiders, he brought with him an emphasis on the team concept to use as the basis for rebuilding the football program. It was soon evident that he was looking for unselfish players who were willing to give their all to achieve success on the field. Coach Elrod also emphasized the positive impact the team concept could have in other areas of life beyond simply football. There was no "I" in "team," thus preventing a dependency on extremely talented players from controlling the outcome on the field. As an average player, I took great pride as being labeled a team player. The majority of my playing experience came on special teams, although I was able to experience additional playing time as an offensive back. I think this emphasis on working together to achieve a unified goal also played a role in my subscribing to an open-door political philosophy as a councilman.

The open-door policy to which I subscribed promoted open communications between an elected representative and his constituents, motivating the involvement of all who were to be impacted by certain issues, thus allowing input from a wide variety of sources. When urban sprawl emerged and the rapid pace of growth intruded into our community, the open-door policy allowed me to consider input from various community interests, especially those to be immediately impacted, as a key factor when determining the position to take on a proposal.

From 1987 to 1995, I worked in conjunction with other resident citizens of the Donelson-Hermitage Neighborhood Association to address issues of growth. My interaction with business owners and developers was vital to understanding their position on growth. Finally, this interaction was important in further determining my philosophy of the role local government was to play in the lives of citizens.

The following organizations represent those in which I was active from 1987 to 1995. These organizations were instrumental in educating me on various municipal procedures involved in the local political process and the role that individual citizens could play in preserving and protecting the community in which they had invested.

Gateway Steering Committee

Prior to serving as a councilman, the initial service I provided to the community was as a member of the Gateway Steering Committee. Gateway was an extensive mixed-use development proposed for 609 acres in the bend of the Stones River. It included three million square feet of non-residential uses; 1,370 residential dwelling units; and three hundred housing units for the elderly. It was to generate approximately eight thousand to eleven thousand automobiles onto Lebanon Pike at peak morning and evening hours.

The committee was organized in 1987 following the election of Larry McWhirter to the Metropolitan Council. The committee was part of the Donelson-Hermitage Neighborhood Association, Inc., and played an important role in influencing Councilman McWhirter as to what position he would take regarding Gateway.

Other members of the committee included Lee Thomas, president of the Donelson-Hermitage Neighborhood Association; Edward Nave, chair; John Marshall, area director; Rosemary Stanley, coordinator;

Bob Sheehan, Ray Speer, James S. Matthews, Tom Friddell, Joe Wilson, Bill Stupak, Bernard Harrell, Illona Leeper, and William Brewington. This steering committee was organized to work with Meritbanc officials in an attempt to satisfactorily address the issues raised by the community.

District 14 Councilman Larry McWhirter and wife, Janet (Photo courtesy of Larry McWhirter)

The major categories reviewed by this committee in cooperation with the Meritbanc officials were:

1. the density of houses in the project and construction of homes with comparable values of existing homes in the community;

2. traffic problems associated with the project, mainly centering around Lebanon Pike traffic congestion;

3. a review of the total project of six hundred acres and its impact on the community;

4. a review of the connector roadways from Lebanon Pike to the Gateway project, concentrating on ways to relieve pressure on current homeowners;

5. methods of minimizing disruption and negative impacts of the actual construction, especially in the areas of earth-moving equipment, dump trucks, and dust; and

6. the maintenance of the natural beauty of the area, including bluff areas; the creation and preservation of green acres, such as parks, to enhance the beauty of the community; and the establishment of buffer areas between commercial and residential areas.[3]

Ultimately, the review of these categories illustrated the overwhelming adversity projected by Gateway and brought about its defeat on May 17, 1988.

Aerial view of the six-hundred-acre undeveloped floodplain proposed for the Gateway mixed-use development

Rezoning Petition

In July 1988, a residential single-family home was purchased in Stanford Estates, situated on the west side of Belding Drive near Jenry Drive. Similar to the vast majority of parcels within Stanford Estates, the parcel upon which the house was constructed exceeded the minimum lot size required by the Metropolitan Zoning Code. The parcels of Stanford Estates were required to be no smaller than ten thousand square feet, or roughly a quarter of an acre, but because this subdivision was constructed between 1958 and 1960, the lots were much larger than the required minimum.

A month later, in August 1988, the parcel upon which the house was situated was subdivided into two separate parcels. A small, white, wood-frame duplex was brought in and placed on the newly subdivided parcel during the late hours of the night.

The duplex was inconsistent with existing homes in Stanford Estates. It was a mere twelve hundred square feet in size. That was in direct contrast to the existing homes, which averaged twenty-three hundred square feet in size. The house was also inconsistent in construction, as it was a wood-frame structure while the existing homes in Stanford Estates were a minimum of 90 percent masonry. Finally, the nature of the house was also at odds with the neighborhood. Duplexes represented a rental, transient environment that was incompatible with a single-family subdivision. Such incompatibility

The wooden duplex that was installed in Stanford Estates following the subdividing of a single-family parcel

would adversely impact the existing homes and the investments that their owners had placed in them over the years.

The action needed to curb future subdividing was outlined in conversations with Councilman Larry McWhirter. The general residential zoning of Stanford Estates (R10) allowed for single-family and duplex structures in the subdivision. The Metropolitan Zoning Code allowed up to one quarter of the existing homes in a subdivision to be duplexes under the general residential (R) zoning category. To prevent any further subdividing and installing of rental duplexes in Stanford Estates, a rezoning of the entire subdivision was necessary.

The rezoning would be to residential single-family (RS). This zoning allowed for only single-family houses to be included in Stanford Estates. To accomplish this rezoning, it was required that a thorough majority of the existing homeowners sign an instrument calling for the Metropolitan Council to rezone Stanford Estates. As a community representative, I agreed to begin circulating such an instrument to achieve the desired rezoning. McWhirter agreed to sponsor the rezoning before the council once the appropriate signatures were obtained.

From October 1988 to August 1989, I circulated a petition calling for the rezoning of Stanford Estates. When the circulating of the petition was complete, 233 homeowners, or 90 percent, had signed the petition calling for the rezoning. In January 1990, the rezoning was approved by the council. The successful rezoning stabilized the residential environment of Stanford Estates. It represented a positive experience in that it promoted my close interaction with fellow neighbors and metropolitan officials whose cooperation was required to achieve the rezoning.

FROM THE NASHVILLE BANNER

July 17, 1990

One-man Campaign Helps Neighborhood Maintain Its Charm

Bruce Stanley became upset in 1988 when a neighbor legally sold a part of his lot in Stanford Estates on Lebanon Pike to a developer for a duplex.

He mounted a one-man campaign, going door-to-door in his spare time for 10 months with a petition to get the subdivision rezoned from residential to single-family homes.

"I wanted to maintain the area as it was for the 28 years I've lived here," Stanley said. Until the lot was sold for the duplex, Stanford's 270 homes were each occupied by a single family.

There was nothing illegal about the duplex deal, Councilman Larry McWhirter said.

The property owners had 10,000 square feet, and that met the zoning requirements, he said.

The problem started years ago, McWhirter said, when there were fewer zone changes. The zoning jumps normally were in 10,000 square feet.

"Properties zoned R10 (minimum of 10,000 square feet) might actually be just below the next (R20) range," he said.

Stanley got 233 of the 270 homeowners to sign the petition and got the zoning changed with the help of McWhirter, who took it to the Metro Board of Zoning Appeals and the Metro Council.

The bill for the zoning change was $1,000, according to Metro staff planner Jerry Fawcett.

Fawcett said Stanford and a small rezoning proposal in Belle Meade are the only two recorded instances of neighbors seeking a zoning change.

"If the Planning Commission wants something rezoned they have to pay the fee like everyone else," Fawcett said. "If a councilman wants something rezoned he either has to get the property owner to pay it or pay it himself."

Action last week by the Metro Council Planning Committee to waive rezoning fees for neighborhood groups will enable the Planning Commission to implement the land-use plans being developed through subarea planning by rezoning the necessary areas, Fawcett said.

Fees range from a minimum of $400 to $5 per acre for plots up to 100 acres in size and $2.50 per acre over that, Fawcett said.

Councilman John Summers said the proposal, already approved by the Metro Planning Commission, will be considered tonight by the full council.[4]

—Used by permission, the *Nashville Banner*, July 17, 1990

Metropolitan Nashville Greenways Citizen Advisory Committee

The Metropolitan Greenways Commission and a citizen advisory committee (CAC) were officially created by an amended ordinance approved by the Metropolitan Council on January 21, 1992. The citizen advisory committee was responsible for advising the Greenways Commission and was to include one representative from each of the thirty-five council districts as appointed by the councilmember from that district.

Councilman McWhirter appointed me to serve as the District 14 representative on the citizen advisory committee. My role on the citizen advisory committee brought me in conversations with owners of riverfront property. Such owners did not have a negative view of greenways in general. However, by asking for the donation (or simple sell) of their riverfront property for use in the designated greenway, metropolitan officials had presented an unacceptable situation to the private landholders. This prevented a number of floodplain parcels along the Stones River from being acquired by 2001.

Interaction with riverfront property owners educated me on the benefits an open-door policy had when dealing with the public. The open communication eliminated public suspicion of government programs and officials and allowed for a more cooperative relationship to exist between private citizens and public officials.

Ultimately, the advantages derived from open communication would have long-term benefits for Metropolitan Nashville. Finally, interaction as a member of the CAC of the Metropolitan Greenways Commission provided me with a keen learning experience that proved beneficial when I served on the Metropolitan Council.

Nashville's Agenda

The Nashville's Agenda was organized in the fall of 1992 by the Leadership Nashville Alumni Association to set municipal goals for the immediate future. The process used to determine municipal goals was known as visioning. It involved literally hundreds of citizens from Metropolitan Nashville engaging in historical conversations that spanned many weeks and were centered in several locations throughout Davidson County. Included among those communities involved was Donelson, which had felt the adverse impact of urban sprawl.

The primary objective of Nashville's Agenda was motivating citizens to work together to develop obtainable goals benefiting Metropolitan Nashville. The organization's chair, Keel Hunt, believed that, "People of all races, classes, interests and backgrounds are encouraged to come to open meetings and talk about what they want their city to be. Goals emerge from the city's design, growth, social conditions, economy, government, environment, and anything else on which enough people agree. Goals emerge that the government and community leaders are compelled to pursue, because that's an inherent mandate to take action."[5] Indeed, the organizations and individuals involved in Nashville's Agenda included business interests, residential associations, municipal department heads, state government officials, labor representatives, and private university administrators.

Launched in the fall of 1993, Nashville's Agenda received a $136,000 grant from the HCA Foundation, as well as vocal praise from Mayor Phil Bredesen, leaders of the Chamber of Commerce, and numerous councilmembers. The Nashville's Agenda Steering Committee consisted of Chairman Hunt, vice chairs John Stern and Brenda Wynn, Sue Peters, Sherry Winn, Ellen Bradbury, Gwen Harris, Stan Scott, Hershell A. Warren, Nelson Andrews, Dart Gore, Brenda McCoy Hunter, the Reverend Marcel Kellar, A. Vernon

Peterman, Dr. Sheila Peters, Joanne Pulles, Ken Roberts, Cynthia Morin, Andrea Edwards, and Debbie Reaves.

To assist in the goal setting and ensure citizen involvement, Davidson County was divided into separate areas. Each area was headed by a coordinator who then named co-chairs from the specific area. The coordinator was responsible for working with the co-chairs to schedule vision sessions. During the vision sessions, input from area citizens was recorded. Such input included suggested improvements that the city needed to stabilize and enhance the urban environment of Metropolitan Nashville as the twenty-first century approached.

Charlie Howell was appointed coordinator of Area 4, which included Donelson, Hickory Bend, Pennington Bend, and Stewart's Ferry. In the summer of 1993, Howell appointed me as co-chair of the area, along with Peggy Watson and Leighton Bush. My appointment was centered on addressing numerous growth issues faced by our community since the emergence of urban sprawl.

On October 7, 1993, a committee meeting was scheduled for Area 4. The meeting was required to organize the upcoming vision session for Area 4 and to provide the appropriate notification to the community of the meeting. The vision session for Area 4 was held on October 14, 1993, at the Donelson Senior Citizens Center. During the session, numerous needs were brought to our attention and recorded. Some of the more notable needs included the establishment of mass transit, environmental protection and preservation, increased police protection, and opening safe neighborhood schools to serve the public. The needs voiced by the public at the October session further familiarized me with issues that demanded attention to promote a stabilized urban environment and enhance living in our growing city. Conversations with resident citizens about their specific needs brought to my attention the importance of having these needs addressed.

In January 1994, the Steering Committee of the Nashville's Agenda project created a list of twenty-one goals for the twenty-first century. These goals were derived from the approximately thirty-five hundred needs voiced at numerous vision sessions that occurred across the city in the fall of 1993. More than two thousand Nashvillians were involved in the brainstorming sessions.

The goals set by the Nashville's Agenda project were viewed by the general public as appropriate. They addressed the needs of Metropolitan Nashville in a comprehensive manner. The goals were to be reached through the cooperative efforts of the citizens and their elected representatives. Nashville's Agenda promoted open communication and cooperation between diverse voices throughout the city. It was clearly a project whose success was dependent on the open-door policy that was adopted by resident citizens who were adversely impacted by uncontrolled growth associated with urban sprawl.

In the years following Nashville's Agenda, a number of its goals were achieved. Some of the goals were achieved by action of the Metropolitan Council during my tenure. Among these goals were the release of the Metropolitan Nashville Public School System from the federal busing mandate, the opening of the Frist Center for the Visual Arts in the renovated U.S. Post Office building downtown, the pending construction and opening of a new symphony hall near the Gaylord Entertainment Center to house both the visual and performing arts for Metropolitan Nashville, and my sponsorship of Ordinance No. BL2002-1021 and its passage by the Metropolitan Council, regulating floodplain development to an extent previously unknown in Nashville.

Nashville's Agenda had also prioritized goals that were questioned by the public. Goal number sixteen called for establishing Metropolitan Nashville as home to professional and amateur athletic teams and providing state-of-the-art facilities from whence these teams could operate. Ultimately, the agreement of professional football and hockey franchises to move their operations to Metropolitan Nashville involved sizeable municipal incentives, including the giving of naming rights to the professional sports franchises. Such incentives prevented the public from witnessing the projected positive return on their investments.

My involvement in Nashville's Agenda promoted an interaction with all sections of Metropolitan Nashville. This interaction educated me on the needs and desires of differing interests throughout the city and of the importance of the open-door policy. Finally, I found that Nashville's Agenda represented a project that increased my understanding of issues burdening our city in 1995, and led to my election to the Metropolitan Council.

Chapter Two

The Metropolitan Council

I, (councilmember name), do solemnly swear that I will support the Constitution of the United States of America and the State of Tennessee, that I will faithfully and impartially discharge the duties as a member of the Metropolitan Council without fear or favor and solely for the public welfare, so help me God.

Oath of Office
Metropolitan Council

Upon the adoption of the Metropolitan Charter in June 1962, there were notable changes promoted by the new metropolitan government. Included in those changes was the replacement of the old thirty-one-member city council with a new forty-member Metropolitan Council. The Metropolitan Council was given the responsibility to legislate the new metropolitan government. That legislative authority included being responsible for governing 533 square miles of Davidson County, not simply the 73-square-mile city of Nashville.

In addition, the Metropolitan Council was to be representative of the community. Its membership was never designated to be exclusionary. In essence, the Metropolitan Council was to include elected citizens from all walks of life. The forty-member legislative body was derived from concerns voiced by citizens residing in the suburban communities of Davidson County. Citizens wanted a larger representative body. The size of the Metropolitan Council was such that it would be representative of the entire Metropolitan Nashville and Davidson County populace.

Local government was the final level of American government where input from individual citizens was truly considered when developing policy. A sizeable local legislative body was required to ensure individual representation in the ever-growing Metropolitan Nashville and Davidson County urban area.

There were attempts to revise the charter from the time of its adoption. Between 1964 and 2003, one of the most sought-after revisions called for a reduction in the size of the Metropolitan Council. Business interests were the primary sponsors of such revisions. The reasoning used by businesses for proposing a reduction in the size of the Metropolitan Council centered on the streamlining of local government. Such streamlining was proposed to make local government more cost effective and less of a burden on the resident citizens. In addition, it was believed that making the Council smaller would allow the hiring of a larger professional staff that would provide notable assistance to the councilmembers in legislative matters. However, these arguments favoring the reduction in the size of the Council had numerous shortcomings.

The argument favoring the streamlining of our government and making it more cost effective was based on suspect projections. Reducing the number of councilmembers would enlarge the area of each district and increase the number of constituents represented by each elected member. In 1995, the Metropolitan Council districts averaged approximately eleven thousand constituents each. Such an average illustrated an immense number of citizens each councilmember was to represent. The reduction of the Metropolitan Council would have each individual member representing a substantially greater number of citizens.

Under such a proposal, the increase in the number of constituents each councilmember was elected to represent would adversely impact the representation provided to individual citizens by our government. (From the start, there were various aspects of the original Metropolitan Charter that were highly questioned by the Davidson County voting citizens. One of the most notable areas of controversy was the failure to provide appropriate legislative representation to the citizens, specifically those residing in the suburban communities of Davidson County. Ultimately, this controversy caused the original Metropolitan Charter referendum to be defeated at the polls in 1958.)

Following the defeat of the original charter referendum in 1958, the Charter Commission began concentrating on developing a Metropolitan Charter that adequately addressed the size of the local legislature. In the end, the Metropolitan Council was to be a forty-member legislative body that included five at-large members who represented the entire county, and thirty-five district members who represented a specific area of the city.

The adoption of the new Metropolitan Charter referendum in June 1962 quelled the representation question. The continued growth in population of Metropolitan Nashville over the years necessitated the maintenance of the Council at the forty-member limit.

However, as the city continued to grow, and regional and national commercial interests began to infiltrate Metropolitan Nashville, there were requests to have the Metropolitan Council reduced in size. Such a reduction required an amendment to the charter. Amending the charter required a resolution of council or a petition from the public and then adoption by popular vote of the citizens of Metropolitan Nashville.

An amendment or amendments to the charter could be proposed by "the adoption of a resolution by the council favoring the same and submitting it or them to the people for approval."[1] In addition, an amendment could be proposed "upon petition filed with the metropolitan clerk, signed by ten (10) percent of the number of the registered voters of Nashville-Davidson County voting in the preceding general election, the verification of the signatures to be made by the Davidson County Election Commission and certified to the metropolitan clerk."[2]

The forty-member Metropolitan Council represented the second largest municipal legislature in the nation in 1995. During my eight-year tenure on the Metropolitan Council, there were attempts to reduce the size of the Council. The councilmembers who sponsored resolutions requesting the reduction in size were closely allied with business interests. The Metropolitan Council meeting of June 3, 2003, included a number of amendments to the Metropolitan Charter. The amendments included a number specifically calling for the reduction in the size of the Metropolitan Council.

I opposed each of these amendments. My opposition was based firmly on concerns resident citizens had with reducing the size of the Metropolitan Council. One of the key concerns was the lack of representation a smaller council would present to the citizens of our continually growing city. In addition, there was a legitimate argument that members of a smaller council would easily be controlled by special interests, especially the commercial lobby. The Metropolitan Council could not be controlled by a specific special interest or it would lose its status as a representative governmental body.

The Metropolitan Council was presided over by the vice mayor. According to the Metropolitan Charter, the:

> vice mayor shall be elected for a term of four (4) years and until his successor is elected and qualified. He shall possess the qualifications of the mayor and shall be compensated at the rate of forty-two hundred ($4,200) dollars per annum, payable semimonthly. In the event the office of mayor becomes vacant, the vice mayor shall serve as mayor and be compensated as such until the vacancy is filled at a special election or at a general election, as provided in section 15.03 of this Charter. During the time that the vice mayor shall serve as mayor, he shall cease to act as presiding officer of the council.[3]

The responsibilities of the vice mayor as presiding officer of the council included appointing the councilmembers to standing committees and designating the chairs of each committee. The Planning, Zoning, Historical and Port Authority and the Traffic and Parking Committees were exceptions to this rule. The councilmembership elected the chairs of those committees to serve annually on the Planning Commission and the Traffic and Parking Commission.

In order to legislate efficiently, the members of the Metropolitan Council were asked to serve on committees. The size of these committees averaged eight to twelve members. Such committees allowed a thorough review of legislation prior to its appearance before the entire Metropolitan Council. In addition, members of the committee voted on each piece of legislation following its review. The vote could be in support, in opposition, or for deferral. The vote of the committees would influence the action taken by the entire Metropolitan Council when considering legislation. The standing committees of the Metropolitan Council from 1995 to 2003 included:

- Airport Noise Mitigation
- Budget and Finance

- Charter Revision
- Codes, Fair and Farmers Market
- Education
- Federal Grants Review
- Health, Hospitals and Social Services
- Parks, Library, Recreation and Auditorium
- Personnel, Public Information, Human Relations and Housing
- Planning, Zoning, Historical and Port Authority
- Public Safety, Beer, Wine and Whiskey
- Public Works
- Rules, Confirmations, and Public Elections
- Traffic and Parking
- Transportation and Aviation

The committees on which I served included Education; Parks, Library, Recreation and Auditorium; Planning, Zoning, Historical and Port Authority; Transportation and Aviation; and Airport Noise Mitigation. I served as chair of the Education Committee (2001–2002); the Parks, Library, Recreation and Auditorium Committee (1997–1998); and the Airport Noise Mitigation Committee (1996–1999). In addition, I was appointed to specific governmental bodies organized to address certain issues. Included among those were the Stormwater Management Task Force, the Tornado Recovery Board, and the Courthouse Commemoration Committee.

Stormwater overflow represented one of the more adverse issues facing the citizens of Metropolitan Nashville in 1995. Uncontrolled overflow promoted flooding, which had a devastating effect on residential properties throughout Metropolitan Nashville. The source of the overflow problem could be traced in many instances to poor planning on the part of metropolitan authorities over the years.

Prior to the emergence of sprawl and the rapid growth with which it was associated, metropolitan officials gave little consideration to either short- or long-term impacts of new developments on the established community. One of the key impacts that should have been considered was increased stormwater runoff forced on the existing community by new developments. Metropolitan policy had refused to address drainage or flooding that was off the public right-of-way.

Upon my election, one of the key policies I requested metropolitan authorities to address was the public funding of drainage and flood relief off the public right-of-way. There was no annual allocation of public funds in the budget to address such projects; the Department of Public Works was the agency with which I needed to cooperate to have this addressed. I maintained open communications with the Public Works officials in an attempt to have the drainage and flooding problems addressed. The Public Works officials with whom I worked included Director Marlin Keel and engineers Mark Macy, Tom Palko, and Joey Broussard. However, until there was an allocation of public funds to cover the cost of the projects, none would proceed.

Throughout my first few months on the Metropolitan Council, I was an ardent advocate for the adoption of a new, more comprehensive policy that would offer a solution to the drainage and flooding problem. However, funding for such drainage projects was to remain static. Because there was no specific allocation in the metropolitan budget for each fiscal year, funding was to be obtained by councilmembers tapping the unappropriated fund balance.

On August 20, 1996, the Metropolitan Council adopted Resolution No. RS96-381. The resolution requested the allocation of $5,075,000 from the unappropriated fund balance of the General Services District to fund drainage activities, street paving activities, and sidewalk construction and repairs. It was unanimously passed by the Metropolitan Council. The five million dollars was to be equally distributed among the thirty-five council districts, thus giving each district councilmember approximately $145,000 with which to fund designated infrastructure projects. However, the allocation was not designated specifically for any particular type of project. In addition, the capital was to be administered by the Department of Public Works in cooperation with the district councilmembers.

Working with the engineers from the Department of Public Works and impacted citizens, I was able to target a substantial number of drainage projects in District 14 that were in desperate need of repair. In fact, the vast majority of District 14 infrastructure funds were to be used for drainage projects.

Maintaining open communication with constituents adversely affected by drainage was essential in assisting metropolitan engineers to prioritize the projects once appropriate funding was obtained. The 1997–98 budget by the Metropolitan Council included approximately $7 million for infrastructure upgrades or maintenance. The allocation gave each council district approximately $200,000 each for infrastructure upgrades. I immediately began conversations with the administrators and engineers of Public Works to designate the District 14 projects that were to be addressed. The overwhelming number of projects pertained to drainage. The additional drainage projects to be funded with the allocation had been brought to my attention by individual citizens adversely affected by flooding and stormwater overflow.

By April 1998, Metropolitan authorities still had no plans to address drainage in a comprehensive manner. A tornado swept through Metropolitan Nashville on April 16, 1998. The adverse affects of the tornado accentuated the flooding and drainage problems of the area. Hermitage represented one of the suburban areas heavily hit by the tornado.

Resulting from the catastrophic effects of the tornado, "a task force that will try to solve the city's drainage problems—including the periodic flooding of some neighborhoods—was appointed"[4] by the Metropolitan Council with the passage of Resolution No. R98-1273 on October 6, 1998. The members of the task force included councilmembers Leo Waters (chairman), Don Majors, Charles Fentress, and me.

A wide-ranging group of citizens was appointed to the task force to assist the council in its investigation of the existing Metro stormwater program, the growing Metro flooding and environmental problems, and to determine an appropriate course of action. Citizens appointed to the task force included Joe Edgens (vice chairman), C. Michael Allen, Rosetta Davis, Dewayne Duhon, Cynthia Fitzgerald, DeCosta Jenkins, Mack Prichard, Ed Rumage, Stan Scott, John Sheley, and Nick Wargo. In addition, Metropolitan Nashville contracted with Ogden Environmental & Energy Services, Inc., and the Ingram Group to assist the task force. Finally, we worked closely with the Department of Public Works since it had the most experience in dealing with drainage problems over the years.

The task force regularly met for ten months to address drainage issues and to develop a program that would bring about a more rapid

Mother Nature's Fury

I didn't expect one of the events that I was forced to face as a council member. On April 16, 1998, I had an afternoon appointment with Don Jones, legal advisor to the Metropolitan Council, to discuss legislation that was being considered. The council staff office was located on the first floor of the courthouse. In addition, I planned to go through my council mail and visit the state archives before driving home.

On the afternoon of the sixteenth, I left my Donelson home around 2:00 P.M. to make my appointments. The weather was clear and sunny. After taking approximately twenty minutes to drive to the downtown courthouse, I parked in the lot designated for, among others, members of the council.

After meeting with Don Jones, I reviewed my mail and interacted with members of the council staff, as well as fellow Councilman David Kleinfelter. I then left the council staff office and was about to exit the courthouse, when downtown Nashville was engulfed by a tornado. The security officers normally monitoring the entrances to the courthouse refused to allow anyone to exit or approach the glass doors.

The view of the front parking lot clearly illustrated the effect of the heavy winds brought by this tornado. The trees situated in the grass knolls of the parking lot were bent to a horizontal position. In addition, many citizens who were caught outside attempted to enter the courthouse. It was difficult for them to maintain their balance, much less open the heavy doors. Security personnel helped these people get inside the courthouse for shelter. Citizens that succeeded in entering the building were physically spent and emotionally strained from fighting the powerful force of the tornado.

Prevented from leaving the courthouse by security personnel, I returned to the council staff office while the tornado swept through the downtown area. Being a strong granite structure, the courthouse represented an extremely safe environment in which to wait while the tornado passed. Within fifteen minutes the tornado and its damaging weather had moved through downtown Nashville.

When I exited the courthouse, I witnessed the substantial damage left in the tornado's wake. A large percentage of the cars in the parking lot had windshields blown out by the extreme pressure of the tornado. Luckily, because I had parked in a depressed area of the lot, my car had no damage and I was able to drive the approximately eight miles back to Donelson.

However, the tornado caused severe damage to a large portion of the downtown business district. The closing of these businesses prompted citizens to flee the downtown area for their homes in suburban communities of Metropolitan Nashville and surrounding counties. The extremc volume of traffic seeking to exit downtown overwhelmed the highways and caused traffic to limp along at a snail's pace. In addition, the loss of electricity and the heavy winds caused numerous traffic signals to go out, adding to further traffic congestion.

During the drive home, I saw substantial damage done to the community by the tornado as it cut a path through Metropolitan Nashville. I heard radio stations notifying the public of the damage that occurred. One of the areas hit hardest by the tornado was Hermitage. Although a portion of Hermitage was in District 14, the most intense damage in Hermitage occurred on the grounds of the Andrew Jackson home; over one thousand trees were uprooted on the Hermitage plantation grounds. I arrived home at approximately 6:00 P.M. The drive home, which usually took no longer than twenty minutes, had taken approximately two-and-a-half hours.

Ultimately, the cost of this natural disaster to Metropolitan Nashville was approximately $100 million. The experience that I had with the tornado, and the subsequent Tornado Recovery Board, educated me further on the role council members were to play in stabilizing and enhancing the municipal environment of Metropolitan Nashville.

Trees uprooted and destroyed by the 1998 tornado

solution to the drainage problems of our city. During those meetings, we worked with municipal officials of the cities of Charlotte, North Carolina, and Louisville, Kentucky. Those cities were similar in size to Metropolitan Nashville, and had adopted stormwater management programs allowing for an annual allocation of capital with which to address drainage and flooding issues within their boundaries. Metropolitan Nashville spent approximately $9.2 million annually on stormwater management, not counting the combined sewer and sanitary sewer programs. In contrast, Charlotte spent approximately $46 million per year, and Louisville spent $20 million per year on drainage projects.

Conclusions that were reached by the task force included:

1. Metro had an estimated $20 million backlog in unresolved drainage maintenance needs;

2. there was a $20–$40 million backlog in more minor capital construction needs for projects the current infrastructure program could not deal with;

3. there was a potential of over $10 million in major creek flooding capital needs identified by master plans; and

4. there was conceivably $5 million to support stormwater problems caused by combined sewer and infiltration problems or programs.

Additional facts brought to our attention included:

1. drainage system complaints were growing at a rate of approximately 1,500 per year;

2. the state recognized more than two hundred miles of impaired streams in Davidson County;

3. the flood of September 1979 resulted in more than $40 million in damages;

4. there were more than five thousand buildings located in the floodplain;

5. Metro entered the Federal Emergency Management Agency (FEMA) flood insurance program in 1982. As of May 31, 1999, 2,266 flood insurance policies had been issued, with 886 flood claims paid in Davidson County totaling more than $4.7 million; and

6. sixty-seven properties in Davidson County had filed two or more flood insurance claims, with one property having filed fourteen claims in thirteen years.

Furthermore, the task force was informed that the current Metro maintenance program addressed only 30 percent of the drainage system. In addition, it was noted that the unresolved infrastructure program type project backlog was growing at a rate of about $2–$3 million per year.

Finally, we were notified that the ability to protect surface waters from increased flooding, sediment, and other pollution was greatly hampered by the lack of engineering and inspection staff resources.

With the information in hand, the Stormwater Management Task Force laid out a plan to address the drainage problems faced by the citizens of Metropolitan Nashville. An eight-point plan was developed to address the worst of the problems. The plan included:

1. provision of off right-of-way maintenance support;

2. resources to construct major capital improvements to solve long-standing flooding problems along the larger streams;

3. increase the number of construction/erosion control inspectors;

4. increased support for water quality efforts in anticipation of expanded regulatory mandates;

5. expansion of support for minor capital construction;

6. increase in engineering support for construction, rezoning support, plans review, and watershed planning;

7. better support to the sanitary and combined sewer programs; and

8. some increase in administrative capabilities to support the expanded program and make it more responsive to customer needs.[5]

The task force recommended that municipal government take the lead in developing and initiating a comprehensive stormwater drainage program. It was noted that there was:

> a part of the drainage system that the individual property owner should maintain. But construction and maintenance of the parts of the system that drain significant public street water, or drain a number of properties, are *beyond the capability of an individual property owner to maintain*. Government must take the lead in insuring that this "public" drainage system is well constructed and maintained. Metro has not fully assumed this responsibility in the past—stormwater has been the "forgotten utility," and thus the problems.[6]

Many benefits would be derived from the implementation of such a program. The benefits included:

1. safer streets during storms;

2. increased property values along streams;

3. maintenance needs that are a public responsibility but are not just along the roadways will be better addressed;

4. minor or nuisance local flood problems will be addressed at double the current rate;

5. more maintenance needs will be met *before* property owners suffer flood damage;

6. long-standing major stream flooding problem solutions will be solved through accelerated capital construction;

7. Public Works will be able to support sanitary sewer separations from other related work;

8. streams will be better protected from pollution; and

9. downstream flooding impacts from new development will be reduced.[7]

One of the final recommendations made by our task force was that the new mayor and council that were to take office in the fall of 1999 review and accept the findings of our task force and use those findings to implement the required drainage program.

Upon his election in 1999, Mayor Bill Purcell did not waiver in his position to implement a new comprehensive drainage relief program. The primary purpose of such a program was to correct the drainage and flooding issues that had adversely affected the citizens of Metropolitan Nashville over the years. It was to have city officials formally address the problem that they had been unwilling to recognize, thus providing municipal funding and engineering to correct the problem.

In the meantime, the Purcell administration was working on developing a comprehensive drainage program to service the entire Davidson County area. The administration considered the findings of the Stormwater Management Task Force to be one of the key sources for developing such a program. In discussions with the mayor, I was able to impress upon him the clear understanding of our task force pertaining to countywide drainage issues and the need to include our findings in the final proposal.

Finally, on January 30, 2002, Mayor Purcell announced the creation of such a drainage program. A key element of the program was the establishment of a new stormwater division in the Metro Water Services Department. The new division was to deal specifically

Mayor Bill Purcell

An attorney by profession, Purcell received his law degree from Vanderbilt University and received the 2004 Distinguished Alumnus Award from Vanderbilt Law School. Beginning in 1986, Purcell served five terms in the Tennessee House of Representatives. During this tenure, Purcell was the House majority leader and chair of the Select Committee on Children and Youth. Purcell's work in the legislature positioned him in the forefront of education, health care, workers compensation, and criminal sentencing reforms. Prior to being elected mayor, Purcell served as director of the Child and Family Center at the Vanderbilt Institute of Public Policy Studies, a nationally recognized center building a bridge between academic research, politics, and practices to benefit children and their families.

Purcell was the fifth mayor of the Metropolitan Government of Nashville and Davidson County, elected first in 1999 and reelected to a second term in 2003, with a record-setting 84.8 percent of the vote. As mayor, his priorities are good schools in every neighborhood, safe neighborhoods in every part of the city, and a quality of life shared by all Nashvillians.

During Purcell's tenure, Nashville has also seen unprecedented economic expansion, with the location of four corporate headquarter operations in 2003 and another in early 2004. The companies range from Clarcor, a one-hundred-year-old filtration business from Rockford, Illinois, to the Taiwan-based computer manufacturer, Quanta. Caremark RX is a Fortune 300 company that left Birmingham, Alabama, for Nashville. Louisiana-Pacific moved its headquarters from Portland, Oregon, to Nashville, and Asurion, an enhanced services provider for the wireless industry, left Silicon Valley for Music City. Purcell continues his efforts to bring more people and businesses to Nashville's downtown and to the nearby Gulch and Rolling Mill Hill areas through infrastructure improvements and new venues like the Schermerhorn Symphony Center.

His efforts on behalf of schools have drawn national attention as a model for mayors across the country. The Mayor's First Day Festival kicks off the opening of each school year and brings attention of the whole city and region to the importance of education. In his first term, Purcell increased the annual funding for schools from $397 million to $503 million and provided $165 million in capital funds for new schools, school renovations, and repairs. He visited every school in the city during his first year in office and continued the practice throughout his first term, visiting every school twice.

Purcell also provided increased funding for public safety. He fully staffed police positions with 1,312 officers, opened a new police precinct in Hermitage, and built a new precinct in North Nashville.

Prior to the terrorist attacks of September 11, 2001, he ordered the construction of a backup Emergency Communications Center. He upgraded fire and emergency services to increase the number of EMTs serving the Metro Fire Department.

Purcell has also been focused on improving the city's infrastructure and amenities. The Shelby Avenue Bridge, a newly renovated walking bridge linking downtown and East Nashville, has become an icon for the city with its brightly lit girders shining against the evening sky. Following the completion of a strategic plan for sidewalks and bikeways, the city has added one hundred miles of new sidewalks and new bikeways in East Nashville and along Music Row. A new recycling program serving more than one hundred thousand households in the city's urban services district ranks among the most successful new voluntary programs in the country. Purcell also created an Office of Affordable Housing to spur the development of 11,103 affordable housing units in his first term. He is focused on increasing the availability of downtown residential units and preserving housing stock in the city's historic neighborhoods.

Purcell, his wife, Debbie Miller, and their daughter, Jesse—a student at Hume Fogg High School—live in the historic Lockeland Springs neighborhood of East Nashville.

with the flooding, pollution, and erosion associated with the stormwater drainage problems of our city.

Additionally, specific annual funding was required for the program to be successful in addressing drainage problems. Mayor Purcell designated that funding would come from the existing general fund revenues and the water fund revenues, and increase from $7 million in 2002 to $21 million by fiscal year 2007.

Purcell credited the Metropolitan Council for focusing the city on the stormwater issue and providing the authority for the stormwater plan in the budget in June 2001. He claimed that stormwater drainage was "a problem in neighborhoods all across this city and it will become a greater problem as we grow. By acting now, we can reduce storm water flooding and move proactively to prevent flooding in homes and neighborhoods in the future."

Purcell noted that this program "will begin to address the nearly 50 years of unmet needs across Metro." He said that the program "will begin to address concerns of both funding and responsibility for a system that is currently divided between the Water Services and Public Works departments." He stated that the program "responds to the issues of resources and the issues of management. It gives us one place to look when the issue is storm water."[8]

The new program was to take effect by March 31, 2002. The program was to follow "the recommendations of a report by AMEC Earth & Environmental, Inc., and the findings of a 1999 Metro Stormwater Task Force. The report found Metro's stormwater system is currently fragmented, reactive and underfunded." The report stated the "drainage system is deteriorating, capital needs are unmet, a growing number of residences are expanding in the floodplain, citizen and council frustrations are great and growing." In addition, the report said that Metro "responds to only 40 percent of the legitimate drainage complaints—due to a lack of resources and restrictive policies."[9] The proposed program was to provide initial relief from the drainage problems that burdened Metropolitan Nashville throughout the years.

The Metro Stormwater Management Program was officially moved from the Public Works department to the Metropolitan Department of Water and Sewerage Services on April 1, 2002. The new Stormwater Division was established to address stormwater issues throughout the community. Engineer Tom Palko, formerly of the Public Works Department, became the director of the new division. Upon its establishment, the Stormwater Division cooperated with district councilmembers and area citizens to be made aware of any drainage problems in existence. In the final seventeen months of my service on the Metropolitan Council, I worked continually with District 14 constituents and Stormwater Director Tom Palko to address additional drainage issues within the community. In addition, I kept Mayor Purcell informed with the numerous drainage projects associated with District 14.

There were additional complaints made to the employees of the Stormwater Division by either impacted resident citizens or me between March 8, 1999 and October 30, 2002. These complaints were recorded with the Stormwater Division and inspected by its employees at the earliest possible date. Upon determining the work needed to alleviate the drainage problem, each site was assigned a project number. The project was then placed on the division's priority list. When considering that District 14 represented only one of thirty-five council districts in our city, and that many of the other council districts suffered from as many drainage projects as District 14, it was easy to understand why all District 14 projects did not receive top priority status from Stormwater officials. Furthermore, the costs associated with each project varied widely, with many such projects considered minor by employees of the Stormwater Division.

The creation of a comprehensive drainage program was instrumental in eliminating the drainage problems that had hampered the communities of Metropolitan Nashville and Davidson County over the years. The factual findings of the Stormwater Management Task Force, of which I was a member, educated municipal authorities on the effects of drainage and flooding on our city. It also outlined the long-term merits a comprehensive drainage program would have on the citizens, as well as the infrastructure serving our city.

The annual allocation of capital to fund drainage projects represented the first attempt by municipal officials to address stormwater overflow and drainage issues. The Purcell administration and the Metropolitan Council realized the need to institute such a program for the benefit of Metropolitan Nashville's population.

Upon the completion of my tenure in office in September 2003, I had worked with resident citizens, municipal officials, and fellow councilmembers to provide relief from drainage or flooding problems. During my eight years on the Metropolitan Council, there were eighty-six drainage projects in District 14 that were either completed or in the planning stages. Costs associated with these projects were wide ranging, but they did represent approximately half a million dollars for District 14 citizens. In fact, such costs were further minimized by the beneficial impact that these projects would have on the district or community in general. I was willing to cooperate with others of the community and the representatives of our city to initiate a program that would bring closure to the drainage and flooding problems that the citizens of Metropolitan Nashville had faced over the years.

The Tornado Recovery Board was organized to regulate our recovery from the tornado that swept through Metropolitan Nashville and left substantial damage in its wake in April 1998. Cooperation between the board, department representatives, and private citizens allowed a quick recovery from one of Mother Nature's most devastating natural events.

Finally, I was elected by the Parks, Library, Recreation and Auditorium Committee to represent the Metropolitan Council on the Metropolitan Nashville Greenways Commission from 2001 to 2003.

In November 1994, the voting citizens of Metropolitan Nashville further defined a council representative's term of service. The citizens adopted term limits for the councilmembers with this vote. Councilmembers were to be allowed to serve no more than two consecutive terms. After serving two consecutive terms, and the passage of one full term of four years, former councilmembers were again eligible to run for a seat on the Metropolitan Council.

The adoption of term limits by the citizens of Metropolitan Nashville brought some harsh criticism. Seen as unnecessary to promote proper governing of the city, the opponents felt this "amendment would force a turnover where no force is needed. Since the creation of Metro, the voters of this city have done a fine job of creating turnover themselves at the voting booth."[10] However, those supporting the term limit amendment to the Metropolitan Charter did so because of their belief that incumbents were almost impossible to remove from office, even if they had misrepresented their constituency on certain issues. Ultimately, voters approved the amendment by an overwhelming 3 to 1 margin in the vote.

The Metropolitan Council had been presided over by six vice mayors during its existence. The longest tenured vice mayor was David Scobey, who presided over the Metropolitan Council for six terms (twenty-four years). Scobey had firm control over the council meetings, the councilmembers, and the development of municipal policy during his service to our city. His retirement coincided with my election to the Metropolitan Council in 1995. In fact, unique during the eight years that I served, there were three vice mayors who presided over the Metropolitan Council. That was in direct contrast to the twenty-four-year tenure of Scobey. The three vice mayors that presided during my tenure on the Metropolitan Council were Jay West (1995–1999), Ronnie Steine (1999–2002), and Howard Gentry (2002–2003).

Jay West, who had served as a council-at-large member since 1983, was elected as vice mayor in 1995. His legislative experience was invaluable for the incoming councilmembers. In 1995, there were nineteen candidates elected to their first term. The first-time councilmembers represented 47.5 percent of the entire Metropolitan Council. This was the largest legislative turnover since the adoption of the Metropolitan Charter in 1962, and the first council elections of November 1963.

It was feared that inexperience in the legislative body would ultimately have an adverse impact on all issues affecting the city. One of the more potent arguments raised regarding this inexperience was whether the newly elected Metropolitan Council would be controlled by the mayoral administration or special interests, specifically downtown businesses. These arguments also raised questions as to whether the first-term councilmembers, specifically those elected to represent suburban communities affected by urban sprawl, would be true representatives of the individual citizens in their district. Would they be openly accessible to their constituents and hold open community meetings that addressed issues facing those constituents, or would they be inaccessible to their constituents and make decisions affecting their district behind closed doors with little or no input from their citizens?

Such questions raised concerns that were viewed by Vice Mayor West as serious enough to necessitate educating these new

Vice Mayor Jay West (Photo courtesy of Metro Government of Nashville and Davidson County/Gary Layda)

Vice Mayor Ronnie Steine (Photo courtesy of Metro Government of Nashville and Davidson County/Gary Layda)

Vice Mayor Howard Gentry (Photo courtesy of Metro Government of Nashville and Davidson County/Gary Layda)

councilmembers on the legislative process within the first few weeks of their election. In response to these concerns, Vice Mayor West and the Vanderbilt Institute for Public Policy Studies sponsored an orientation workshop for the councilmembers recently elected to serve on the Ninth Metropolitan Council. The first purpose of the workshop was to offer an opportunity for experienced and newly elected councilmembers to get to know each other in a relaxed, informal setting. The second purpose was to promote a discussion of all aspects of the Council's activities and responsibilities.

To accomplish these purposes, the workshop was to address the following topics:

- How the Council Works. This topic included the basics of the committee structure, the Council's rules, the budget process, the passage of an ordinance, the role of the Council staff, and the procedures and issues concerning Councilmembers' expenses.
- The Zoning Process. This included the steps, mechanisms, and flow in the zoning process, the preparation for and conduct during community meetings by members of the Council, and dealing effectively with developers.
- How Metro Pays for Capital Improvements. This topic included educating the councilmembers on the various types of municipal bonds and how each was to be used, the assignment of Metro's bond rating, the affect bond issues had on the property tax, and the roles of the administration, independent bond counsel, and the Council in the bonding process.
- The Council on Camera. This included a definition of the rules of the game between the media and elected officials, dealing more effectively with the media, and the public opinion of televised Council meetings.
- Survival Kit for Freshmen Councilmembers. This topic laid out what tricks of the political trade new councilmembers should know.

The speakers at the orientation workshop represented both the public and private sectors. They were experienced in certain workshop topics and shared their experiences through open discussions. This shared experience proved invaluable in that it gave us a clear definition of the inner workings of the metropolitan government. The speakers included: T. Jeff Browning, executive director and secretary of the Metropolitan Planning Commission; G. Thomas Curtis, private financier and former employee of J. C. Bradford and Company; Joe Huddleston, chief finance officer for Nashville/Davidson County; Donald W. Jones, attorney, director, and special counsel for the Metropolitan Council; Larry J. McWhirter, attorney with Tennessee Department of Corrections and former District 14 councilman; Michael E. Moore, solicitor general of the State of Tennessee and former director of law for Metropolitan Nashville; Pat Nolan, senior vice president of Dye Van Mol and Lawrence, Inc., a local public relations firm; Jeff Ockerman, attorney and former District 6 councilman; Marilyn S. Swing, metropolitan clerk for Metropolitan Nashville and Davidson County; John Van Mol, partner in Dye Van Mol and Lawrence, Inc.; and Jay West, vice mayor of Metropolitan Nashville and three-term councilman-at-large.

The workshop's hands-on political education was to prove invaluable to the newly elected councilmembers and the city as a whole. Such an extensive orientation was the first of its kind organized and offered to the councilmembers that were to represent Metropolitan Nashville.

The next four years witnessed a number of sensitive issues brought before the council (i.e., Houston Oilers relocation/stadium construction deal, Predators deal, Dell Computer deal) that would heavily impact the entire metropolitan area, as well as development and regulatory issues that were to be addressed by individual district councilmembers. The orientation educated each councilmember on the appropriate action to take on any such issues and allowed councilmembers to adequately represent their constituents. Vice Mayor West was always given great respect for taking the initiative to prepare the incoming councilmembers for the responsibilities that their positions demanded of them in order to be effective legislators for Metropolitan Nashville.

Following my reelection to the Metropolitan Council in 1999, a new vice mayor had also been elected to preside over the Council. Vice Mayor West had been a candidate for mayor in 1999. His decision to run for the chief administrative post had prohibited his running for a second term as vice mayor. Ronnie Steine, who had served as council-at-large from 1991 to 1999, was elected vice mayor to replace West.

Steine had an undergraduate degree in history from Vanderbilt University and a law degree from the Vanderbilt School of Law. During his tenure on the Metropolitan Council, he had served on the Budget and Finance, the Planning, Zoning, Historical and Port Authority, and the Charter Revision Committees. He had been the chair of the Budget and Finance and Charter Revision Committees. Chairing such powerful committees of the Metropolitan Council educated Steine on the type of leadership the Metropolitan Council needed to successfully govern the city. In addition, Steine had been appointed to the Metro Greenways Commission and the Task Force on Emergency Management. He was chair of the latter in 1993.

In his role as vice mayor, Steine continued to cooperate with Vanderbilt University to offer an orientation workshop to councilmembers. The twenty first-term councilmembers that were elected in 1999 exceeded by one the number of first-term councilmembers that were elected in 1995. The fact that 50 percent of the Metropolitan Council had never held a legislative office before raised questions and concerns similar to those voiced by the community following the 1995 elections.

To answer these concerns, Steine sponsored a day-long orientation workshop in cooperation with Vanderbilt University. Similar to the one held in 1995, this workshop educated the incoming Council on the inner workings of the metropolitan government. This included familiarizing the new councilmembers with the numerous departments and agencies of Metropolitan Nashville and the procedures associated with each.

The Metropolitan Charter defined the Metropolitan Council:

> The legislative authority of the metropolitan government of Nashville and Davidson County, except as otherwise specifically provided in this Charter, shall be vested in the metropolitan county council, sometimes hereinafter called "Council," which shall have a total of forty (40) members, including five (5) councilmen-at-large, and thirty-five (35) district councilmen. The entire

electorate of the metropolitan government shall elect the five (5) councilmen-at-large and each of the thirty-five (35) councilmanic districts shall elect one (1) district councilman. There shall be thirty-five (35) councilmanic districts in the metropolitan government, which are hereby created and established in accordance with the detailed descriptions thereof by metes and bounds as set forth in Appendix Two hereto attached as a part of this charter.[11]

The taking of the national census every ten years had brought about changes in the Metropolitan Council districts serving Davidson County and with it the Donelson-Hermitage community. Section 18.06 of the Metropolitan Charter stated that:

Redistricting of the councilmanic districts set forth in Appendix Two of this Charter may be accomplished in the following manner: Within six (6) months after the decennial census of 1970 and each one thereafter is published by the United States Census Bureau showing the population in the area of the metropolitan government, it shall be the duty of the planning commission to recommend to the council whether redistricting of the councilmanic districts is necessary to prevent substantial underrepresentation of particular areas as the result of population changes. If the planning commission shall recommend that redistricting is necessary, it shall submit a proposed ordinance designed to accomplish its recommendation.[12]

Section 18.06 of the Metropolitan Charter was "enacted in response to the Supreme Court's decision in *Baker v. Carr,* 369 U.S. 186 (March 26, 1962) since it is designed to ensure that the Metropolitan Government complies with the one person/one vote principle of the Fourteenth Amendment to the United States Constitution after receipt of the decennial census data."[13]

The Metropolitan Charter further addressed the council's period of service, compensation, age, and residence qualifications:

Members of the council shall serve for a term of four (4) years and until their successors are elected and qualified; and shall be compensated at a rate of three hundred ($300) dollars per month. No person shall be eligible to serve as councilman-at-large or district councilman unless he shall have attained the age of twenty-five (25) at the beginning of his term and unless

> he shall have been a resident of the area of the metropolitan government for a period of one (1) year and shall continue to reside therein during his period of service. No person shall be eligible to serve as district councilman unless he shall have been a resident of the district for which he is elected for a period of six (6) months and shall continue to reside therein during his period of service. Members of the council shall hold no other elective or appointive office in the metropolitan government or employment by said government, except as expressly provided in this Charter.[14]

Throughout the years, the rate of compensation increased steadily with the fluctuation of the national economy. However, unlike private professions, the increase in pay for metropolitan councilmembers, who were public servants, was minimal throughout the years. During my eight years of service on the council, I received a net income of approximately $5,100 per annum, or $500 per month. In addition, each member of the Metropolitan Council was given a monthly expense account of $450. The expense money was to fund legislative activities engaged in by the councilmembers, such as mileage reimbursement and community advertisements.

I used the expense funds available to me to pay for quarterly newsletters in the local newspaper. I had entered into a contract with Jack Soodhalter, the owner and editor of the *News Herald,* that allowed the placement of a half-page newsletter every three months in the community paper at a cost of $350. Such a newsletter was informative to the constituents of District 14 and kept them updated on the issues facing our community and the actions taken by me to address such issues.

The newsletter was the only expense for which I sought reimbursement through my expense account during my tenure on the Metropolitan Council. In addition, because the newsletter was quarterly, and not monthly, I was required to file my expense account forms every three months with the Metropolitan Council staff. This meant that a substantial percentage of the capital used to fund my council expenses would be returned to the Metropolitan General Fund and subsequently reinvested in other areas of our community.

The citizens of Metropolitan Nashville voted in August 2003 to increase the annual pay for the Metropolitan Council. The vote increased the annual salary that councilmembers were to receive to three times what I had received during my service to the community. The Metropolitan Council that took office in September 2003 was to receive an annual salary of approximately $15,000, minus the $450 monthly expense accounts that each councilmember had received over the years.

Questions were raised as to whether councilmembers would be willing to pay the costs associated with their legislative work from their annual salary rather than accessing expense accounts. However, I believed that the elected councilmembers, in general, would ultimately fund any appropriate action that would benefit their constituents. Those that were unwilling to expend the needed funds to accomplish their legislative responsibilities would bring undue suffering on their constituents and face defeat when seeking reelection.

From 1995 to 2003, the professions represented by the councilmembers of the Ninth and Tenth Metropolitan Councils included business, engineering, law, divinity, education, plant administration, pipefitting, firefighting, funeral service, artistry, state civil service, pharmacy, nursing, charitable administration, and communications. In turn, the various professions presented differing views on issues that were to be addressed by the Metropolitan Council.

While serving on the council, I considered such different views as educational sources. There were always views that directly contradicted the position of the constituents of District 14. Therefore, I could not support the positions on specific issues that were supported by extreme views. However, I did consider the variety of positions voiced on the council floor when debating legislation. Taken into consideration, these opinions assisted the councilmembers in determining the position they would take on the issue being debated.

Ultimately, the Metropolitan Council was given the responsibility of governing our city. To obtain the needed support for proposed legislation, it was necessary that councilmembers maintain open communication with the citizens of the district they were elected to represent. The open communication notified councilmembers of issues faced by their constituents and outlined the appropriate legislative action needed to address such issues. To ensure the passage of legislation, alliances were created between councilmembers.

In general, local government remains the last level of American government that promotes individual citizen input and involvement in developing policy for the community. When faced with controversial issues, it is vital to have representation providing for public input to more thoroughly address the benefits or detriment of a particular issue. Citizen activity in the governing process requires the election to the Metropolitan Council of those candidates whose platforms promote citizen input. Such platforms require candidates to be openly accessible to constituents and willing to sponsor open public meetings to address issues that faced the community.

The emergence of urban sprawl clearly illustrated that the majority of elected councilmembers subscribed to the old school of political practices. This was obviously unacceptable to many resident citizens of the community who brought about the defeat of old-school politicians beginning with the 1987 council elections. It also began a continual struggle to determine who would represent the community in the coming years.

Council Campaigns

1995

In 1995, I was informed that the District 14 seat was to be open. Councilman Larry McWhirter had decided against running for a third term. Although the electorate had decided in November 1994 in favor of installing a two-term limit upon councilmembers and McWhirter was nearing the end of his second term, the term limit law was worded so that those councilmembers serving at the time of its passage were eligible to seek election to the council for a final four-year term. McWhirter had decided that he had served the community for eight years and his recent passing of the Tennessee Bar Exam required him to concentrate on his future legal career. With that in mind, I decided to run for the District 14 council seat.

Upon hearing of McWhirter's decision, Sam Underwood, a former district councilmember, once again placed his name on the ballot in an attempt to be elected as District 14 councilman. Underwood "offered his prior eight-year council record as evidence of his ability to perform the job of councilman."[15] However, this argument would be costly as many citizens of Donelson-Hermitage remembered the airport and Gateway issues that burdened Underwood during his final term on the Metropolitan Council. In addition, his inactivity in local political issues during his eight years out of office had an adverse impact on his campaign.

I placed my name on the ballot for the 1995 District 14 council election. I was a candidate and neighborhood activist who supported citizen input on all issues, especially land-use and zoning proposals. In contrast to my opponent, during McWhirter's two-term tenure on the Metropolitan Council, I had been involved in issues that faced the community. The printed media took the position that "Stanley, who has been active in neighborhood groups, has an impressive understanding of this district and a real commitment to listen to constituents."[16] My eight years of community activism played an important role in the 1995 election.

The campaign saw me and members of my campaign committee combing the residential streets of District 14. There were approximately two thousand homes in District 14 in 1995; thus, resident homeowners represented an overwhelming majority of those casting their votes on election day. The face-to-face interaction that I was able to have with the voting citizens as we addressed the citizens door-to-door was vital in introducing myself to those unfamiliar with me. In addition, such interaction allowed me to have an open dialogue with the citizens to become familiar with issues that each citizen needed to have addressed. Although I had received McWhirter's endorsement, I realized that obtaining support from the voting public required that I meet face-to-face with the residents of the district I desired to serve and to answer any questions or concerns presented to me.

I was assisted in my door-to-door strategy by members of my campaign committee. Their assistance would prove vital in my being elected to the District 14 council seat. The members of my campaign committee included Tom Stanley, Mike Sturm, David and Alice Quaintance, Jim and Betty Cannon, Betty Richardson, and Rosemary Stanley.

Many members of the community helped support my campaign. Mr. and Mrs. Luther Aiken were longtime residents of the historic Bluefields subdivision. Their support for my candidacy was evidenced

Treasurer Tom Stanley poses by his brother's political yard sign in June 1995

Candidate Stanley and nephew Matt pose by political yard sign in July 1995

Luther Aiken, Etta Aiken, Rosemary Stanley, and Candidate Stanley at the political coffee sponsored by the Aikens in July 1995

through their hosting a political coffee in July 1995. (Coffees are communal gatherings in the home of a resident citizen.) It allowed me to meet individual citizens of the district, listen to their concerns, and provide appropriate feedback. Ultimately, coffees served as promotional tools for the campaign, as members of the community who attended spread the word of my candidacy and political philosophy throughout the local community.

My campaign did not depend on sizeable contributions from commercial interests, which was pivotal in my election to the Metropolitan Council. The citizens of the district wanted a representative that was familiar with issues that had burdened them. My refusal to accept sizeable contributions from commercial and development interests was looked upon by a majority of voting citizens of the district as a guarantee that my claim to consider residents' input as a priority when addressing controversial proposals was legitimate.

The Campaign Financial Disclosure Statement as provided by the Tennessee Registry of Election Finance was filed by my campaign treasurer on September 7, 1995. According to that report, my campaign had "raised $1,590.06 and spent $1,145.43, bringing his totals to $2,640.06 in contributions and $1,987.90 in expenses."[17]

The majority of the money raised by my campaign was small donations made by individual residents. The largest donation was made by Tom Stanley, treasurer of my election campaign, who contributed eight hundred dollars. Thus, I was not obligated to any special interest and I was prepared to represent the citizens of District 14 in an equitable manner.

The campaign money was used to fund numerous informational advertisements and brochures. The half-page advertisements were taken out in the local newspaper, the *News Herald*. Such advertisements were $367.50 each. The brochures were printed by Donelson Printing, and included information about my personal and professional life. These brochures also included my political philosophy and my involvement in community issues over the years. The cost of these brochures was $124.49. The brochures played a pivotal role during the campaign as they were distributed to residents either by myself or my campaign committee. The residents could then review my history in the community and ask any question of us at that time.

The *News Herald* covered the political debate that took place at the Donelson Senior Citizen Center on June 20, 1995. The debate, which was for those candidates who sought election to the Metropolitan Council from District 14, was sponsored by the Donelson-Hermitage Neighborhood Association, Inc. It was attended by "approximately 50 people, with Bob Sheehan moderating."[18]

The coverage given to this debate gave the constituents of District 14 a clear view of the candidates seeking election to the Metropolitan Council. Each candidate was responsible for answering questions asked by the moderator or individual citizens. The answers given by the candidates were an indication of their familiarity with the community and the issues which the citizens of the community faced at that time.

There were numerous interest groups that had scheduled an interview with me as candidate for the District 14 council seat. Among the more notable was the local news media. Of particular importance was the print media. The awareness associated with the interviews that were ultimately published in the countywide newspapers proved invaluable to me as a first-time candidate. The answers that the candidates gave to the questions asked during the interview were printed for all citizens to view. In addition, the article contained a profile of each candidate, including the address, age, occupation, political hero, political experience, and organizations and memberships of each candidate. The newspapers could endorse a candidate that they felt would best represent the district and the city.

In early July 1995, I was interviewed by both the *Tennessean* and the *Nashville Banner*. The *Tennessean* interview was printed on July 10, 1995. The *Banner* interview was in the July 14, 1995, edition. Among the questions asked were "Why are you running?", "Why do you feel you can make a difference?", "Key issues facing your district?", "Key issues facing Metro in the next four years?", "Where do you stand on the recent controversy over whether the Nashville Arena should be allowed to sell beer?", "Should Nashville continue to burn trash at the Thermal Transfer Plant and should the city build a landfill at Bell's Bend?", and "What would you do if a district councilmember asked for support on an issue that required council action within his or her district?" These questions were asked to probe each candidate's understanding of his district and Metropolitan Nashville in general.

Following the interviews, the papers endorsed the candidates of their choice. In the July 17, 1995, edition of the *Tennessean,* the editorial staff endorsed me for the District 14 seat, believing that "Stanley has already proved himself as a community-minded, neighborhood activist. His election to the council would give him an opportunity to take a broader view of the city."[19]

The election was held on August 3, 1995. I received 571 votes, or 36 percent of those voting in District 14. My opponent received 770 votes, or 48.5 percent of the votes cast. A third candidate, Steve Murff, obtained 245 votes equivalent to 15.4 percent of those cast. The results were somewhat ominous for Underwood in that he had obtained less than 50 percent of the votes, forcing a runoff between the first and second place finishers in September. It was believed that the third candidate had been coaxed into running to siphon votes from me. But the fact that the citizens of the community still remembered specific controversies associated with Underwood during his last term in office prevented his obtaining the needed votes to win outright. The runoff pitted Underwood against me, and my campaign did its best to define the political differences between my opponent and myself.

Advertising in the community newspaper was among the more prominent ways in which the public was informed of the different political attitudes of each candidate. In addition, my campaign committee continued to comb the streets of District 14 in an attempt to educate the voting populace about me and inform them of the importance of casting their votes in the runoff election.

I received the endorsement from both the *Tennessean* and the *Nashville Scene.* These were countywide newspapers whose endorsements were open advertisements to the voters as they explained their reasons for granting the endorsement. In the August 25 edition of the *Tennessean*, the editorial staff explained that "Stanley, who has been active in neighborhood groups, has an impressive understanding of this district and a real commitment to listen to constituents. The runoff pits him against Sam Underwood, a former councilmember."[20]

The *Nashville Scene* predicted my victory in the runoff election in their September 7 edition. In that edition, Editor Bruce Dobie predicted the winners; in District 14, he predicted "James Bruce Stanley over Sam Underwood."[21]

In the runoff election held on September 14, 1995, I obtained 677 votes (51.9 percent) to Underwood's 627 (48.1 percent). My election to the Metropolitan Council was evidence that the citizens did not feel comfortable with an old-school politician representing them. There were numerous land-use controversies in District 14 that demanded a representative whose position on such controversies was to be determined by input from area citizens, not behind closed doors by the order of powerful political figures or large contributors to whom the old-school politicians felt obligated. My election to the Metropolitan Council extended the representation of District 14 to that candidate who would take on certain municipal issues that had burdened the citizens, and not simply because the political and business heavyweights of downtown Nashville gave their permission.

1999

My election in 1995 did not extinguish the old-school political movement. The firm stance that I took when addressing rezoning and development proposals forced many developmental interests to attempt to bring about my defeat for reelection in 1999. This was in spite of the needed improvements that I had provided in general to the District 14 community and Metropolitan Nashville during my first term.

Among the more notable of these improvements was funding for a new Hickman Elementary School, a renovated Donelson Middle School, the new Hermitage Police Precinct, a number of paving projects totaling $50,000, and numerous drainage projects totaling $350,000. The political experience I gained during my first four years on the Metropolitan Council was supplemented by my eight years of political activity prior to being elected to the Council in 1995.

However, the old school mounted a challenge in the 1999 election. "The race for the District 14 seat on the Metro Council pits age versus youth. A political novice versus an incumbent. But in this election, it's the younger candidate who has the political experience."[22] Harold White was the political novice that challenged for the District 14 council position. The sixty-two-year-old had no previous political experience, particularly in local affairs. His understanding of the local political process and ways to remedy community issues was severely limited. This was best illustrated during an interview with the local media. White "said he will work to reduce water rates but admitted he has no specific answers."[23]

Ultimately, White's political inexperience and inactivity prevented his acceptance by the community. In addition, White had resided in District 14 only since 1995. He did not reside in District 14 during the time when the Donelson-Hermitage community was experiencing the effects of urban sprawl. White was unfamiliar with the adverse effects urban sprawl would have on the local community. In addition, his lack of involvement in community issues illustrated his inexperience with metropolitan authorities and led to his misunderstanding of the local political procedure.

In contrast, I had been thoroughly involved in issues affecting the community for approximately twelve years, the final four as District 14 councilman. In addition, my interaction with various metropolitan agencies provided me with an understanding of local procedure. These municipal agencies included the Department of Planning, the Planning Commission, the Department of Public Works, the Metropolitan Nashville Public School System, the Codes Administration, the Metropolitan Health Department, and the Department of Water Services. This interaction, in turn, provided me with valuable experience to address issues that faced the community. This experience proved an extremely positive asset in my favor.

Unlike the 1995 campaign, which witnessed campaign committee members and me combing the streets of District 14 for face-to-face meetings with individual citizens, the 1999 campaign saw me as the incumbent. The members of my 1999 campaign committee included Tom Stanley, Sid Matthews, Mike Sturm, Dart Gore, Larry Keeton, Bob Sheehan, Betty Richardson, David and Alice Quaintance, and Rosemary Stanley.

Dart Gore and Larry Keeton were new members of this reelection committee. Gore was an officer with the AFL-CIO and Keeton was the owner of Dick's Flowers and an active member of the Donelson-Hermitage Chamber of Commerce. Throughout my first term, I gained their support by cooperating closely with both to address issues affecting the community.

It was believed that the community was familiar with me and those issues that I intended to concentrate on upon my reelection.

However, the responsibilities associated with my being an elected councilmember seeking reelection restricted my one-on-one involvement with the individuals residing in District 14.

Although there were a few campaign workers who combed the streets of the district, the treasury of my reelection campaign was spent primarily on advertisements in the local *News Herald*, as well as printing personal brochures and paying for campaign yard signs. These expenses caused my campaign costs to be greater than the costs associated with the 1995 campaign. The capital expenditure used by my reelection campaign in 1999 totaled approximately fifty-four hundred dollars. It still represented a small war chest in comparison to other council candidates at the same time.

The small size of my campaign treasury was due to my refusal to take substantial contributions from special interest groups. As a result, I was able to appropriately and equitably represent the resident citizens of District 14 without interference from special interest groups. Instead, my treasury was made up of small to moderate contributions from resident citizens of District 14, similar to my campaign in 1995.

The Donelson-Hermitage Neighborhood Association, Inc., had been inactive during the years since 1995. This was primarily due to the splintering of such a broad-based resident organization into numerous homeowners associations that represented specific subdivisions. Unlike previous elections, the lapsing of the Donelson-Hermitage Neighborhood Association did not allow for its sponsoring of district debates to familiarize the citizens of the community with the candidates that were seeking to represent them on the Metropolitan Council. Such debates would have been covered by the local media and would have clearly illustrated the differences between the candidates' experience and their political philosophy.

The lack of debates allowed old-school politicians to gain support for their election by making promises to citizens and claiming they had been actively involved in the community since the emergence of urban sprawl. In the majority of instances these claims were proven to be false and exposed the old-school politicians as inappropriate representatives for the citizens of our community.

By the 1999 campaign, the *Nashville Banner* had ceased publication, leaving the *Tennessean* as the most prominent newspaper covering the elections. On June 15, 1999, the *Tennessean* covered the two candidates running for the District 14 seat on the Metropolitan Council. In answer to the questions asked by the paper, I outlined some of the more positive accomplishments that I had brought to our community during my first term in office. Among the accomplishments mentioned in the article was that I was "a member of the Metro Stormwater Management Task Force, which is working toward a comprehensive stormwater drainage plan for the entire county."[24]

I stated that, "I'd like the next administration to adopt a comprehensive plan for addressing flooding issues on both private as well as public property." In addition, it was mentioned that I had cooperated to bring the new police precinct to the area, to renovate Donelson High School for its reopening as a middle school, to construct a new Hickman Elementary School, and regulated certain activities to stabilize residential subdivisions in the area. It was important to note that the cooperation with citizens of the district, along with metropolitan and state officials, was vital in witnessing these accomplishments. Finally, I stated that, "I have a great deal of experience in community issues and I believe that with my four years' experience, I know the procedures that need to be followed."[25]

The election was held on August 5, 1999. The final count saw me obtain 52 percent of votes cast. White received 48 percent. My reelection to the Metropolitan Council in 1999 was illustrative of the suspicions that Donelson-Hermitage citizens had toward old-school politics. In addition, the rapidly increasing intrusion of urban sprawl into Donelson-Hermitage dictated the need to elect politically experienced individuals who gave citizen input priority consideration in issues addressed as they represented the community. During my first term on the Metropolitan Council, I had provided the type of open, acceptable representation necessary to curb urban sprawl by more thoroughly regulating growth.

2003

My reelection to the Metropolitan Council in 1999 prohibited my seeking a third term in 2003, as dictated by the council term limits.

Approximately eighteen months prior to the 2003 local elections, I was informed that old-school politics was to play a critical role in the district council races. Specifically targeted were council districts that had no incumbent seeking reelection. The Nashville Business Coalition was the principal organization that would support candidates in these district races. It was organized in an attempt to retake the Metropolitan Council and return the politics of Metropolitan Nashville to the closed-door days. The candidates were to have primary allegiance to the commercial and developmental interests of our city. Their campaigns were overwhelmingly funded through large contributions by various business interests. Such monetary contributions were viewed by old-school candidates as obligating them to give priority allegiance to those business interests that had invested the most in their campaign. They refused to give due consideration to the input of individual resident constituents who faced certain adversity regarding controversial issues. It was not surprising when District 14 was designated as one of the council districts to be targeted by the old-school politicians.

The Nashville Business Coalition executive director, Charles Fentress, labeled those who did not support its position as "anti-business." The municipality that the Metropolitan Council was responsible for legislating was a complex society represented by a wide variety of interests. However, the coalition wanted the Metropolitan Council to give priority consideration to business interests while governing the city. It was also a clear indication that the business coalition wanted to elect members to the Metropolitan Council that were going to be guided, not by the constituents who they were elected to represent, but by business interests.

In response to the old-school political activity in July 2002, I organized a candidate search committee for District 14 to give resident citizens a stronger voice in the upcoming council elections. In addition, the organization of the committee was in response to the lapsing of the Donelson-Hermitage Neighborhood Association, Inc., and the splintering of the residential interests of the community into separate residential groups, representing individual subdivisions and including homeowners associations and neighborhood watches.

Historically, the political involvement of these groups varied, with some neighborhood watch groups refusing to get politically involved. A number of neighborhood watch groups believed that political

FROM THE TENNESSEAN

July 29, 2003

Group Seeks to Elect Candidates it Views as Backing Business

Former Metro Councilman Charles Fentress makes no bones about the ambition behind his efforts to influence the outcome of the Aug. 7 council elections.

He wants a legislative body that is more pro-business than the current forty-member council.

Fentress is executive director of one of the busiest political-action committees this season, the Nashville Business Coalition—a group that is spreading money to candidates it sees as carrying its pro-business banner.

The group wants to stem what Fentress says was a push by anti-business interests in 1999 to select more sympathetic members to the council.

The group's goal is to inject about $75,000 into this year's elections with hopes of getting its candidates elected.

Of the 30 candidates the group has endorsed, only seven are incumbents. One is running unopposed.

"There have been some issues there that were certainly not helpful to business," said Fentress, referring to the current council. "Such as a living wage; such as (Metro employee labor union) binding memorandums of understanding; such as anything that would create the opportunity for people to block economic development or block incentives. We would not have a lot of the businesses we have if there had not been economic incentives. A lot of people on the council, if they're not pro-business, would not be for economic incentives. We just want some people that run a business, understand a business."

Some of the coalition's big contributors include Gaylord Entertainment Co., HCA, SunTrust Bank, Gulch investor Steve Turner, and businessmen Lee Beaman and Ray Danner.

Fentress has taken an active role "to get the business community to wake up and do all they can to get their friends elected to the council."

Labor advocates say the coalition's focus on labor issues is really just a masquerade of its real intent, extending taxpayer subsidies to big business.

The coalition's candidate questionnaire asks about tax breaks to business, labor issues and the "so-called 'living wage'"—an effort to raise the minimum salary for the lowest-paid city employees. The business community fought it fiercely in 2001 and won.

The questionnaire asks candidates if they support accepting contributions from Service Employees International Union, which represents some Metro employees, and the teachers' union.

Fentress said it is not just unions that are anti-business. "There are a lot of people out in this community who think business is ripping everybody off," Fentress said.

"There are a lot of people out in the community who think that the business people want to asphalt every square inch of land and build something on it. That's crock. It's not true, but that's what they think. Those are also anti-business people."

"There's a lot of people in this community who today would never vote for a referendum to bring the Titans in. There are a lot of people in this community who think we made a big mistake when we brought the Titans in, when we built the arena. Those are nonbusiness people as far as I'm concerned. And they're not all labor."

Don Driscoll, executive director of the SEIU local, which represents about 5,800 Metro employees, said he thinks the coalition views anyone who isn't for subsidizing big business with taxpayer dollars as anti-business.

Driscoll said the 2001 defeat of the living-wage proposal is clear evidence that the business community still carries a big stick in Nashville politics.

The agenda of the council over the past four years has been to fund schools, improve the city's infrastructure, public safety and

(continued)

make sure employees of the government are paid a fair wage—initiatives that are good for all of Nashville, including business, Driscoll said.

Driscoll points to questions on the coalition's survey about contributions to labor unions as a direct shot at unions.

"They're picking a fight," Driscoll said. "We weren't looking for a fight. They use the living-wage issue to say they're not what they're really about, which is corporate welfare."

Despite the sharp rhetoric of the two sides, both concede that in some races they support the same candidates, including at large candidates David Briley, Dianne Neighbors and Buck Dozier and District 10 incumbent Bettye Balthrop.

Joe Hall, a coalition board member and lobbyist with the Ingram Group, called Driscoll's assertions "baloney" and rhetoric to stir his base of union voters to the polls.

Hall said the group isn't anti-labor but is interested in electing educated, business-minded candidates.

Hall said the group wants council members who will practice smart fiscal management and be open to policies that help grow the economy. He said that means incentives "when it makes sense." He said the coalition also supports improving education and public safety.

"Business has to participate in the election process, and if we don't, we can't gripe about its outcome."[26]

—Copyrighted, the *Tennessean*, July 29, 2003

involvement was beyond their scope, and their primary objective was to curb criminal activity in their subdivisions.

In addition, there were numerous residential subdivisions that had no neighborhood groups organized in their area. If an issue arose in their neighborhood, it was the responsibility of individual homeowners to contact and inform the councilmember representing them of the issue. This exemplified the need to elect a councilmember who would be easily accessible and was willing to work with the resident citizens to address any adverse issue.

It was my experience following the 1999 campaign, which had seen the extinction of the Donelson-Hermitage Neighborhood Association, Inc., that there had been no residentially sponsored candidate debates in any of the council districts serving our community. Such debates, attended by voting citizens and covered by the local media, were vital in familiarizing the public with the candidates seeking office.

It was important to actively involve the resident citizens of District 14 in an attempt to elect the most appropriate member of our community to represent us on the Metropolitan Council. The residents that agreed to serve on the search committee were representative of each of the five precincts of District 14.

When organizing the search committee, those individual residents who had played a key role in issues that they had faced during my two terms on the Council were considered. Residents that I had been privileged to work with when addressing zoning or development proposals, or developing regulatory legislation, were given priority consideration. Ultimately, there were thirteen citizens that agreed to serve on the candidate search committee. Ten of the members resided in subdivisions throughout the Donelson and Hermitage communities that represented District 14. The members represented a wide range of professions whose experience in addressing community issues would be invaluable in reviewing the candidates seeking election.

The ten members of the committee from District 14 included Bob Taylor, Donna Vaughn, John Marshall, Doug McMahan, Jim Schleicher, Steve Sykes, Kim Wall, Bob Ferry, Betty Richardson, and Roberta Walter.

There were also three committee members who resided just over the district boundaries. These three members, and the council districts of which they were a part, included Mary Ann Hoffmann, District 15; Bill Tucker, District 13; and Andy Shivas, District 13.

The members of the committee had experienced a wide range of community issues. Such issues included industrial and commercial encroachments and development proposals. To assist in guiding our community into the twenty-first century, the members were prepared to serve on this search committee. The members were not anti-development. Instead they would support proposals that were truly progressive for the community. (Such proposals were considered progressive when they included specific upgrades to the public infrastructure.)

In addition, proposals would not be approved behind closed doors. Instead, it was essential that such proposals receive input from the existing community, specifically those that were to be immediately impacted. The committee was looking to elect a councilmember who would not make closed-door decisions but would involve the resident citizens in the planning process. The committee was thus prepared to hold meetings and recommend to the citizens the best possible candidate for District 14 as the 2003 council elections approached.

The objective of the committee was to "be responsible for identifying the individual citizen that will represent Council District 14 in the manner most acceptable to the constituents of the Donelson-Hermitage district, recruiting that individual to run for this legislative office, and supporting the campaign of this candidate to enable his/her election to the Metropolitan Council."[27]

To reach the objective, specific goals were adopted and included:

1. meeting monthly to share information pertaining to identifying and/or recruiting possible candidates for this office;

2. inviting potential candidates to address the committee and answer questions pertaining to their political philosophy; and

3. supporting the campaign of the candidate the committee has endorsed.[28]

The search committee meetings were held in the Community Room of the Hermitage Police Precinct and were open to the public and media. Representatives from the print media were invited to attend these committee meetings. In fact, reporters from several newspapers attended meetings and were given access to all committee members. Among the more notable newspapers covering these meetings were the *Tennessean,* the *News Herald,* and the *City Paper*.

The openness of these meetings illustrated that the candidate search committee was not an old-school organization. This was particularly disturbing for the old-school advocates who had targeted

District 14 to be retaken in 2003. It seemed that the candidate search committee was undermining old-school political philosophy.

The first meeting of the search committee was on August 29, 2002. The final meeting of the committee was March 17, 2003, and resulted in our formal endorsement of a candidate for the District 14 council seat. During its seven months of existence, the regularly scheduled meetings witnessed the discussion of a wide range of campaign topics, including the adoption of a candidate requirement list. The list set out numerous requirements that would be used to guide the committee toward an acceptable candidate. Meeting these requirements would assist the candidate to obtain the endorsement of our committee and ensure capable representation for District 14. The requirements included on the list were:

- Representation—Councilmember will truly represent the needs of the constituents who elected him/her to office. The councilmember will not be influenced by special interests or political heavyweights located outside the council district.
- Experience—Councilmember is required to have experience addressing issues associated with the district. The historical interaction a council candidate has had with different departments/agencies of the metropolitan government provides vital initial experience needed by the newly elected councilmember to obtain rapid relief for constituent issues.
- Accessibility—Councilmember is required to be openly accessible to the constituents. This accessibility will allow for an open communication between councilmember and the constituents and a more rapid and thorough relief for the constituents.
- Understanding—Councilmember is required to have an understanding of the various procedures associated with different metropolitan departments and programs. In addition, it is required to have a strong understanding of the district needs (i.e., infrastructure, zoning). This understanding will be used as the foundation upon which government experience can be expanded for the benefit of the constituents.
- Association—Councilmember will not be closely associated with outside special interests or political heavyweights that do

not represent the citizens of the district. Decisions on the council floor affecting the constituents of the district should not be decided behind closed doors without input from the district constituents. The councilmember will not be allowed to become a "rubber stamp" for special interests at the expense of the established community he/she was elected to represent.

- Leadership—Councilmember is required to cooperate with various metropolitan department/agencies and initiate any legislative action needed to relieve and stabilize the suburban community represented by District 14.

In addition, numerous individuals who had influence in the creation of public policy were either invited to attend and address our committee or were informed and updated on the selection process instituted by the committee. Among those contacted were Nancy Holland of the Metropolitan Nashville Education Association (MNEA) and John Stern, president of the Nashville Neighborhood Alliance.

There were three candidates that had shown an interest in running for the District 14 council seat. Candidates Greg Rodriguez, Deborah Swartwood, and Harold White were invited to address the search committee. It was important for the committee to know what other organizations sponsored each candidate, and thus be able to identify where the candidate's allegiance was directed.

Rodriguez was president of the Tennessee Hispanic Chamber of Commerce and was on the board of the Nashville Hotel/Motel Association. The Nashville Business Coalition was an initial supporter of his campaign.

White, who had lost the 1999 campaign, had established business alliances supportive of his council run in 2003. Such alliances included the Nashville Business Coalition and the Donelson-Hermitage Chamber of Commerce. Because of such close ties to the commercial sector, it was feared that either of these men, if elected, would give priority consideration to commercial proposals regardless of the adversities such a proposal projected on the community.

This pro-business position was best exemplified by Rodriguez when he claimed to the committee that "there needs to be a balance:

pro-business, pro-labor, adding that the current Metro Council seems to lean heavily on the side of labor."[29] In addition, White had made campaign promises that seemed unlikely to be able to be fulfilled. The most notable of these promises was his sponsoring quarterly meetings in each of the five precincts making up District 14. This promise meant he would sponsor a minimum of twenty community meetings per year. Such a promise was illustrative of White's political inexperience, since it was unlikely he could hold so many meetings.

Although the council was considered a part-time position, the wide variety of municipal issues and constituent demands that each council-member was responsible to address required full attention by the councilmember. The time required to address such issues prohibited a district councilmember from sponsoring at least twenty community meetings a year. This campaign promise by White appeared to be an attempt to sway residential voters and was highly questioned by members of the committee.

In contrast to both White and Rodriguez, Swartwood had no ties to the Nashville Business Coalition. Thus, she was not expected to be controlled by outside business interests which favored rezoning and development at the expense of area residents. Swartwood was a resident of Hermitage for ten years. She owned and operated a business, and was a member of the Donelson-Hermitage Chamber of Commerce. She was an active participant in the education of her two children, having served as president of the Hermitage Elementary PTA from 2000 to 2002. In addition, her residence on Hickory Hill Lane put her in close proximity to a developmental hot spot. Her interaction with others of the community facing similar developmental controversies educated her on the importance of citizen input when debating such controversial proposals.

When addressing the search committee, Swartwood promoted citizen input on all issues involving the community and said she would maintain open communications with the citizens of District 14. She claimed that "being PTA president for two years, that's the main experience that's kind of along this line. It taught me how to deal with public issues. You have to learn to deal with people."[30]

The March 17, 2003, meeting saw the District 14 Council Search Committee openly endorse candidate Swartwood for election to the Metropolitan Council. "The committee chose Swartwood because she had more of a pro-constituent stance than the other candidates." The committee felt that "Swartwood has been actively involved in the community, particularly at Hermitage Elementary." In addition, the committee was "impressed with how she was willing to give priority consideration to constituent input regarding development,"[31] of specific areas such as the 220-acre Brown's Farm, the 285-acre Binns property, and portions of the Ravenwood Club. It was important to elect the appropriate representative for District 14 to adequately address these issues.

The failure of either Rodriguez or White to obtain the endorsement of the search committee was viewed by the Nashville Business Coalition as undermining its attempts for a pro-business candidate to retake District 14. The coalition endorsement of Harold White guaranteed the removal of Rodriguez from consideration. Further exemplifying his association with old-school politics was the attempt by White to discredit the search committee.

Such a political maneuvering was best illustrated by a mailing that White sent to the citizens of District 14. It was funded through the White campaign, which included a number of corporate donors and real property investors. In this mailing, White referred to the search committee as "backroom politics at its worst" and openly criticized the endorsement of Swartwood. He referred to the committee's endorsement as a "coronation" and demanded an "election" to determine who would be the best representative for District 14.

Finally, the defining of "election" by *Webster's Dictionary* in this mailing was indicative that White and his campaign viewed the voting resident citizens of District 14 as uneducated people. A number of voting citizens contacted me about their outrage of this mailing and informed me of their support for Swartwood.

In the following weeks, both Swartwood and White campaigned for election to the Metropolitan Council. Swartwood's campaign involved a loyal group of residents combing the streets of District 14 and meeting face-to-face with the citizens of the community.

In early July, both candidates were interviewed by the *Tennessean*. These interviews, which included probing questions by the editorial board of the paper, revealed the candidates' understanding of the community they were seeking to represent and their knowledge of the local political procedure. In late July, the *Tennessean* announced that Deborah Swartwood received the paper's endorsement for District 14. The editorial board stated that "Swartwood is a stay-at-home mother who is active in local school activities. Over the past months, she has taken it upon herself to learn about Metro procedures. She also has some impressive ideas about staying connected with constituents."[32]

In response to the failure of White to obtain the endorsement of the local print media in the upcoming election, a third candidate was recruited to run for the District 14 council seat. Sarah Moore was a teacher at Mt. Juliet High School in Wilson County.

Moore had resided in District 14 a short time. Thus, she had not been actively involved in addressing any controversy impacting District 14. Her interaction with the local resident population and metropolitan authorities was completely lacking. This hindered her understanding of local procedures used by metropolitan authorities when addressing issues. Her claim to "bring classroom experience to the council"[33] further illustrated a lack of political experience which was necessary to address local issues and adequately represent the citizens of District 14.

Her sudden candidacy was questioned by members of the district. Many believed her candidacy was to simply siphon votes from Swartwood, the other female in the District 14 race. Her endorsement by the Republican Party further raised questions about her association with the Nashville Business Coalition. The third-party candidate recruitment technique was old-school maneuvering prevalent throughout the history of politics in Metropolitan Nashville. It was used to splinter the votes cast in a particular race and allow the election of a candidate who had the backing of a particular section of the community.

The election was held on August 7, 2003. Upon the closing of the polls, White was elected with 844 votes (51 percent) of those cast. Swartwood received 568 (35 percent) of the votes cast. Moore finished last with 222 votes (14 percent). The old school had succeeded in electing their candidate to the District 14 Metropolitan Council seat. This election undermined the sixteen years of open representation that District 14 had witnessed since 1987; demanding that the neighborhood groups of District 14 be extremely involved in upcoming issues facing the community.

Such involvement included keeping a close eye on rezoning and development proposals that were to be made by nonresident interests. Resident input was vital in determining the developmental direction of the community, especially when represented by a politician with strong business ties.

Conclusion

The Metropolitan Council served as the representative body to ensure that citizen input was given priority consideration when faced with controversial issues. Metropolitan Nashville was an extremely diversified urban environment, continually growing as the city entered the twenty-first century. A strong, independent voice was required in the municipal legislature to equitably represent the position of various interests on issues that faced the community.

The advent of urban sprawl on the suburban communities of Metropolitan Nashville caused citizens to question the existing political machine that controlled policy at the time. Numerous shortcomings were uncovered in the old-school political machine as a result of this questioning. One of the primary shortcomings was the use of closed-door decisions to adopt policy for the city. It clearly showed the overwhelming influence the business lobby and political heavyweights exercised on district councilmembers. Many council-members were viewed as simply pawns for powerful downtown interests. A number of old-school politicians were not re-elected as a result, and a new era of government was begun in Metropolitan Nashville.

The new councilmembers of the new era subscribed to the open-door manner of developing policy. Open communication and cooperation motivated invaluable input and ensured the adoption of policy that was to have a progressive impact on the entire community.

However, the new era of government for Metropolitan Nashville did not force the extinction of old-school political tactics.

For approximately sixteen years, the Metropolitan Council was comprised of members that endorsed the open communications concept. The political complacency developed by citizens during that time was a belief that the community would no longer support candidates that subscribed to the old school of political thought.

The active involvement of business in council elections of 2003 represented a rude awakening to the citizens of Metropolitan Nashville. The desire of the business interests to return to the good old days of politics resulted in their making substantial contributions to candidates for the Metropolitan Council. The result was the election of a number of candidates who were heavily supported by the local business community.

The sponsoring of closed meetings by members of this Council brought controversy. In debating issues associated with the city's $1.35 billion budget in 2004, a core group of councilmembers sponsored private meetings. Noticeably absent from these meetings were the local media and the public. Many of the councilmembers aligned with these meetings were heavily influenced by business interests. Closed-door meetings of this type were a clear indication that business-controlled councilmembers were attempting to revert to politics of old.

These meetings violated the state Sunshine Law requiring meetings that determine policy and are attended by numerous elected officials to be made public. "When council members shut the door, they shut out not only some of their own colleagues, but all of their constituents."[34]

It is important to remember what circumstances drove us away from this former network of politics. Only time will tell if the resident citizens of Metropolitan Nashville will rise up again to remove those councilmembers who are heavily controlled by business interests. This will ensure that the Metropolitan Council will once again be a responsible legislative body and be representative of the entire Metropolitan Nashville.

Chapter Three

Legislation

The Metropolitan Council represents the legislative branch of the Metropolitan Government of Nashville and Davidson County. The Council is the popularly elected legislature for the municipality. The role of the legislature is to make statutory laws for the area over which it has jurisdiction. Such laws are enacted through the legislative process by legislators. A legislator is defined as "one who makes laws; a member of a legislative body."[1]

The councilmembers are responsible for regulating activities throughout the city. Such regulation works to control everyday activities, thereby protecting the environment of the city and the investments made by citizens in Metropolitan Nashville. Legislation is "the act of giving or enacting laws."[2] The approval of legislation by the popularly elected Metropolitan Council creates new laws to govern the city as well as representing a uniform position the councilmembers have taken on a specific topic or issue.

There are two types of legislation involved in the politics of Metropolitan Nashville. The first type of legislation is the ordinance. A municipal ordinance is defined as "a law, rule, or ordinance enacted or adopted by a municipal corporation for the proper conduct of its affairs or the government of its inhabitants; e.g. zoning or traffic ordinances, building codes."[3] These ordinances represent formal laws which the city and its citizens are required to follow.

The adoption of ordinances by the Metropolitan Council requires sincere consideration of the impact it will have on all areas of the community. The benefits such an ordinance will have on the community must outweigh the detriments.

The legislative process involved in the consideration and passage of an ordinance is complex. The process requires the ordinance to be reviewed by numerous metropolitan departments or agencies, various council committees which have jurisdiction over the issue being addressed by the ordinance, the local citizens, and the Metropolitan Council. The ordinance must be brought before the Metropolitan Council for three separate readings, with the vote of the Council on the final reading designating whether it will be passed or defeated. Finally, following its passage by the Metropolitan Council, the legislative process requires the ordinance to be signed into law by the mayor for it to become effective.

The second type of legislation is the resolution. Resolutions are defined as "a formal expression of the opinion or will of an official body." In addition, resolutions are "usually employed to denote the adoption of a motion, the subject-matter of which would not properly constitute a statute, such as a mere expression of opinion." Finally, a resolution "denotes something less formal than 'ordinance'; generally, it is mere expression of opinion or mind of council concerning some matter of administration, within its official cognizance, and provides for disposition of particular item of administrative business of a municipality."[4]

Due to its being less formal than an ordinance, a resolution is required to be heard only once by the Metropolitan Council. Prior to its being heard by the entire Council, the resolution is required to be reviewed by the appropriate metropolitan departments or agencies, as well as those council committees that have jurisdiction over the matter being addressed by the resolution.

The two forms of resolutions include general resolutions and memorializing resolutions. General resolutions are requests to either public or private entities to take a particular action on a certain issue. Memorializing resolutions honor individual citizens or groups for the positive impact that they have had on the local community. Throughout my tenure on the Metropolitan Council, I sponsored numerous ordinances and resolutions in response to the citizens of Metropolitan Nashville in general, and of District 14 specifically. The legislation was initiated in an attempt to more thoroughly regulate activities in our community, request specific action be taken by different departments on issues, and honor those citizens who had offered their professional service to the community over the years.

The legislative process guiding legislation through the Metropolitan Council is clearly defined in the *Rules of Procedure of the*

Council of the Metropolitan Government of Nashville and Davidson County. Upon my election to the Metropolitan Council in 1995, I became extremely familiar with the rules of procedure so that I could responsibly legislate the activities in both Metropolitan Nashville and District 14. Addressing concerns raised by area citizens required drawing up an appropriate bill, either a resolution or an ordinance.

To author such a bill involved researching the issue to be addressed by the legislation, which, in turn, promoted an interaction with numerous parties affected by the bill. Those parties included individual citizens, other councilmembers, and various government departments or agencies. Such interaction motivated an open communication and cooperation between all parties to be affected by the bill. This promoted legislation free of controversy.

The formal authoring of the bill was the responsibility of the council sponsor and the legal advisor to the Metropolitan Council. The completed bill was then ready to be filed with the metropolitan clerk. The rules designated that "all bills and resolutions shall be filed in triplicate with the Metropolitan Clerk, the original to be retained in her office at all times subject only to withdrawal for signature by the Mayor."[5]

Such bills "shall be filed with the Metropolitan Clerk's Office not later than 4:00 P.M. on Tuesday, immediately preceding a regular meeting of the Council and not later than 11:00 A.M. of the third day, excluding Saturdays and Sundays, preceding the day of any other Council meeting." In addition, it was designated that "no late bill or resolution will be considered by the Council except on an emergency basis. Any sponsor of a late bill or resolution must state on the introduction thereof that an emergency exists and must further state the nature of the emergency."[6]

The metropolitan clerk was required to "restrict all matters on the first meeting during each odd month to bills on public hearing and to bills on introduction and first reading provided the sponsor is present at the Council meeting and no objection to passage on first reading is made; the Clerk shall exclude bills on public hearing from any other Council meeting."[7] Bills requiring a public hearing were almost exclusively restricted to zoning matters. However, prior to the adoption of the city budget each summer, a public hearing was required so that citizens could weigh in with their opinions on budgetary issues.

After filing a resolution or bill, the metropolitan clerk places them "on the agenda in the order in which they are filed, provided however, the Metropolitan Clerk may arrange resolutions or bills according to their subject matter at the discretion of the Metropolitan Clerk." In addition, "the agenda for each meeting shall be prepared by the Metropolitan Clerk and mailed by her to each member not less than two days, excluding Saturdays and Sundays, before the meeting at which it will be considered. For regular meetings the agenda is to be mailed not later than Friday prior to such meetings." Finally, "the agenda shall show on all planning and zoning and mandatory referral matters listed thereon the vote of the Planning Commission on its action on such matter and shall similarly indicate the vote of all other boards and commissions of their recommendations of such matters which were referred to such boards and commissions."[8]

The rules dictated that "all ordinances must be referred to the appropriate committee by the President of the Council after first reading, and except for zoning matters, budget, revenue service charges or tax measures, no ordinances may be amended after second reading." Similarly, resolutions were to be referred to the appropriate committee or committees. In addition, "no vote will be taken on any resolution until a committee has considered same." Finally, "the committee to which an ordinance or resolution has been referred shall make a report to the Council at the next regular meeting after its referral unless an extension of time shall be granted by the President for good cause shown."[9]

When dealing with departmental referrals, it was required that no resolution or ordinance that had to be "referred to the Metropolitan Planning Commission for a recommendation shall be filed with the Metropolitan Clerk unless evidence of submission to the Metropolitan Planning Commission is filed together with the legislation or the legislation has noted upon it the recommendation of the Metropolitan Planning Commission."[10]

The rules further outlined the required procedure that bills were to take on all land-use or zoning ordinances. "Upon introduction of any zoning ordinance not accompanied by a recommendation of the

Metropolitan Planning Commission, such ordinance shall be referred to the Planning Commission and the Planning, Zoning, Historical and Port Authority Committee of the Council. The Metropolitan Clerk shall advertise such ordinance for public hearing and second reading; however, no action shall be taken by the Council on second reading and no public hearing shall be held by the Council until the recommendation of the Planning Commission has been submitted to the Metropolitan Clerk."[11]

The recommendation from the Planning Commission pertaining to any land-use or zoning bill before the Metropolitan Council played a necessary and vital role in determining the position the Council was to take on such a bill. The rule also promoted an open interaction between councilmembers and representatives of the Planning Commission to ensure that land-use or zoning legislation would be addressed in the most appropriate manner.

The progression of a bill through the legislative process oftentimes required its deferral. A deferral is best defined as the "act of delaying, postponing or putting off."[12] The deferral of a bill was the responsibility of the sponsor. A deferral of a bill before the Metropolitan Council provided time for the sponsor to obtain answers to questions raised pertaining to the bill. Such questions were raised in response to concerns councilmembers and citizens had about the effects a bill would have on the community.

In addition, if the questions or concerns voiced over a specific piece of legislation were too extreme, a withdrawal was available to the sponsor, which formally removed a bill from further consideration by the Metropolitan Council. In many instances, withdrawing a bill motivated the sponsor to begin working immediately on similar legislation that would eliminate the questions raised pertaining to the original bill.

The length of time for a requested deferral varies widely, the determination of which is the responsibility of the sponsor. The length of deferral should involve the appropriate time to research the questions associated with the legislation and provide acceptable answers to the Metropolitan Council to insure its passage. In addition, all ordinances on second or third reading and resolutions that have been deferred twice by the sponsor "shall automatically be removed by the Clerk from the agenda for the succeeding Council meeting."[13]

However, "any bill or resolution which has been removed from the agenda, either pursuant to this rule or because the sponsor has requested indefinite deferral, shall be placed on the agenda only at the written or oral request of the sponsor which shall be made to the Metropolitan Clerk by the Tuesday preceding the Council meeting at which time the matter can be considered."[14] The sponsor can make the request to have the resolution placed for further review after all questions and concerns have been adequately addressed. Such answers are intended to assure those who raised the questions will be placated and ultimately supportive of the legislation.

When the Metropolitan Council ultimately considers an ordinance or resolution at its meeting:

> the first person to be recognized by the President shall be one of its sponsors. The second shall be the chairman or one spokesman of the committee to which the matter has been referred. No action may be taken on any ordinance or resolution (except ordinances on introduction and first reading) at any meeting of the Council or at any meeting of a committee of the Council to which such ordinance or resolution has been referred unless a sponsor is present or a sponsor has informed the President or chair of the committee, in writing, of the action to be taken and of the member of Council designated to handle the matter in the sponsor's absence.[15]

During deliberation of legislation by the Metropolitan Council, a councilmember "shall speak no more than once on the same subject until all members have had an opportunity to speak on it, and for no more than eight minutes, except that one sponsor of an ordinance or resolution and one spokesman of the committee to which the matter has been referred shall each have the right to speak twelve minutes. This restriction may be waived by a majority of the members present."[16] In addition, "the Mayor or his authorized representative shall have the privilege of the floor for the purpose of discussing matters under consideration by the Council."[17]

The end of open debate on an ordinance or resolution requires the motion to be made by the sponsor pertaining to the action requested of the Metropolitan Council. Such motion may be for approval, disapproval, deferral, or withdrawal. However, a motion to table the legislation may be made by a councilmember that is not supportive of the motion made by the sponsor.

When a motion to table has been made, the Metropolitan Council will vote on such motion only after they understand the reasoning behind the tabling motion. "A motion to table may be debated only by the maker of the motion and by one proponent of the bill or resolution involved."[18] In the vast majority of instances, the proponent is the sponsor of the legislation. However, the sponsor may wish to have a cosponsor, or a fellow proponent of the bill, speak in opposition to the motion to table.

Upon the completion of the debate on the motion to table, the Metropolitan Council must vote on that motion specifically. If the motion to table receives the necessary twenty-one votes, the bill is tabled, thereby prohibiting further action be taken on the legislation. Ultimately, that position taken by the Metropolitan Council will result in the defeat of the legislation.

However, the tabling motion is defeated upon its failure to receive twenty-one votes in support. The Metropolitan Council is then obligated to consider the original motion made by the sponsor on the bill. The passage of the bill is achieved with the casting of at least twenty-one votes in support.

If the recommendation of the Planning Commission is for disapproval of the legislation, the sponsor is required to have at least twenty-seven affirmative votes on third and final reading to obtain its passage. Finally, "any affirmative action of the Council may be rescinded by ⅔ vote of the full membership of the Council (27 votes)."[19]

The open involvement in debate over legislation is an extremely educating experience. Such involvement promotes a close interaction between councilmembers, metropolitan officials, lobbyists, and the private citizens of Metropolitan Nashville. The interaction involves open communication between all parties to be affected by the legislation; this promotes an awareness of the various positions taken by different parties on the legislation and the reasons such positions are taken. Such differing positions necessitate the cooperation between all parties with an interest in the legislation. This cooperation should ultimately lead to the presentation and adoption of an ordinance or resolution that will have a positive impact on the citizens and environment of Metropolitan Nashville.

Upon my election to the Metropolitan Council in 1995, there were a number of issues that had been brought to my attention by constituents or that I had experienced personally as a citizen of Metropolitan Nashville over the years. These issues demanded solutions as quickly as possible and were to have both immediate and long-term benefits for the city and its individual resident citizens.

One of the most important issues was the adoption of a policy to more thoroughly regulate floodplain development. In my role as district councilman for Metropolitan Nashville, I was prepared to sponsor the appropriate ordinance to regulate floodplain development for the benefit of the city in general. I also sponsored a number of resolutions that requested different governmental departments or agencies to review their policies on specific issues and provide relief to the local citizens adversely affected by those policies.

In addition, I sponsored a number of resolutions that honored specific individuals for their services to the citizens of Donelson-Hermitage and Metropolitan Nashville in general.

Ordinances

Throughout my tenure on the Metropolitan Council, numerous issues were brought to my attention either by constituents or through personal experience. Overwhelmingly, these issues were associated with land-use controversies. The conflicts resulting from such controversies had an adverse impact on the community by undermining the stability of the local environment. In many instances, the instability projected upon the community included depreciation in property values, which, in turn, had a detrimental effect on the investments individual citizens had placed in their properties.

In response to concerns voiced to me by the local citizens, I determined the most appropriate manner in which to bring closure to the issues and prevent their reemergence in the future. As a resident citizen, I understood the importance of finding a solution to them as soon as possible.

In the majority of instances, it became evident that these problems could be solved through the passage of an ordinance that would more thoroughly regulate the specific activities from whence the controversies emerged. Such regulation would substantially eliminate the controversies underlying the issues adversely affecting the community and promote a more stable environment in which citizens could invest. For instance, I sponsored ordinances to regulate consignment sales, excessive noise from entertainment establishments, and floodplain development.

The development of the most appropriate ordinance to address controversial issues required open communication and cooperation with professional officials and impacted citizens. In my position as a member of the Metropolitan Council, I had access to expert professionals employed by the metropolitan government. Their expertise was wide-ranging and included the vital areas of law, land-use planning, engineering, and finance. The advice and input these professionals provided played a vital role in directing the path of the ordinance as it made its way through the legislative process.

In addition, the resident citizens impacted by controversial issues represented a knowledgeable public who desired to be openly involved in the legislative process. Citizen involvement was embraced and considered an extremely important criterion in developing the most effective ordinance to address the issue with which they were faced.

Regulating Floodplain Development

The rapid pace of growth and development associated with the emergence of sprawl into Metropolitan Nashville in the mid-1980s brought many land-use issues that had been floundering over the years within the local political scene to the forefront of issues demanding immediate attention. Primarily, these issues concentrated on the outdated infrastructure serving the city. There was a need to have such infrastructure upgraded prior to approving newly proposed developments.

In addition, the unrelenting growth of Metropolitan Nashville necessitated the development of new programs to assist in alleviating the adverse impact further development forced upon the city and its citizens. These programs regulated development throughout Metropolitan Nashville and were created with the adoption of new legislation by the Metropolitan Council. The programs represented an acknowledgment by metropolitan officials of the need to more comprehensively address the issues of growth. A failure to acknowledge the issues associated with substantial growth would further burden the established community and motivate long-term problems for Metropolitan Nashville.

Floodplain development became one of the most important issues regarding our rapidly expanding city. Floodplains were defined as "the relatively flat or lowland area adjoining a river, stream, watercourse, lake, or other body of standing water which has been or may be covered temporarily by floodwater." Additionally, the floodplain was defined as "the 100-year floodplain having a one percent chance of being equaled or exceeded in any given year." Floodplains were considered extremely sensitive sites due to their likelihood of flooding. In addition, the floodplains were situated directly contiguous with natural floodways. Floodways were defined as "that portion of the stream channel and adjacent floodplain required for the passage or conveyance of a 100-year flood discharge."[20]

The advent of sprawl into Metropolitan Nashville witnessed sizable tracts of property either noticeably encumbered, or completely encompassed, by the one-hundred-year floodplain. These floodplain tracts remained either semi-developed or undeveloped. However, in that state, they were an attraction to developers, which resulted in extremely dense developments being proposed for the floodplain areas. Such proposed developments represented a wide variety of land uses including residential single-family, residential multi-family, commercial retail, commercial office, mixed-use, and industrial warehousing. In addition, these various types of developments promoted differing levels of stormwater displacement that would adversely impact the established community.

Floodplain acreage was distinct in many ways from other acreage outside the floodplain. The primary distinction was the fact that it was prone to extensive flooding caused by the adjacent floodways overflowing their banks and saturating the floodplain site. An additional source of flooding involved the heavy levels of stormwater runoff from developed property contiguous with the floodplain as it flowed toward and emptied into the natural waterway.

Another distinct characteristic of floodplains was the weak, erosive sediment that was created by a continual saturation of the land by stormwater runoff or overflow flooding. That type of soil undermined the attempt to create a firm, stable foundation upon which developments could be constructed.

Floodplains continually serve the local community in important ways. According to an environmental Web site, "They temporarily store floodwaters, improve water quality, provide important habitat for river wildlife, [and] create opportunities for recreation."[21]

Floodplains act as a natural sponge for heavy levels of rainfall or stormwater runoff. "During periods of high water, floodplains serve as natural sponges, storing and slowly releasing floodwaters. The floodplain provides additional 'storage,' reducing the velocity of the river and increasing the capacity of the river channel to move floodwaters downstream." In addition, "natural floodplains also help improve water quality. As water courses through the floodplain, plants serve as natural filters, trapping sediments and capturing pollutants. Nitrogen and phosphorous (found in fertilizers) that wash off farm fields, suburban backyards and city streets ignite a chemical chain reaction which reduces the amount of oxygen in the water, suffocating fish and other aquatic organisms. But, many floodplain plants will use nitrogen and phosphorous before they can reach the river, improving water quality." The trees and plants of a floodplain "anchor the river's banks, preventing bank erosion, and providing shade which reduces water temperatures." Finally, natural floodplains act as a habitat for fish and wildlife, as they "provide fish and wildlife the places they need to feed and reproduce. Nearly 70 percent of all vertebrate species rely upon the land along the river's edge—called the 'riparian' zone by scientists—during their life cycle. Healthy riparian zones create a vegetated transition zone between rivers and upland habitats, providing shelter, food, and migration corridors for river wildlife."[22] The vital role played by natural floodplains in the local community necessitated a thorough regulation of development proposed for these extremely sensitive areas.

On August 15, 1978, an ordinance introduced by Councilman Robert L. Reasoner was adopted by the Metropolitan Council. The purposes of Substitute Ordinance No. 78-840 were to control storm drainage facilities, grading, excavation, clearance, and other alteration of the land to limit the dangers of personal injuries or property damage caused by stormwater runoff. The bill was viewed as necessary to secure eligibility for flood insurance.

Ultimately, this bill established stormwater regulations, which were codified in the Stormwater Management Manual. The manual set standards for development activities in the floodway and floodplain. The basic standards set for floodplain development included requiring residential development to be elevated a minimum of four feet above the floodplain; requiring commercial development to be elevated a minimum of one foot above the floodplain; establishing "cut and fill" policy for Metropolitan Nashville which required new development must balance all "fill" in the one-hundred-year floodplain with an equal volume of "cut;" and establishing the requirement for submission to and review of development plans by the Department of Public Works.

Finally, this ordinance created the Stormwater Management Committee, which was established to hear variances to the floodplain regulations. In addition, Ordinance No. 78-843 was also placed into effect on January 1, 1979. That bill, sponsored by Councilman Earl C. Shacklett, amended the text of the Zoning Regulations as it related to the Floodplain Overlay District.

However, shortcomings to the regulations established by these ordinances soon became evident with the emergence of sprawl into

View of single-family home being constructed on elevated "fill" ground. The erosive cuts visible in the ground illustrate an unstable foundation upon which these homes were built.

Metropolitan Nashville and the ever-growing numbers of developmental proposals with which it was associated. Exemplifying the shortcomings of the ordinances was the overall authority given to the Stormwater Management Committee and the director of the Department of Public Works to determine which proposed floodplain developments were to receive ultimate approval. Numerous floodplain developments had met the requirements set forth by bills 78-840 and 78-843 and, thereby, received approval to proceed. However, with the emergence of sprawl, many of the floodplain developments approved and completed under these ordinances were beginning to adversely impact the neighboring community in which they were contiguous.

A more restrictive development policy for floodplains was needed to set modern standards pertaining to the developmental density of floodplains and restrict the land uses allowed in these environmentally sensitive areas. These restrictions would work to reduce stormwater runoff into the natural waterways from floodplain developments.

In addition, controlling the amount of the stormwater runoff from floodplain developments would guarantee a reduction in the amount of unnatural pollutants entering the natural waterways that the citizens of Metropolitan Nashville and its neighboring communities depended upon for drinking water.

Finally, it was essential in considering more modern standards for floodplain development to review the almost exclusive role that the Stormwater Management Committee and the Department of Public Works had in either approving or disapproving floodplain development. The Stormwater Management Committee represented an administrative body that did not give adequate consideration to the opinions of impacted citizens when considering a floodplain development proposal. It was essential that citizen input be given greater weight in the developmental review process to ensure the approval of the most stable floodplain development proposals.

Floodplain developments approved and constructed in the era of sprawl from 1985 to 1999 failed to include noticeable input from impacted citizens, and were based almost exclusively on the outdated regulations adopted in 1979. A large percentage of the floodplain developments constructed at that time were extremely dense and promoted heavy volumes of stormwater runoff into the natural waterway.

This heavy volume of stormwater runoff was directly attributed to an increased impervious surface created with the development of the property. Impervious surface was defined as "any ground or structural surface that water cannot penetrate or through which water penetrates with great difficulty"[23] and included roads, parking lots, and buildings (e.g., single-family residences, multi-family buildings, industrial warehouses). The covering of the natural floodplain acreage that was saturated by stormwater displaced large volumes of stormwater onto neighboring developments that were situated outside the floodplain. Ultimately, the voluminous stormwater increased flooding and drainage problems throughout the city with the passage of time.

Throughout the years, floodplain developments were allowed to proceed with the acquisition of the required permits. The Department of Public Works was responsible for issuing grading permits to developers if there was to be any land disturbance activities such as filling or excavating soil, the installation of pipes or digging ditches, and alterations to drainage channels. The Codes Administration was responsible for issuing building permits to developers for any improvements or additions to existing structures as well as for any new structures to be constructed within the floodplain.

Obtaining these permits was not extremely difficult. The developer was simply required to show that any residential structures included in the development proposal were to have a finished floor elevation of four feet above the one-hundred-year floodplain level. Conversely, all commercial buildings included within a development were to have a finished floor elevation of one foot above the one-hundred-year floodplain level. The soil used to elevate proposed structures was required to come from the same floodplain within which the construction was to take place. The soil was obtained by cutting into the floodplain and using the excavated ground as fill upon which the structures were to be constructed.

Upon my election to the Metropolitan Council in 1995, the adoption of more thorough floodplain development regulations by the metropolitan government was a high priority on my agenda. The entire Davidson County area consisted of 51,468 acres of one-hundred-year floodplain. "Of that total, 9,201 acres is vacant—about 18 percent."[24]

Undeveloped or semi-developed tracts of floodplain acreage saturated District 14 and adjacent council districts. There were approximately 450 acres of totally encompassed floodplain in District 14 alone, and approximately 700 acres of property heavily encumbered by the floodplain. Both the totally encompassed and heavily encumbered floodplain acreage was located in the bend in the Stones River, behind the Clover Bottom Developmental Center on Stewart's Ferry Pike, or along numerous residential arteries including McCrory Creek Road, Cloverwood Drive, Truxton Court, and Boulder Park Drive.

The floodplain tracts situated throughout Donelson-Hermitage were aligned with the Cumberland River, Stones River, Mill Creek, McCrory Creek, and Stoner Creek. These natural waterways, and the floodplains with which they were contiguous, represented unstable environments for development. The interaction that I had with resident citizens whose homes were situated within, or on the periphery of, the floodplains clearly illustrated the overwhelming flooding issues they had to face each year.

The residence of Joe Turley was situated just off the banks of McCrory Creek. He explains, "When we get a substantial amount of rainfall . . . sometimes the creek expands from 6 feet wide to 60 feet wide and overflows the banks. It [water] has at times gotten so high it's gotten into our crawl space under the house. It's happened about five times in the last 10 years."[25] This represented only one of a large number of flooding and drainage problems that was brought to my attention.

The overwhelming source of these problems could be directly attributed to floodplain development and the heavy volume of stormwater displacement on neighboring developments. Such floodplain development had obtained approval through the approximately twenty-year-old regulations. This further demonstrated the need to adopt more stringent floodplain regulations to protect the established community and preserve the natural environment of the floodplain.

In 1998, the first attempt to address floodplain development standards for Metropolitan Nashville was initiated by District 12 Councilman Phil Ponder. "Ponder got involved in the issue when Wal-Mart wanted to build a store on Old Hickory Boulevard in his

Hermitage district, but was stymied by complicated zoning codes dealing with the amount of impermeable surface—such as paved parking lots—allowed in floodplains."[26]

The site targeted by Wal-Mart, upon which it was to construct a massive super center, fronted Old Hickory Boulevard, south of the Juarez Drive intersection. However, one of the main problems associated with constructing an approximately two-hundred-thousand-square-foot super center on the acreage was the location of the natural Stoner Creek on the back part of the site. The floodplain aligned with Stoner Creek encompassed about one-third of the total acreage of the site.

The existing floodplain development standards included specific setbacks and buffers for proposed construction. The Old Hickory Boulevard site was simply too small to meet the setback and buffer requirements for floodplain development to allow for the approval of such a large commercial proposal. According to Ponder, Wal-Mart was "trying to get this OK'd and they finally just said, 'This is too much.' They just couldn't overcome it."[27]

Ponder then organized a Floodplain Review Committee to address the issues associated with existing floodplain development standards and develop legislation that would amend the existing floodplain development standards of Metropolitan Nashville. Members of the Floodplain Review Committee included Department of Planning Director Jeff Browning, District 15 Councilman Roy Dale, District 10 Councilman Tim Garrett, Shain Dennison of the Metropolitan Parks and Recreation Department Greenways Division, Doug Delaney of the Development Office of the Metropolitan Development and Housing Authority, Tom Palko of the Metropolitan Department of Public Works, Lon (Sonny) West of the Metropolitan Codes Administration, Alan Jones of the Tennessee Environmental Council, John Stern of the Nashville Neighborhood Alliance, Mickey Sullivan of Gresham Smith & Partners, Bill Acree, and Barry Sulkin. Ponder served as chairman of the committee.

Although not a member of the committee, I attended a number of its meetings held at the Metropolitan Planning Commission Conference Room and listened intently to the discussions, which

Councilman Phil Ponder (Photo courtesy of Phil Ponder)

involved greenway interest in floodplains, review of Stormwater Management regulations, review of floodplain/floodway maps, and amendments to the existing Code of Laws addressing floodplains.

One of the more important topics the committee failed to debate was the acceptable developmental density of floodplain development and the short- and long-term consequences that extremely dense floodplain developments would have on the neighboring community and the natural floodplain environment. That failure to address the developmental density issue illustrated the underlying goal of the committee, which was to liberalize the floodplain development standards of Metropolitan Nashville.

Following months of deliberation within the committee, Ponder was prepared to introduce the appropriate legislation that would address the findings of the Floodplain Review Committee.

Councilman Ponder introduced an ordinance to amend various sections of Title 17 of the Metropolitan Code of Laws, the zoning code of the Metropolitan Government of Nashville and Davidson County on February 1, 2000. This legislation ultimately referred to as Substitute Ordinance No. BL99-117 amended numerous sections of the Metropolitan Zoning Code.

The overwhelming number of amendments proposed by the ordinance had my full support. They represented a streamlining in governmental procedure from which the city would reap both short- and long-term benefits. However, the sections of the ordinance proposing amendments for floodplain/floodway development standards received my utmost attention.

The existing procedure for addressing floodplain development was in desperate need of overhauling. And yet the proposed amendment worked to liberalize the city policy. Such liberalization of the floodplain regulations was in direct contrast to what was needed

Figure 3-1

How the Metropolitan Council Voted on Substitute Ordinance No. BL99-117 on March 21, 1999

Supported

- Chris Ferrell
- Leo Waters
- Howard Gentry
- Brenda Gilmore
- Melvin Black
- Lawrence Hall
- Eileen Beehan
- Earl Campbell
- Lawrence Hart
- James Dillard
- Bettye Balthrop
- Feller Brown
- Phil Ponder
- Tony Derryberry
- J. B. Loring
- Amanda McClendon
- Ludye Wallace
- Morris Haddox
- Edward Whitmore
- Norma Hand
- Bob Bogen
- Jim Shulman
- Michelle Arriola
- Janis Sontany
- Jason Alexander
- Saletta Holloway
- Michael Kerstetter
- Don Knoch
- Craig Jenkins
- Ron Turner
- Lynn Williams
- Vic Lineweaver

Opposed

- Carolyn Baldwin Tucker
- James Bruce Stanley
- Ronnie Greer
- Ginger Hausser
- John Summers

Abstained

- David Briley

by Metropolitan Nashville as it was being adversely impacted by sprawl.

According to Ponder, the deletion of the existing floodplain tables from the Metropolitan Zoning Code was necessitated when the Stormwater Management Review Committee recommended strengthening the Stormwater Management Manual in 1999. The recommended new provisions were signed into law by Mayor Phil Bredesen on September 17, 1999. The primary new provision prohibited development in the floodway and established a fifty-foot buffer on each side of the floodway that was ineligible for development.

Ponder believed these restrictions more than offset what he considered were lenient restrictions provided by the zoning code which permitted floodplain disturbance and provided no buffer area. Ponder also noted that the Floodplain Review Committee had recommended the removal of the floodplain tables from the Metropolitan Zoning Code at its meeting on October 27, 1999.

The new provisions to the Stormwater Management Manual, however, addressed only nonresidential development. These provisions failed to regulate residential developments, specifically multi-family complexes which represented extremely dense developments.

In effect, the amendment to the floodplain/floodway development standards eliminated the regulation of both multi-family and nonresidential developments (e.g., churches, day care centers, community facilities, commercial, and industrial establishments) in the floodway/floodplain from the Metropolitan Zoning Ordinance and permitted the Stormwater Regulations administered by the Stormwater Management Committee (Department of Public Works) to exclusively address such dense development proposals; removed the Metropolitan Council and the Metropolitan Planning Commission and/or Department of Planning from regulating floodplain/floodway development proposals; and designated only a fifty-foot undeveloped buffer from the floodway into the floodplain for proposed developments.

The remaining floodplain acreage situated outside this buffer was considered eligible for development and promoted an increased impervious surface ratio for development in the floodplain by permitting any type of land use, regardless of density, to be developed in the floodplain. An increase in the impervious surface ratio eliminated open ground into which stormwater is absorbed. The substantial reduction in open ground promoted a greater volume of stormwater runoff into the natural waterways and onto neighboring developments.

Following its passage on first reading by the Metropolitan Council on February 1, 2000, Substitute Ordinance No. BL99-117 was heard by the Planning Commission on March 2, 2000. The bill in its entirety, including the section amending the review process for floodplain/floodway development, was approved by the Planning Commission six to zero. It was then scheduled to be heard by the Metropolitan Council on second and third readings. After being approved by the Metropolitan Council on second reading, the bill was scheduled to be heard on third and final reading on March 21, 2000.

During the debate by the Metropolitan Council over this bill, I informed the councilmembers that my opposition to the bill was associated with the proposed amendments to Chapter 17.28 (environmental and operational performance standards). The proposed amendments would liberalize the floodway/floodplain development standards by removing residential multi-family and nonresidential development proposals from the zoning code.

Instead, such high-impact developments were to be addressed almost exclusively by the Stormwater Management Committee. The Planning Commission and its staff of professional land-use planners, along with the Metropolitan Council, would be substantially removed from the floodplain review process. Ultimately, the elimination of the Metropolitan Council from this process removed public input as a key factor to be used in determining the acceptability of a floodplain proposal.

Also, the establishment of only a fifty-foot undisturbed buffer from the floodway into the floodplain raised serious questions as to its ability to preserve and protect the natural environment of the floodplain, reduce heavy volumes of stormwater displacement, and assist in controlling the impact of flood waters on neighboring developments.

The close of debate brought a motion for the adoption of the bill on third and final reading. The motion was seconded and the bill was adopted by a vote of 32-5-1. The approved bill was signed by Mayor Bill Purcell on March 27, 2000, and became effective on March 29, 2000.

The passage of Substitute Ordinance No. BL99-117 motivated me to begin researching the issue of floodplain development and the impact this less-than-restrictive law would have on the natural environment of the floodplain and the existing developments situated in close proximity to the floodplains. The research of this issue began in April 2000.

My personal experiences with floodplain development, flooding, and stormwater drainage accentuated the information uncovered by the research. Prior to my election to the Metropolitan Council, I had served on numerous neighborhood steering committees addressing development proposals. The 1987 Gateway mixed-use proposal was situated in the six-hundred-acre bend in the Stones River. Approximately 40 percent, or 240 acres, of the property targeted for construction by this proposal was located in the one-hundred-year floodplain.

As a member of the Gateway Steering Committee, I experienced firsthand a lackadaisical attitude of both private developers and metropolitan officials in addressing realistic concerns raised by resident citizens pertaining to the development of the floodplain acreage and the subsequent flooding which it promoted. I also became very familiar with the metropolitan land-use review process and witnessed a failure of metropolitan officials to give priority consideration to either the flooding or drainage issues associated with floodplain development.

Having been appointed to serve on the Stormwater Management Task Force (1998–1999) permitted my interaction with both private and government engineers while addressing the severe drainage problems of Metropolitan Nashville. I learned of numerous sources of stormwater drainage overflow. A substantial number of the drainage problems were attributed to the development of floodplains and the stormwater displacement with which they were associated.

Finally, I was obligated as an elected representative of the citizens of Metropolitan Nashville to address the shortcomings of the new floodplain policy that became effective with the passage of Substitute Ordinance No. BL99-117. The liberal policy toward floodplain development contrasted directly with the regulatory needs of the city.

Floodplains represented extremely sensitive areas of the city. Such sensitivity required that floodplain development be more thoroughly regulated. Restricting the types and density of developments allowed in floodplains would work to control stormwater displacement and overall flooding forced on the established community. It would also work to ensure stable additions to the community.

One of the initial steps taken in my research of floodplain development issues was a meeting in April 2000 with Interim Director Karen Nicely of the Department of Planning and Director Randall Dunn of the Department of Public Works. During the meeting, issues raised by councilmembers and private citizens over Substitute Ordinance No. BL99-117 were discussed.

It became evident that neither Nicely nor Dunn were receptive to the idea of introducing a more thorough ordinance to regulate floodplain development. However, within two months of the meeting, the Department of Planning had hired a new director, Rick Bernhardt. He would play a vital role in developing and adopting a much more restrictive floodplain development policy dictated by the recent growth trends of Metropolitan Nashville.

Over a twenty-one-month period, my research involved platting both semi- and undeveloped floodplain parcels situated along the Cumberland River, Stones River, Harpeth River, McCrory Creek, and Mill Creek. Criteria used to include a parcel in the floodplain table were that each parcel was a minimum of ten acres in size, each parcel was either undeveloped or semi-developed, at least 25 percent of each parcel was encumbered by the one-hundred-year floodplain, each parcel lacked direct access to a major thoroughfare, and access to the closest major thoroughfare from these parcels was obtained along minimally sized residential arteries serving established residential districts.

Even with the criteria restricting inclusion on the table, the platting of these floodplain parcels resulted in an eleven-page, seventy-eight parcel floodplain table totaling 5,504 acres of property that was either totally encompassed or substantially encumbered by the one-hundred-year floodplain. The parcels were located in the Old Hickory, Donelson, Hermitage, Madison, Bellevue, and Inglewood suburban communities of Metropolitan Nashville.

The table designated that approximately thirty-seven established subdivisions were situated directly contiguous to the undeveloped or semi-developed floodplain parcels. They would be adversely impacted by the approval and construction of dense developmental proposals on neighboring floodplain acreage. The adversity forced on the existing subdivisions involved increased flooding or stormwater overflow. In addition, the projected increased levels of commuter traffic onto the narrow residential arteries would be a detriment to the quiet residential environment of the established subdivisions. Ultimately, this table served as an evidentiary tool when making my arguments for a more restrictive floodplain development ordinance.

The floodplain table illustrated many areas of Metropolitan Nashville that would be adversely impacted by the dense floodplain developments to be approved under the recently passed liberalized review process. The areas of the city that were to be most adversely impacted included highway infrastructure, public schools, and neighboring residential subdivisions. I toured many of these properties in order to familiarize myself with the topographical layout of the parcels as well as the existing developmental landscape and the infrastructure (e.g., highways, schools) serving the properties.

In the vast majority of instances, the floodplain parcels represented isolated acreage that was served by inappropriate infrastructure. The approval of proposed development on such properties demanded an extensive review of the proposed plan and the impact it was to have on the established community. In addition, the large size of many of the floodplain properties included on the table necessitated the adoption of a much more restrictive floodplain policy by Metropolitan Nashville. Finally, regulating the developmental density on the large floodplain parcels would reduce the impact of new development on the already outdated infrastructure.

In June 2000, the new director of the Department of Planning Rick Bernhardt and I toured District 14. During the tour, Bernhardt was informed of my working toward a more restrictive policy toward floodplain development.

One of the key areas that we viewed during the tour was the massive bend in the Stones River. It was noted there was inappropriate access to this acreage, and that at least 40 percent of the total acreage was situated within the one-hundred-year floodplain of both the Stones River and Cumberland River. Bernhardt informed me of his desire to review the existing policy toward floodplain development and amend the policy where it was needed. The open communication promoted with Bernhardt's tour of each council district in Metropolitan Nashville clearly initiated a new era in the relationship between the Department of Planning, the Planning Commission and the Metropolitan Council.

On August 25, 2000, Councilmen Bob Bogen and J. B. Loring and I met with Bernhardt to discuss the issues associated with floodplain development and the current metropolitan policy regulating such development. Bogen represented District 23 which included Bellevue and the Harpeth River. Loring represented District 15 which included

Council member Carolyn Baldwin Tucker (Photo courtesy of Metro Government of Nashville and Davidson County/Gary Layda)

Councilman Bob Bogen (Photo courtesy of Metro Government of Nashville and Davidson County/Gary Layda)

the Pennington Bend of the Cumberland River as well as Mill Creek. The natural waterways and floodplains located in these council districts designated the need for a stronger, more restrictive floodplain development policy in Metropolitan Nashville.

It was determined during the meeting that the professional land-use planners from the Department of Planning would play an active role in the development of an ordinance restricting floodplain development. The meeting also allowed me to make known to key officials of my desire to have metropolitan officials more actively regulate floodplain development in our city.

On September 18, 2000, I corresponded with key councilmembers who had raised concerns over the floodplain policy adopted with the passage of Substitute Ordinance No. BL99-117. The councilmembers included Carolyn Baldwin Tucker, Ronnie Greer, Ginger Hausser, and John Summers. The mailing updated the councilmembers on the status of the research I had begun approximately five months earlier. In addition, they were informed of the plan to file legislation in the near future that would amend bill No. 99-117. Finally, they were notified of upcoming meetings that would be scheduled with attorney

Don Jones and director Rick Bernhardt to address the floodplain issue. Their input on this issue was vital. Therefore, their attendance at these meetings was requested.

The first meeting to address city policy governing floodplain development was scheduled for the afternoon of November 14, 2000. The meeting was held in Rick Bernhardt's office in the Planning Commission building. The councilmembers invited to attend the meeting included Carolyn Baldwin Tucker, Ronnie Greer, Ginger Hausser, John Summers, Bob Bogen, and J. B. Loring. Also invited to attend were John Stern, president of the Nashville Neighborhood Alliance, and Stan Scott, with whom I had served on the Stormwater Management Task Force.

Although not all invited were able to attend the meeting, the open discussion promoted by the meeting clearly designated the desire on the part of both councilmembers and private citizens to have a more restrictive policy in Metropolitan Nashville. It was agreed that a more restrictive floodplain development policy should concentrate on either regulating developmental density on floodplains or designate a certain percentage of floodplain acreage be maintained as open space.

However, it was believed that an attempt to amend the existing policy that had only been previously adopted in March would be severely opposed. It was decided to delay any formal attempt to amend the existing policy. This gave me the opportunity to interact more closely with numerous and varied individuals and groups that had an interest in the floodplain development issue.

In January 2002, Mayor Bill Purcell introduced the Stormwater Management Master Plan to the Metropolitan Council. The plan was based on the findings of the Stormwater Management Task Force and included the creation of a Stormwater Division of the Department of Water Services. The Stormwater Division was to work with members of the Metropolitan Council and private citizens to relieve drainage problems throughout Metropolitan Nashville.

The funding for the drainage projects was to come from an annual budgetary allocation. Such an allocation represented the first formal funding for flooding and drainage projects in the history of Metropolitan Nashville. The projected cost of flooding and drainage projects at the time of the implementation of the Stormwater

Management Master Plan ranged from $20 million to $70 million. In addition, it was my belief that "simply because we have a plan in place doesn't mean we should continue detrimental development. Such development will only increase the cost of this comprehensive storm water drainage program on an annual basis."[28]

Based upon the adverse impact intense floodplain developmental density would have on the annual expenditures of the newly adopted Stormwater Management Master Plan, I began concentrating on regulating floodplain development through restricting the density of developments allowed on the environmentally sensitive floodplains. This strategy involved amending Title 17 of the Metropolitan Code of Laws, the zoning code of the Metropolitan Government of Nashville and Davidson County.

In cooperation with attorney Don Jones, legal advisor to the Metropolitan Council, Section 17.28.040 (floodplain/floodway development standards) represented the codes section that was to be amended to achieve a more restrictive policy. In order to restrict developmental density in floodplains, it was determined during numerous meetings with Jones that only the least intense zoning districts of the Metropolitan Zoning Code should be considered eligible for floodplain development.

The legislation to amend the policy of Metropolitan Nashville governing floodplain/floodway development was introduced to the Metropolitan Council on April 2, 2002. The Ordinance No. BL2002-1021 was to amend Section 17.28.040 floodplain/floodway development standards by providing new restrictions on development in floodplains and floodways. The ordinance included the following:

> WHEREAS, some zoning districts are proper for floodplain/floodway development as such propriety is based upon: (1) the low intensity development associated with these districts, (2) a reduced impervious surface ratio (ISR) permitted by this less intense development, and (3) conformance to the natural conservation policy for environmentally sensitive floodplain/floodway parcels; and
>
> WHEREAS, other zoning districts are improper for floodplain/floodway development such impropriety is based upon: (1) the high density

> development associated with these districts, (2) an increased impervious surface ratio (ISR) permitted by this more intense development, and (3) nonconformance to the natural conservation policy for environmentally sensitive floodplain/floodway parcels; and
>
> WHEREAS, permitting development in certain zoning districts which feature the above requirements while prohibiting development in certain zoning districts which demonstrate impropriety, and prohibiting variances or exception to these provisions protect land and property values while promoting the health, safety and welfare of the citizens of metropolitan government.[29]

Ultimately, the proposed ordinance did not prohibit floodplain development, but concentrated on restricting the developmental density allowed on acreage encumbered by floodplains by classifying zoning districts as either proper or improper. The zoning districts that promoted less dense developments were considered proper. Those that were considered improper promoted extreme density of development. It was believed that by restricting the developmental density of floodplains, much more open ground would be preserved and would prevent the covering of the natural floodplain acreage by an unnatural impervious surface.

For example, the RS80 single-family district was classified as proper for floodplain development and required each residential lot to be no smaller than eighty thousand square feet, or two acres in size. The construction of large single-family residences on two-acre lots allowed for the preservation of a substantial percentage of natural floodplain as open ground.

In contrast, the RS10 single-family district was classified as improper. This district required each residential lot to be a minimum of ten thousand square feet, or one-quarter of an acre. A proposed RS10 subdivision on floodplain acreage allowed for four homes per acre. The construction of the single-family residences on these small lots promoted the covering of a larger percentage of natural floodplain by an unnatural impervious surface. Such covering reduced the amount of open ground available for stormwater absorption and created greater volumes of stormwater displacement and flooding onto neighboring properties.

The ordinance was co-sponsored by thirty fellow councilmembers, clearly illustrating a county-wide concern pertaining to the floodplain development issue. The co-sponsors were Bob Bogen, Michael Kerstetter, Phil Ponder, Tony Derryberry, Lawrence Hall, Don Majors, Lawrence Hart, Carolyn Baldwin Tucker, Brenda Gilmore, Feller Brown, Bettye Balthrop, Ron Nollner, Earl Campbell, J. B. Loring, Morris Haddox, Edward Whitmore, Norma Hand, Amanda McClendon, Ronnie Greer, Janis Sontany, Michelle Arriola, Jim Shulman, Ludye Wallace, John Summers, Saletta Holloway, Jason Alexander, Craig Jenkins, Ron Turner, Lynn Williams, and Ginger Hausser.

In time, a number of the co-sponsors to this original ordinance would prove to be valuable allies in the legislative battle that occurred over the attempt to more thoroughly regulate floodplain development.

Immediately following the introduction of Ordinance No. BL2002-1021, concerns were raised over the bill. The primary argument raised by opponents of the bill was centered on differing criteria to be used to regulate floodplain development. Developers believed that the regulation of floodplain development should be performance based, rather than limiting developmental density on floodplains based on zoning categories.

Roy Dale, former councilmember and civil engineer with Dale & Associates, favored "more flexibility in the criteria." In addition, John Sheley, executive vice president of the Home Builders Association of Middle Tennessee, believed "flexibility in current regulations lets developers do off-site improvements to stormwater systems when they build in floodplains."[30]

However, allowing a liberal flexibility in floodplain development regulations would undermine the attempt to adopt a more stringent growth-management plan for Metropolitan Nashville.

John Stern, president of the Nashville Neighborhood Alliance, concurred with that position. Stern believed that there was "a desire to increase the level of protection of natural areas." He further stated that "our biggest problem is not dealing with hydrology, water being filtered or moved. It's growth management."[31]

In April 2002, I opened dialogue with a private environmental group that had a definite interest in preserving the natural environment of floodplains. The Cumberland River Compact (CRC) is a "unique non-profit group that believes we can have both a strong economy and a healthy environment."[32] The correspondence that I had with Margot Farnsworth of the CRC included a fax that had substantial information I had uncovered during my research.

I was invited to address a meeting of the Board of Directors of the CRC to inform them of the ordinance that was pending before the Metropolitan Council and to answer any questions about the legislation. One of the topics raised during the meeting included a discussion of the ordinance promoting less-dense development on floodplain acreage. Ultimately, the board members of the Cumberland River Compact voiced their support of the pending ordinance.

Due to the substantial number of concerns raised and the wide variety of opinions given on how best to restrict floodplain development, when the bill came before the Metropolitan Council for second reading on May 9, 2002, I moved to have it deferred indefinitely and re-referred to the Planning Commission. The motion was seconded and adopted by voice vote of the Metropolitan Council.

The action taken by the municipal legislature of Metropolitan Nashville on this bill brought sincere attention by appropriate metropolitan authorities on this issue. The viability of the policy in place to regulate floodplain development was questioned and debated for the following six months.

One of the meetings scheduled to address the floodplain issue occurred on September 30, 2002, in the Metropolitan Council Office. Those in attendance were legal advisor Don Jones, Planning Department Director Rick Bernhardt, District 11 Councilman Feller Brown, and I. The meeting lasted no longer than one hour.

The hour-long conversation, however, was very informative, specifically for Bernhardt, as a wide variety of developmental issues were discussed. Councilman Brown clearly voiced his desire to have more restrictive floodplain development standards in place. His position was based primarily due to the flooding and stormwater overflow experiences he had as council representative for the Hadley Bend area of the Cumberland River. Brown would become one of the more vocally supportive fellow councilmembers for the legislation regulating floodplain development.

The Planning Commission heard Ordinance No. BL2002-1021 on November 14, 2002. The professional staff provided its analysis of the ordinance to the Commission following months of both independent and cooperative review of the legislation. During the review process, I had informed the staff that an amendment would be filed to reclassify the RS20 and R20 zoning districts as improper rather than proper.

The recommendation that the professional staff gave to the Planning Commission was their belief:

> that the approach to floodplain regulation proposed by this text change proposal is artificial and not sufficiently focused on preserving the natural floodplain. Rather than dividing up existing zoning districts and permitting unrestricted development in certain districts, staff would recommend a regulation that preserves a certain percentage of floodplain in all zoning districts. This is the approach reflected in the current cluster lot provisions. While this text change proposal would further limit development of lands within the floodplain, staff does not believe this is either the appropriate approach or goes far enough. Therefore, the staff recommends disapproval.[33]

Following the staff review of the issue, a number of councilmembers addressed the Planning Commission and voiced their support for the more restrictive legislation. The councilmembers were responding to written notice that I had sent to them on November 6, 2002, informing them of the current status of the floodplain legislation and the fact that the Planning Commission was to hear the bill on November 14. As a result of my letter, councilmembers J. B. Loring and Feller Brown addressed the Commission to voice their support of the bill. They informed the Commission of the wide variety of developmental issues associated with the current floodplain development policy.

When addressing the Commission, I informed them of an amendment to the ordinance that would change the categories of "proper" and "improper" to "permitted" and "prohibited."

Following the close of the public hearing, the Commission debated the bill. It was determined that there remained certain specific aspects of the legislation that needed to be addressed and, until they were, the Planning Commission unanimously voted to defer the bill

Councilman Feller Brown (Photo courtesy of Feller Brown)

until the first meeting in January. The two-month period would provide enough time to have the necessary metropolitan officials cooperate in developing a more effective and protective policy regulating floodplain development in Metropolitan Nashville. Also, I would be able to inform environmental groups of the ordinance and request their open endorsement of the change in metropolitan policy.

A key environmental group that was informed of the ordinance was the Tennessee Environmental Council (TEC). In late November, I had contacted the TEC and specifically outlined the purposes of the legislation.

On December 3, 2002, I received a letter from the TEC openly endorsing the Bill No. 2002-1021. Executive Director Will Calloway stated in the letter that the attempt to control development in floodplain areas represented a "type of proactive growth management" and that it was "very valuable for communities." He further stated that "development in floodplains causes problems both in economic and environmental terms. Damage and loss because of persistent flooding of homes and businesses leave many individuals without adequate insurance or with significant financial constraints. In many instances, better zoning restrictions would have prevented building in these areas. Additionally, reducing the natural area that serves to accommodate flood waters often redirects these waters elsewhere, creating a new area prone to flooding. The value of floodplains as natural retention basins cannot be measured simply on a dollar per acre basis. Finally, these open spaces serve as a habitat for wildlife, provide recreation areas for communities and add to the aesthetic value of any neighborhood." The letter ended with the statement that "TEC endorses Bill No. 2002-1021 and encourages the Metro Council to pass the improved zoning regulations during its next legislative session."[34]

The Tennessee Environmental Council represented one of the most influential environmental organizations in the state of Tennessee. Obtaining its open endorsement of the ordinance played a positive role in the ultimate passage of a more restrictive floodplain developmental policy for Metropolitan Nashville.

A meeting was scheduled for December 13, 2002, at the Planning Commission conference room to discuss further the floodplain ordinance. I was reminded by legal advisor Don Jones of the importance of including all interested parties in the debate over the bill. Such open communication and cooperation would assist in creating an acceptable regulatory ordinance for floodplain development. Those that attended the meeting were "representatives from the Metropolitan Planning Department, developers, Metro Attorney Don Jones, representatives of the Metro Water Services Department and other council members."[35]

The information shared between different community interests, including governmental, developmental, residential, and legislative, played a vital role in determining which direction the ordinance should take to provide more thorough guidelines for floodplain development. During the meeting, regulations governing floodplain development in other cities were discussed. The areas included Tulsa, Oklahoma; Carroll County, Maryland; and Rockville, Maryland. The examples were used to determine how Metropolitan Nashville should regulate floodplain development.

On December 20, 2002, I received a letter from Bernhardt that included the first full draft of alternative text amendments addressing floodplain development and cluster lot options. The text amendments were intended to expand the preservation of 50 percent of the floodplain rule currently for cluster lots to all development, except downtown and industrial uses; clarify that the 50 percent rule is a "no-touch zone" and establish the appropriate parameters for use; limit the cluster lot option to planned-unit developments only; and clarify the purpose of the cluster lot option.

These amendments represented a revision to the original bill that guaranteed the preservation of a substantial percentage of floodplain acreage as undisturbed open space. This would preserve wildlife habitat and act as a buffer between the developed floodplain acreage and the natural waterway. In that role, it would work to filter stormwater runoff from the floodplain developments, thereby substantially reducing the amount of unnatural pollutants released into the natural waterway. Finally, the undisturbed open space represented a much larger area in the floodplain that was prohibited from development than the minimal fifty-foot buffer established under the existing guidelines.

On January 7, 2003, a public hearing was held on Ordinance No. BL2002-1021 before the Metropolitan Council. The public hearing witnessed citizens that both supported and opposed the bill addressing the council. During the hearing "some residents said the bill was on target for addressing the county's extensive flooding and drainage problems, while others complained that the measure would significantly decrease the value of their vacant properties in floodplain areas." In addition, members of "the development community criticized it as being overly strict."[36]

In response to the variety of opinions on the bill, I moved that it be deferred until the February 4, 2003, council meeting. The motion was seconded and approved by a voice vote of the Metropolitan Council.

On February 4, 2003, the bill was further deferred to the February 18 meeting of the Metropolitan Council. That deferral was requested by me because the revisions to the original bill had just been completed and the revised ordinance was scheduled to be considered by the Planning Commission at its February 13 meeting. David Kleinfelter, manager for the Land Development and Design division of the Metropolitan Planning Department claimed that "this is a definite compromise." In addition, he believed "this proposal increases the protection significantly in a way that's evenly distributed."[37]

The revised bill was designated Substitute Ordinance No. BL2002-1021. The substitute ordinance amended development standards by providing new restrictions on development in floodplains and floodways. The bill amended the floodplain/floodway development standards by constraining development, limiting encroachment, and protecting the floodway and floodplain areas of Metro Nashville. It also regulated residential and non-residential development in Metro Nashville.

On March 18, 2003, the substitute ordinance was amended by councilmembers John Summers, Feller Brown, and me to further clarify the 50 percent "no-touch zone" and thereby work to preserve and protect the natural floodplain areas of Metropolitan Nashville.

The amendment involved the deletion of the first paragraph of Substitute Ordinance No. BL2002-1021 in its entirety, and substituting it with the following:

> A.1. Preserved floodplain. Except as otherwise noted below, all development proposed on property that is not developed, as defined herein, encumbered by natural floodplain or floodway, as of the effective date of this ordinance, shall leave a minimum of fifty percent of the natural floodplain area, including all of the floodway area, or all of the floodway area plus fifty feet on each side of the waterway, whichever is greater, undisturbed and in its original, natural state. The preserved floodplain shall be adjacent to the floodway or, as otherwise approved by the zoning administrator or by the metropolitan planning commission if the property is the subject of a subdivision or rezoning application. The clearing of trees and brush within the undisturbed area shall be prohibited. For purposes of this subsection, a portion of the lot is improved with any material that substantially reduces or prevents the infiltration of stormwater by the total horizontal area of the lot including, but not limited to, roofs, streets, sidewalks and parking lots paved with asphalt, concrete, compacted sand, compacted gravel or clay. Evidence that a portion of the property is developed shall include grading or building permits and/or aerial photographs. Absent grading or building permits, a lot shall not be deemed developed under this section if the use of the property was for agricultural activities.[38]

The revised substitute ordinance eliminated the concept of proper and improper zoning districts; expanded the requirement that 50 percent of the floodplain be preserved in its natural state from residential cluster lot subdivisions to all development, except in six intensive zoning districts used in the most urban parts of the city; required 50 percent of the natural floodplain/floodway remain as a "no-touch zone" without any manipulation of the floodplain; and established exceptions to the no-touch zone for variances approved by the Stormwater Management Committee, greenways, and compliance with flood insurance standards and FEMA to maintain Metro's eligibility for federal flood insurance.

Councilman John Summers (Photo courtesy of Metro Government of Nashville and Davidson County/Gary Layda)

Ultimately, the revisions to Metropolitan Nashville's floodplain development standards were as effective in controlling developmental density and preserving open space along the one-hundred-year floodplains as prohibiting certain types of land uses.

On February 10, 2003, the Honey Brook Homeowners Association expressed their appreciation of my working to address the issue of floodplain development. The Honey Brook subdivision was "up in arms over this issue." It was relayed to me that "the community has had 28 of its 94 homes placed in the one-hundred-year floodplain with the updating of the FEMA flood maps." In addition, the president of the association claimed that she was "in the process of learning as much as possible to protect our property values as Nashville in their short sighted way develops us underwater." Finally, the Honey Brook homeowners let me know that "if we can help you please do not hesitate to let us know."[39]

Similarly, on March 18, 2003, Councilman John Summers, a co-sponsor of the floodplain bill, distributed a letter from the Board of Directors of the Lion's Head Homeowners Association strongly favoring the passage of the substitute ordinance. In the letter, the homeowners claimed that they were "currently experiencing storm water runoff problems resulting from over development along Richland Creek and its tributaries." Furthermore, they expressed their opposition to "any further development in the floodplain/floodway and any amendment that will weaken the restrictions provided by this bill."[40]

Such written correspondence by adversely affected resident citizens was greatly appreciated by me and those with whom I had been working on the issue and strengthened the arguments favoring a more thorough regulation of floodplain development in Metropolitan Nashville.

The Planning Commission recommended approval of the substitute ordinance on February 13, 2003. It was passed on second reading before the Metropolitan Council on February 18, 2003, and scheduled to be heard on third and final reading on March 18, 2003.

In preparation for the final vote by the Metropolitan Council on this bill, I corresponded with all councilmembers on March 10, 2003, requesting their support for the bill's passage.

Included in the mailing was an outline of the thirty-two-month legislative process that brought us to that point. The process involved substantial research of the existing policy governing floodplain development and the platting of both semi- and undeveloped floodplain parcels within Metropolitan Nashville and Davidson County.

In addition, a list of those interested parties with whom I had cooperated since April 2000 to develop the most comprehensive and acceptable legislation to address floodplain development was attached. This list included Director Rick Bernhardt and the staff of the Department of Planning, Director Scott Potter of the Water Services Department, Stormwater Division Director Tom Palko, the Tennessee Environmental Council, the Cumberland River Compact, the Home Builders Association, the Nashville Neighborhood Alliance, the Metropolitan Council, and the Purcell administration. It was also noted that all of the parties mentioned had endorsed the ordinance.

It appeared that Substitute Ordinance No. BL2002-1021 would receive final passage without controversy. However, opponents of the legislation that had remained quiet throughout the process suddenly decided to voice their opposition.

In a mailing from Rick Bernhardt on Friday March 14, 2003, I was informed of his meeting with representatives of commercial and industrial interests pertaining to the floodplain ordinance. The business representatives attending that meeting included Bill Hawkins, Wood Caldwell, Leslie Shechter, Don Williams, Kim Hawkins, Jimmy Granberry, Dan Barge III, and Berry Holt of St. Thomas Health Services.

They proposed to Bernhardt and his staff that all commercial property be exempt from the bill and that Mayor Purcell veto it until the city undertook a full economic impact of the bill as proposed. In addition, they wanted the removal of the limitation on the potential amount of variance that could be granted by the Stormwater Committee provided the variance would improve floodwater storage and water and environmental quality. Finally, they requested a one-meeting deferral of the bill to see if any additional issues were present in the ordinance.

The deferral of the ordinance was to be my decision as sponsor of the bill. The failure of the commercial and industrial interests to notify me of their concerns pertaining to this bill raised questions about the necessity to act on those concerns. Those interests had been given many chances to voice their concerns during the months of deliberation. Their refusal to raise such concerns until final consideration by the Metropolitan Council questioned the validity of the concerns.

The main concern of St. Thomas Health Services was centered on the restrictions the new policy would place on its attempt to develop a 6.12-acre parcel of property that was known as the Knights of Columbus property. A large percentage of that property was situated within the one-hundred-year floodplain. St. Thomas had planned a major expansion onto that property. However, the constraints placed upon the property by the pending ordinance were considered by St. Thomas to be an overwhelming obstacle to its planned development. St. Thomas had invested approximately $6 million in floodplain property. The development of that property under the pending ordinance required St. Thomas to seek numerous waivers and variances. As a result, the corporate officials viewed the ordinance as effectively condemning their property without receiving compensation.

Deferral of the bill for one meeting was being considered until I received a telephone call from Councilman Feller Brown on the night of Saturday March 15, 2003. During the telephone conversation, Brown informed me of a certified letter that he had received that day from St. Thomas Health Services. The letter notified him of its objections to the pending floodplain ordinance and requested that he vote to defeat the legislation on third reading. Brown voiced to me his frustrations over the manner and time in which the mail was sent by St. Thomas. He was further disturbed when I informed him that I had not received any such mailing from St. Thomas or any other party opposing the legislation. In my role as the primary sponsor of the floodplain ordinance, I should not have been ignored by St. Thomas in its communication with the Metropolitan Council. However, the refusal to include me in the mailings clearly illustrated the motive of St. Thomas to have the ordinance simply defeated. The actions taken by St. Thomas over the weekend ended any further consideration of deferring the bill.

Over the following three days, I contacted a number of other councilmembers and inquired of any mailings they had received from St. Thomas. I was informed by all that they had received the mailings from St. Thomas. The strategy implemented by St. Thomas to have the ordinance defeated represented old-school politics. That political school of thought promoted the interests of one over the interests of the entire city. The rapid pace of growth that had descended upon Metropolitan Nashville with the emergence of sprawl clearly exposed this political method and the means with which it was implemented as selfish policy. The practice of special interests to influence councilmembers did not include a complete picture of the impact their positions would have on the community in general. Ultimately, these political antics raised controversy as to the position the Metropolitan Council was being asked to take on the bill.

Substitute Ordinance No. BL2002-1021 came before the Metropolitan Council on March 18, 2003, for third and final reading. The ordinance provided new restrictions on floodplain/floodway development in the rapidly growing urban environment of Metropolitan Nashville and Davidson County. It gave ultimate authority to the Metropolitan Planning Commission and the Metropolitan Council to regulate and review floodplain development proposals representing any kind of land use including single-family or multi-family residential and nonresidential.

During debate of the bill on the council floor, it was noted that there had been a "last minute plea from St. Thomas Hospital to oppose its passage." The councilmembers were informed of the refusal of St. Thomas officials to include the sponsor of the bill in their communication. This type of political strategy represented an underhanded and unacceptable form of government. The Metropolitan Council was informed that I had "worked for three years on the issue and was offended that St. Thomas did not approach"[41] me as they did fellow councilmembers, specifically since I was the sponsor of the ordinance. The bill was the product of approximately twenty months of open cooperation, communication, and deliberation between public and private entities with floodplain interests. I considered the bill a "positive next step toward regulating flood-plain development."[42]

Among the councilmembers that were vocally supportive of the bill were Feller Brown, Bob Bogen, and Carolyn Baldwin Tucker. I was extremely appreciative of their open endorsement due to the positive role it played in bringing about final passage of the bill. Upon close of debate, the vote was taken on the bill. The Metropolitan Council passed the floodplain ordinance by a vote of 25-1-6.

The table clearly illustrated the more restrictive developmental regulations enacted with the adoption of Substitute Ordinance No. BL2002-1021. Additionally, it showed a more comprehensive applicability of the regulations to types of development, and a greater clarity by which floodplain development was to be regulated. Such

Figure 3-2

How the Metropolitan Council Voted on Substitute Ordinance No. BL2002-1021 on March 18, 2003

Supported

- David Briley	- Tony Derryberry	- Bob Bogen
- Carolyn Baldwin Tucker	- James Bruce Stanley	- John Summers
- Brenda Gilmore	- J. B. Loring	- Michelle Arriola
- Melvin Black	- Amanda McClendon	- Janis Sontany
- Don Majors	- Ronnie Greer	- Michael Kerstetter
- Lawrence Hall	- Ludye Wallace	- Craig Jenkins
- Earl Campbell	- Morris Haddox	- Ron Turner
- Bettye Balthrop	- Norma Hand	- Charles Tygard
- Feller Brown		

Opposed

- Saletta Holloway

Abstained

- Chris Ferrell	- Adam Dread	- Jim Shulman
- Leo Waters	- Eileen Beehan	- Lynn Williams

Figure 3-3

Table Comparing the Previous Floodplain Regulations with the Newly Adopted Regulations[43]

	Old Regulations	**New Regulations**
Applicability	Residential	Residential and Non-Residential
Size of Protected Area (Preserved Floodplain)	None for conventional development. 50 percent if cluster lot option requested.	Minimum of 50 percent of natural floodplain area or all of the floodway area plus fifty feet on each side of the waterway, whichever is greater.
Exemptions	Residential—greater than one acre.	Properties zoned CC, CF, MUI, MUG, IR, IWD, and IG; or that portion of properties previously developed and improved or where a building or grading permit has been issued.
Encroachments Permitted	Streets and utilities by variance.	Streets and utilities by variance, but limited to no more than 20 percent of the protected floodplain area.
Floodplain Uses Permitted	Greenways, parks, playing fields.	Greenways, public parks, private parks, golf courses, and state-certified wetlands.
"No-Touch Zone"	Preserved floodplain to remain in "natural" state.	Clarifies that preserved floodplain is not to be disturbed, including the cutting of vegetation.

legislation was essential to guide Metropolitan Nashville through the extremely rapid pace of development that had descended upon the city with the emergence of sprawl.

On Wednesday March 26, 2003, Planning Department Director Rick Bernhardt hosted a meeting among all parties that had shown an interest in the floodplain ordinance. Those invited to attend the meeting included public officials, private interests, and the news media. The purpose of the meeting was to explore certain issues raised prior to final passage of the bill. The input of the various individuals that were invited was considered essential to address the concerns over the bill in the most comprehensive manner.

During the meeting, the ordinance was summarized for those in attendance prior to the beginning of deliberation. The summary noted that "the new ordinance tightens restrictions on low-lying lands known as flood plains, areas prone to flooding in the wake of heavy rains. Construction in flood plains often leads to costly drainage and flooding problems and generally is frowned upon by local and federal government officials." Those attending the meeting were informed that "Stanley's bill specifically defines the 50% area as a 'no-touch

Figure 3-4

***Article from* Music City Planning Notes**
(Metropolitan Planning Department Newsletter)
***Updating Community on Floodplain Ordinance*[44]**

Floodplain Regulation Update

On Tuesday, March 18, 2003, the Metro Council adopted revised floodplain regulations with Substitute Ordinance BL2002-1021.

Council member Bruce Stanley worked tirelessly to improve the Zoning Code after implementation of the 1998 floodplain regulations showed more of the floodplain could be developed than was intended. While both the Zoning Code and the Stormwater Management Code regulate development within natural floodplain areas, only the Zoning Code contains performance standards for residential and nonresidential development.

zone,' meaning that it can't be developed—and it can't be used as fill ground to elevate the part of the flood plain that can be developed."[45]

Bernhardt made one of the most notable comments at the meeting when he claimed that "the bill takes the next step in providing reasonable protection for flood plains."[46] Bernhardt's statement supported the floodplain ordinance that he played a vital role in developing and having passed. The statement also undermined the claims of St. Thomas to immediately amend the bill, as it was considered a positive change in floodplain development policy for Metropolitan Nashville.

There was a wide range of support for the new floodplain ordinance. One source of support was voiced by resident Jim Dolan of Donelson. Dolan lived on the banks of McCrory Creek and stated that he was "relieved the floodplain bill passed. The basement of his home has been flooded four times—his yard countless times—and he worries that continued development in flood plains near his neighborhood will make it worse." Dolan claimed "I get all the water that comes off the airport runway on the east side of Donelson Pike, and that's just one source. Do you realize how much concrete is out there? All that water comes this direction. It's got to have somewhere to go."[47]

Another source of support came from the printed media. An editorial from the *Tennessean* informed the citizens of the midstate of the importance of having better planning ordinances passed to minimize damage due to flooding. The editorial targeted recent storms and the heavy rainfall with which they were associated. The subsequent flooding was the cause of the death of two young children. "The storm didn't produce a record amount of rainfall for this area, but it shattered lives just the same. There will be much second-guessing now on what could have been avoided. Murfreesboro always has its share of developments caught in flood waters because of poor planning. The storm also calls attention to efforts in the Metro Council to restrict development in flood-plain districts. The bill, sponsored by Councilman James Bruce Stanley, takes on a new urgency when seen in the light of a flooding situation. Planning is something communities can do about the weather."[48]

The floodplain ordinance that was ultimately adopted by the metropolitan government represented a cooperative effort on the part of both

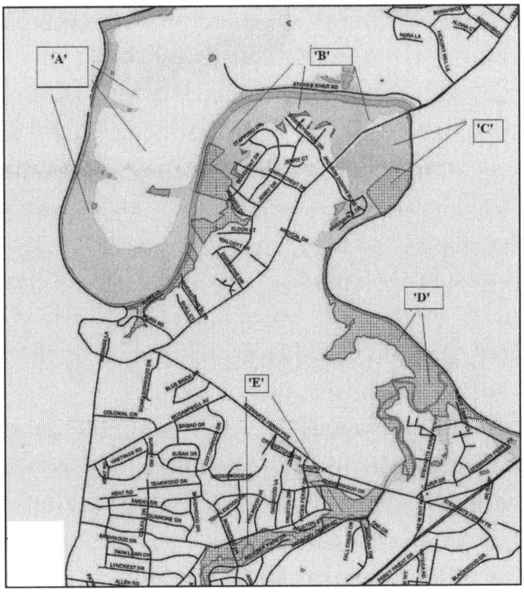

Map 3-1: Floodplain acreage in Council District 14. "A"—The bend in the Stones River; "B"—Floodplain acreage contiguous with Stanford Estates; "C"—Jackson Downs floodplain acreage; "D"—Stones River/McCrory Creek floodplain acreage; "E"—McCrory Creek floodplain. (Source: Metropolitan Planning Department of Nashville and Davidson County.)

public officials and private interests and promoted the preservation and protection of the natural environment and the established community by more thoroughly regulating floodplain development.

Resolutions

During the eight years in which I was privileged to serve on the Metropolitan Council, I sponsored numerous resolutions. The general resolutions that I sponsored were based on concerns raised by affected citizens. Such resolutions were designed to bring about change in policy by public or private entities, provide relief to citizens from specific problems, or assist in bringing needed services to the citizens of the community. In addition, the memorializing resolutions that I sponsored were filed to acknowledge the positive impact certain citizens had made to District 14 and Metropolitan Nashville.

In contrast to ordinances introduced for consideration and approval by the Metropolitan Council, resolutions represented nonbinding legislation that were "generally used to make changes in internal policy or to take commendatory or memorializing action."[49] In addition, resolutions simply stated the position of the Council on a specific issue. In that role, the resolution, unlike an ordinance, did not require the approval of the mayor.

However, the local legislative process did mandate that the mayor be given the opportunity of reviewing and approving the resolution following its approval by the Metropolitan Council. The approval of the mayor obviously gave greater political weight to a resolution, but the refusal of the mayor to endorse a resolution did not invalidate it. A resolution approved by the Metropolitan Council was sent to the party to whom it was addressed. The resolution outlined the actions requested to be taken by the public or private entity for the benefit of the local community.

The numerous resolutions that I sponsored throughout my eight years on the Metropolitan Council were addressed to a wide variety of entities. These included metropolitan departments and utilities, state officials, and federal officials and agencies. The approval of the resolution by the Metropolitan Council substantially improved the possibility of having the appropriate action taken by the specific entity.

Memorializing Resolutions

Resolution No. RS2000-217

A resolution requesting the Metropolitan Board of Education to appropriately recognize Mr. Jimmy Edwards, former principal of Donelson High School, at the Donelson Middle School campus. The resolution was introduced to the Metropolitan Council on May 16, 2000, and adopted by the Council on June 6, 2000. It was approved by Mayor Bill Purcell on June 8, 2000.

Resolution No. RS2001-803

A resolution recognizing the 2001 Donelson Civitan 14 & Under Slow Pitch Travel Team. The resolution was introduced to, and adopted by, the Metropolitan Council on November 6, 2001. It was approved by Mayor Bill Purcell on November 7, 2001.

Resolution No. RS2003-1503

A resolution recognizing Greg Ketteman for his administrative accomplishments and community involvement during his ten-year term as principal of Hickman Elementary School. The resolution was introduced to, and adopted by, the Metropolitan Council on July 1, 2003. It was approved by Mayor Bill Purcell on July 2, 2003.

Those whom the Metropolitan Council formally recognized through these resolutions represented the local community in a positive and beneficial manner. I considered myself extremely fortunate to have had a close interaction with the individuals honored or the programs with which they were associated. In my role as a member of the Metropolitan Council, I was both obligated and pleased to have Metropolitan Nashville acknowledge the accomplishments of the recipients of these resolutions.

General Resolutions

The general resolutions I introduced were addressed to various entities in an attempt to obtain a change in existing policy. This change provided relief to impacted citizens and created a more efficient government for Metropolitan Nashville. The resolutions are categorized according to the entities to which they were addressed.

Metropolitan Board of Public Education

Resolution No. RS2001-643

A resolution requesting the Metropolitan Board of Public Education to create a capital needs committee for public schools.[50]

The resolution was approved by the Council's Education Committee on June 19, 2001. It was then introduced to, and adopted by, the Metropolitan Council on the same date. However, the Board of Public Education failed to take any action on the request.

Resolution No. RS2001-688

A resolution requesting the Metropolitan Board of Public Education and the Metropolitan Planning Commission to cooperate in providing educational needs assessments for proposed residential developments within the area of the Metropolitan Government.[51]

The resolution was approved by the Council's Education Committee and the Planning, Zoning, Historial and Port Authority Committee on August 7, 2001. It was then introduced to, and adopted by, the Metropolitan Council on the same date.

Resolution No. RS2002-950

A resolution requesting the Metropolitan Board of Public Education to provide the Metro Council with a plan to utilize existing classroom capacity.[52]

I co-sponsored the resolution with fellow councilmembers Don Majors and Melvin Black. It was approved by the Council's Education Committee on February 19, 2002. It was introduced to the Metropolitan Council on the same date. During that meeting, the caption was amended by deleting the phrase "a plan to utilize existing classroom capacity" and inserting the phrase "an assessment of existing classroom capacity and alternatives to utilize such existing capacity." The amended resolution was adopted by the Metropolitan Council on February 19, 2002.

Resolution No. RS2002-943

A resolution authorizing the director of public property to exercise an option to purchase real property (Map 98, Parcels 101 and 163—John Hager Road) on which to construct the new Ruby Major Elementary School and a future middle school.[53]

The resolution was introduced to the Metropolitan Council on February 5, 2002. It was approved by the Council's Budget and Finance Committee, Education Committee, and Planning, Zoning, Historical and Port Authority Committee. The resolution was approved by the Metropolitan Planning Commission on February 14, 2002. That approval was followed by its adoption by the Council on March 19, 2002, and approved by Mayor Bill Purcell on March 25, 2002.

Resolution No. RS2003-1477

A resolution requesting the Metropolitan Board of Public Education to establish a political science/history magnet program at McGavock Comprehensive High School.[54]

The resolution was approved by the Council's Education Committee on June 3, 2003. It was then introduced to, and adopted by, the Metropolitan Council on the same date. The Metropolitan Clerk was directed to send a certified copy of the resolution to the mayor, the director of schools, each member of the Board of Education, and each member of the Tennessee delegation to the United States Congress.

The members of Congress were to be included in the mailing due to the substantial federal capital used to fund public school magnet programs.

In July 2003, I made a presentation to the Board of Education outlining the necessity and benefits of having a magnet program operating in conjunction with the general comprehensive courses offered at McGavock Comprehensive High School.

Nashville Electric Service (NES)

Resolution No. RS2002-1202

A resolution requesting Nashville Electric Service and the Tennessee State Department of Health to provide electric service to Warrior Football Field.

The resolution was approved by the Council's Public Works Committee and the Rules and Confirmations Committee on October 15, 2002. It was then introduced to, and adopted by, the Metropolitan Council on the same date. The Metropolitan Council went on record requesting the "Nashville Electric Service and the Director of the Tennessee State Department of Health to provide electric service to Warrior Football Field in the most cost-effective manner."[55] Certified copies of the resolution were then sent to the president of the Nashville Electric Service and to the director of the State Department of Health.

Resolution No. RS2003-1376

A resolution requesting the Nashville Electric Service to review its Vegetation Management Program and address issues and concerns of homeowners and private property owners.

The resolution was approved by the Council's Public Works Committee on March 18, 2003. It was then introduced to, and adopted by, the Metropolitan Council on the same date. The resolution called for a possible amendment to the program "to promote a more thorough utility service and citizen interaction when addressing the extent of needed cut and trim from power lines and should define the specific distance on utility easement the subcontractors are allowed to vary." In addition, it called for the program to "be amended to promote improved communications with NES officials and individual homeowners and should consider both immediate and long term impact on individual resident property."[56]

Davidson County Delegation to the Tennessee General Assembly
Resolution No. RS2002-949

A resolution requesting the Davidson County delegation to the Tennessee General Assembly to introduce and support legislation that allows constructive notice to be given to owners of property who are in violation of building codes and health codes.[57]

The resolution was introduced to the Metropolitan Council on February 19, 2002. It was approved by the Council's Codes Committee and adopted by the Metropolitan Council at the same meeting. A certified copy of the resolution was sent to each member of the Davidson County delegation to the Tennessee General Assembly. It was my hope that state legislators would take action on this resolution, thereby removing a key obstacle to the promotion of a stable and healthy urban environment for Metropolitan Nashville.

U.S. Army Corps of Engineers
Resolution No. RS2001-704

A resolution requesting the U.S. Army Corps of Engineers to amend its present federal regulations to allow leasing of property for local public school facilities.[58]

The metropolitan clerk was directed to send a certified copy of the resolution to the U.S. Army Corps of Engineers, to Senators Thomas Frist and Fred Thompson, and to Congressman Bob Clement. The resolution was approved by the Council's Education Committee and Planning, Zoning, Historical and Port Authority Committee. It was then introduced to, and adopted by, the Metropolitan Council on August 21, 2001.

The Metropolitan Planning Commission
Resolution No. RS2002-1004

A resolution requesting the Metropolitan Planning Commission to adopt changes to its subdivision regulations to provide for notice of public hearings and consideration on developments in floodway and floodplain areas.[59]

The resolution was introduced to the Metropolitan Council on April 16, 2002. Following its approval by the Council's Planning,

Zoning, Historical and Port Authority Committee, it was adopted by the Metropolitan Council on April 16, 2002. The Metropolitan Council was recorded as requesting the Metropolitan Planning Commission to adopt changes to its subdivision regulations to provide for notice of public hearings and consideration on developments in floodway and floodplain areas.[60]

The Stormwater Management Committee
Resolution No. RS2002-1003

A resolution requesting the Stormwater Management Committee to adopt changes to its regulations to provide for notice of public hearings and consideration on developments in floodway and floodplain areas.

The resolution was filed in conjunction with Resolution No. RS2002-1004 and as a supplement to Ordinance No. BL2002-1021. The resolution was approved by the Council's Public Works Committee on April 16, 2002. However, it was deferred until June 4, 2002, to consider concerns of some councilmembers of the impact this resolution would have on the authority of the Stormwater Management Committee.

The resolution was finally adopted on June 4, 2002. It was approved by Mayor Bill Purcell on June 6, 2002. A certified copy of the resolution was then sent to the acting director of the Public Works Department and each member of the Stormwater Management Committee.

The Mayor and the Codes Administration
Resolution No. RS2002-1203

A resolution requesting the mayor and the director of codes administration to request that the Davidson County delegation to the Tennessee General Assembly introduce and adopt legislation providing for constructive notice for enforcement of the Metro Property Standards Code.[61]

The resolution was approved by the Council's Codes Committee and Fair and Farmer's Market Committee on October 15, 2002. It was then adopted by the Metropolitan Council on the same date. A certified copy of the resolution was then sent to the mayor and the director of codes administration.

Conclusion

The legislation sponsored by me throughout the eight years of service on the Metropolitan Council represented a response to concerns brought to my attention by local constituents. The ordinances or resolutions that I sponsored represented a manner in which issues could be addressed for the benefit of the taxpaying citizens of Metropolitan Nashville. The open communication and cooperation of the legislative process promoted the adoption of the most comprehensive and acceptable ordinances or resolutions to be used to regulate activities within Metropolitan Nashville. The legislative process represented an educational experience for all involved as it allowed everyone to become familiar with wide-ranging opinions on differing issues.

Chapter Four

Governmental Interaction

The role of the Metropolitan Council as the municipal legislature obligated each member of this legislative body to openly communicate and cooperate with individuals from other government bodies in addressing communal issues. Such issues varied widely between council districts. However, interaction between the council representatives, their constituents, and representatives from other government bodies ensured a comprehensive review of the issue and a positive solution.

The United States Constitution divided the government into three branches, the administrative branch, the legislative branch, and the judicial branch. In addition, the founding fathers created three levels of government to operate at the federal, state, and local levels. When issues arose from one of the sites in Metropolitan Nashville, the citizens were able to contact the councilmember that represented them and inform the councilmember of the issue and their ultimate concerns. The notification promoted cooperation between the councilmember and the citizens to have the issue addressed. The addressing of many of the issues called for a change in policy from the local, state, or federal level of government. Such a change in policy was both positive and beneficial for citizens in particular and the city in general.

A number of issues were brought to my attention by constituents who were adversely impacted by existing policy. It was my role as the elected municipal legislator to interact with the citizens and the appropriate local, state, or federal government representative to attempt to have the issue addressed. The issues raised were wide-ranging and involved federal, state, and local policies and programs. Amending these policies would promote a much more stable and constructive municipal environment in which the citizens of Metropolitan Nashville had invested. The stability promoted by these policy changes would act as a motivating factor for additional private interests to invest in the local community.

Ultimately, my interaction involved cooperating with government officials to have public infrastructure and services upgraded. In addition, the interaction involved proposed amendments to existing policy and programs. The amendments were proposed to address serious concerns voiced by citizens who had been adversely impacted by government-sponsored programs, or to alter government policy for the benefit of the citizens of Metropolitan Nashville.

Metropolitan Government

Throughout my tenure on the Metropolitan Council, it was my responsibility to have any concerns or issues brought to my attention by the citizens addressed by the appropriate municipal department. To determine the most appropriate and acceptable solution required my openly interacting with pertinent metropolitan officials and the resident citizens. The numerous departments with which I interacted and the issues that we addressed are included in the following manifest.

Metropolitan Nashville and Davidson County Public School System

Public schools have played a vital role in educating the youth of the community, providing extended educational programs for the citizens in general, and promoting positive social interaction among the citizens through a wide variety of organizational meetings held at school facilities located throughout the community. In that role, public schools represent one of the more vital areas of infrastructure serving Metropolitan Nashville.

Since the adoption of the Metropolitan Charter, the public school landscape of Metropolitan Nashville has been subjected to some profound changes. Changes to the public school landscape are the responsibility of the elected officials of Metropolitan Nashville. To ensure such changes are in the best interest of the citizens of the city, members of the Metropolitan Council and the Metropolitan Board of Public Education are required to maintain open communication with each other and their constituents, in part, because of the control the Metropolitan Council has over the city budget.

The vast majority of monies needed to fund proposed changes to the public school system must be approved by the Metropolitan Council. Therefore, including both the Education Committee and the Budget and Finance Committee, as well as councilmembers whose districts will be impacted, are necessary to bring about the changes. The input provides a wide variety of ways to address the needed changes. In addition, the educated guidance from the professional staff of the public school system assists in directing the Metropolitan Councilmembers and the members of the Board of Education to an appropriate solution.

During my service on the Metropolitan Council, the public school system witnessed dramatic changes. The most prominent change involved the release of Metropolitan Nashville from the twenty-seven-year federal busing mandate and a resurgence of citizen enthusiasm for public schools. The reinvigorated enthusiasm directed public attention to areas of the school system that suffered from severe neglect over the years.

The most notable area neglected were school facilities. The school system had lacked the appropriate funding to maintain and improve the existing public schools serving Metropolitan Nashville. There was little or no capital available to construct new public school facilities to relieve overcrowding or to replace aged and irreparable public schools throughout the system. However, the release of Metropolitan Nashville from the federal busing mandate returned the administration of the local public school system to local elected officials.

Ultimately, this increased annual capital assigned to the public school system, specifically for improvements to the public school buildings. The large number of capital improvement projects for public schools required prioritization, which was accomplished through open cooperation between the Metropolitan Council and the Metropolitan Nashville Board of Public Education.

I was very fortunate to be a member of the Council's Education Committee at that time. The involvement of citizens with an interest in public schools was vital. Citizen involvement was encouraged through the organizing of an advisory board to address the

Board of Education and the Metropolitan Council. The members of the advisory board included parents of public school students, the administrator of the public school needing capital improvements, and the councilmembers who represented citizens with children in the school.

An advisory board clearly illustrated to local elected officials the genuine interest the citizens of Metropolitan Nashville had in one public school in particular and the public school system in general. Finally, open interaction between the Metropolitan Council and the Metropolitan Nashville Board of Public Education revealed the much-needed capital improvements to public school facilities. These upgrades to the existing facilities represented positive long-term investments in the extensive public school infrastructure serving Metropolitan Nashville.

In addition, there were numerous instances when, as councilman for District 14, I was invited by the faculty and administration of the public schools in the district to interact with the students. The Read Across America program represented a national effort to promote the importance of reading to students, and the local schools openly embraced the program. It involved having individuals from both the public and private sectors of the community visit local schools and read to students. Another program the local schools participated in was the Mayor's First Day Festival sponsored by Mayor Bill Purcell, and held in the Gaylord Entertainment Center.

Mayor Bill Purcell and teacher Rosemary Stanley with Councilman Stanley at the Mayor's First Day Festival held at the Gaylord Entertainment Center in August 2002

Those attending the festivities included the mayor, students, teachers, administrators, municipal officials, and private entrepreneurs. The primary objective of the celebration was to promote the public schools serving our city and to honor the teachers, administrators, and students associated with the public schools. It was also used to establish a cooperative relationship between private businesses and public schools. The interaction promoted by such programs played a vital role in educating the public and their elected officials on the role of the public schools in our community.

Capital Projects

The New Hickman Elementary School

The 1986 division of the Hickman Elementary School student body into two separate facilities (Hickman on Ironwood Drive and the Hickman Annex on Maplecrest Drive) and the Ironwood Drive facility's location under airplane flight paths motivated the Metropolitan Nashville Board of Education's 1988 decision to construct a new Hickman Elementary School. This new facility was to be at a different location and unify the Hickman Elementary School student body under one roof. However, this proposal did not move beyond the designation stage due to a lack of capital to fund the project. In 1989, the new Hickman project was postponed indefinitely by the Board of Education.

The Metropolitan Council's approval of the municipal budget for fiscal year 1993–94 included a property tax increase. A substantial portion of the revenue obtained from that tax increase was designated for capital improvements to schools. Noticeably missing from the capital improvements list was a new Hickman Elementary School. The status of Hickman Elementary School remained the same with the student body being divided into two separate facilities.

Upon my election to the Metropolitan Council in 1995, I initiated open discussions that addressed proceeding with the new Hickman Elementary School project. In November 1995, I presented the Hickman Elementary PTA with a plan to establish a parent advisory board to promote the completion of the new Hickman project. The PTA agreed to this plan and began organizing the advisory board. Ultimately, I was honored to serve on the Hickman Parent Advisory

Entrance to the original Hickman Elementary School

Board (HPAB) with Rufus Baker, Barbara Brown, Cathy Caldwell, Jill Baker, Mark Edwards, Cheryl McAdams, Danea Wallace, Beth Young, Mike Sturm, Leah Martin, Eloise Robinson, Linda Roland, Dorinda Shachlett, Tony and Kathy Derryberry, and Principal Greg Ketteman.

The HPAB determined that its primary goal was to achieve the consolidation of Hickman Elementary School into one building. In addition, the board was to investigate using the old Donelson High School on Stewart's Ferry Pike as the possible location to house a unified Hickman. Additional issues to be addressed by the HPAB were health-related concerns that included a large infestation of roaches and possible high radon levels at the Hickman Annex. Also, airplane noise levels and airplane fuel dumping affected the Ironwood Drive facility.

On December 18, 1995, Rufus Baker was elected as the board chair/spokesperson and Cathy Caldwell as its secretary. In addition, an action plan was adopted by the HPAB to outline the needs of Hickman.

During the first months of 1996, I opened dialogue with representatives of the Board of Education and other councilmembers to garner their support for this project. The Education Committee met on January 22, 1996, at the old Donelson High School. During this meeting, Director of Schools Richard Benjamin discussed the proposed Commitment to the Future desegregation plan with councilmembers.

In answer to questions raised regarding the unification of Hickman Elementary, Dr. Benjamin stated that a new Hickman had been designated as a top priority project in the Commitment to the Future plan.

However, it was also noted that the acceptance of the proposed plan and the initiation of the capital projects with which it was associated were not to take place for at least five years. By order of both the state fire marshal and the state health department, the older portion of Donelson High, constructed in 1928–29, was to remain vacant until the proper renovations were made to stabilize the site.

It was at that time that I inquired about the Board of Education's support for using the appropriate funds to immediately begin the proper renovations to the old Donelson High to house a unified Hickman. This was the first mention of using the old Donelson High site. The rationale behind the use of this site was that it was centrally located within the Hickman Elementary School zone, it was substantially outside the flight paths of the airplanes, and both Metropolitan Nashville and the state had recently invested heavily in the area with the construction of the new Stewart's Ferry Pike/Lebanon Pike intersection.

However, Dr. Benjamin was unwilling to commit to such a proposal. In the long-term, this noncommittal attitude taken by the Board of Education proved beneficial for the Hickman project.

On February 27, 1996, Chairman Rufus Baker addressed the Board of Education. Baker outlined the existing problems with both facilities then housing the Hickman student body. The most notable of those problems dealt with the high radon level readings taken from the Hickman Annex that housed Hickman Elementary School's third and fourth grade students. These high radon levels promoted an unhealthy environment for the students, faculty, staff, and administration of the facility. Concluding his presentation, Baker requested the Board of Education endorse the plan to relocate the entire Hickman student body in a renovated Donelson High building. The Board took the position of studying the proposal put before them before they could take any firm action.

In April 1996, I met on different occasions with Dr. Bill Wise, deputy superintendent of schools, and Joe Edgens, director of operations for the Board of Education. During these meetings, there was an attempt to determine the feasibility of the renovations to the old Donelson High facility to house a unified Hickman. In addition, I began working with the appropriate metropolitan officials to determine a cost estimate for this renovation project.

It was established that the renovations to the old Donelson High structure would cost $4,017,000. In July 1996, I received approval for an amendment to the capital improvement budget in the amount needed to renovate the old Donelson High facility and unify Hickman at the site. I addressed the Board of Education on October 22, 1996, in an attempt to gain their endorsement for the funds and move forward with the unification and relocation of Hickman.

However, the Board of Education ultimately refused to endorse this allocation claiming that a substantial number of school capital projects remained incomplete and that the board would need the existing capital in their unreserved fund balance to guard against possible cost overruns.

Over the following year, the HPAB and I continued to meet with Board of Education members and other metropolitan officials to press the necessity of addressing the Hickman unification issue. Among the more notable officials targeted were District 4 Board of Education member Charles Gann, chairman Ron Turner of the Council's Education Committee, and numerous other councilmembers with an interest in the project. In the meantime, I met individually with members of the Board of Education to inform them of the importance of this project.

In January 1997, the HPAB elected Barbara Brown as its new chair/spokesperson. Mrs. Brown played a vital role in meeting with members of the Board of Education and its staff to obtain their support for the Hickman project.

Natural vegetation overwhelming the 1928–29 portion of Donelson High School prior to its renovation and reopening

During this time, in meetings with Dr. Bill Wise, now the new director of schools, I determined that a new Hickman Elementary School should be included in the capital improvements budget for fiscal year 1997–98. This inclusion of a new Hickman no longer designated that Hickman be unified in the old Donelson High facility, but that a new Hickman Elementary School be constructed behind the old Donelson High School and share the same campus.

In February 1997, I received a cost estimate of $6,011,000 from the Board of Education for this project. I targeted the old Donelson High site as the location to invest in constructing a new Hickman Elementary School because of the need to stabilize this site, which had been rapidly deteriorating since the closing of Donelson Junior High School in 1986. In addition, the $6-million investment in this site motivated Metropolitan Nashville to designate the renovation of the old Donelson High facility as a top priority project.

Realizing the necessity of gaining the appropriate support for this project, I met with Mayor Phil Bredesen on March 11, 1997. I outlined the Hickman project and the benefits it would have on the community and requested his endorsement of the project. Following a lengthy discussion, Mayor Bredesen agreed to consider endorsing the project.

In May 1997, Mayor Bredesen announced a proposed property tax increase. The revenue from this tax increase was used primarily to fund improvements to the public library system. However, it was also announced that approximately $85 million of this revenue was to be invested in capital improvements to the public school system. Throughout the years that the Hickman project had lain dormant, a lack of appropriate funding was always used as the primary reasoning behind the Board of Education's refusal to take action on the project.

The $85 million designated for capital improvements to the public school system was substantial enough to compensate for the construction of a new Hickman Elementary School. Upon receiving the capital improvements budget from the mayor for fiscal year 1997–98, I noticed that a new Hickman Elementary School was designated as a top priority project. This illustrated Mayor Bredesen's support for the Hickman project, which proved vital in the upcoming months.

Dr. Bill M. Wise

Through his professional life, Wise advised the public on the state of education. His experience in educational issues was invaluable in guiding the Metropolitan Nashville Public School System into a new age substantially free from federal judicial interference. Wise was born October 26, 1935, in Petersburg, Tennessee. He began his education in public schools in Lincoln and Marshall Counties, Tennessee. Following his high school graduation, Wise obtained his bachelor of science (1963) and his master of administration (1965) from the University of North Alabama in Florence, Alabama. He obtained his doctor of education from the University of Tennessee in Knoxville in 1970. He was named a Ford Foundation Fellow when he received his doctorate.

The administrative experiences of Wise included serving in the following capacities for Metropolitan Nashville-Davidson County Public Schools: assistant superintendent for business and facility services from 1970 to November 22, 1994; deputy superintendent from November 22, 1994 to February 25, 1997; interim superintendent of schools from February 26, 1997 to November 25, 1997; and superintendent of schools from November 25, 1997 to June 30, 2001.

During his career in education, Wise consulted on numerous issues ranging from desegregation to school facilities to management studies. Among those he consulted for were the U.S. Department of Justice in Corpus Christi, Texas, and various public school systems throughout the country.

Honors received by Wise included the Bill Wise Award from the Council of the Great City Schools, the Distinguished American Award from the National Football Foundation and College Hall of Fame, the Alumnus of the Year (1986) from the University of North Alabama, and the Outstanding Administrator of the Year (1993–94) from the Tennessee Association of School Administrators.

Bill Wise and his wife, Peggy, have one child and live in Metropolitan Nashville.

The Board of Education had the ultimate authority in determining which school projects throughout the public school system should receive priority status. I met with General William Moore and Tim Campbell of the Metropolitan Nashville Airport Authority (MNAA) on August 6, 1997, to outline the Hickman Elementary situation for them and gain their support.

Following a lengthy meeting, the MNAA agreed to openly endorse the construction of a new Hickman Elementary School as an immediate project. In addition, I made a presentation to the general membership of the Donelson-Hermitage Chamber of Commerce on August 14, 1997, and obtained its open endorsement of the Hickman project. Both the MNAA and the Chamber of Commerce addressed letters to the Board of Education requesting that a new Hickman Elementary School be designated a top priority project.

On November 25, 1997, I presented my arguments to the Board of Education. During the presentation, I requested the inclusion of a new Hickman Elementary School in its next capital allocation. Included among the information submitted to the Board of Education were letters of support from members of the Hickman Parent Advisory Board (HPAB), the Metropolitan Nashville Airport Authority (MNAA), and the Donelson-Hermitage Chamber of Commerce. I reminded the Board of Education of the availability of funds. In addition, I noted that the construction of the new Hickman Elementary School at the proposed location would stabilize the site and lay the foundation for the immediate renovations to the old Donelson High School. Such renovations were necessary for its transformation and reopening as Donelson Middle School. After this presentation, the Board of Education announced its approval of the new Hickman Elementary School project and its inclusion in the board's immediate appropriation.

The new Hickman Elementary School, located at 112 Stewart's Ferry Pike, was designated to be 71,466 square feet in size and house approximately 550 students. Metropolitan authorities designated the firm of Orr/Houk & Associates to be the architects of the project. The general contractor was Robert S. Biscan & Co. The groundbreaking for the new school took place on Wednesday, May 26, 1999. I was honored to speak at the groundbreaking ceremonies with other dignitaries

The new Hickman Elementary School located at 112 Stewart's Ferry Pike

including Director of Schools Dr. Bill Wise, Board of Education Chairperson Betsy Walkup, Board of Education member Charles Gann, and Vice Mayor Jay West. The new Hickman Elementary School opened its doors at the beginning of the 2000–2001 school year.

The new Hickman Elementary School project took approximately twelve years to be completed. However, this project exemplified the influence an organized community effort could have in addressing a project of this magnitude. It also illustrated the positive effects open interaction between officials of different metropolitan departments would have on the public school infrastructure and the community. In addition, this coordinated community effort illustrated both the short- and long-term benefits the student body of Hickman Elementary School and the community were to receive from this project. The most notable benefit, of course, was the establishment of a stable and healthy learning environment that promoted unhindered education of the community's children.

Donelson Middle School

Donelson High and Donelson Junior High School represented the Donelson-Hermitage community admirably throughout its long history. It opened in 1928 on a ten-acre campus along Stewart's Ferry Pike. It expanded through the years, reaching a maximum size of 115,996 square feet situated on a 17.99-acre campus in 1959.

Realizing the historical significance of the Donelson site to the community, the $6-million Hickman investment in the Donelson campus dictated that a renovated and modernized Donelson Middle School be a top priority project with the adoption of the new Commitment to Excellence desegregation plan by the metropolitan government in 1998.

The Donelson Middle School project was scheduled to run in conjunction with the construction of the new Hickman Elementary School that was to take place on the same campus. Ultimately, the new Donelson Middle School project involved the demolition of the 43,000-square-foot 1928–29 structure; its replacement by 37,000 square feet of new classroom space; and the renovation and modernization of the 72,000 square feet of Donelson High School constructed in the 1950s. The alterations to the original Donelson High and Junior High Schools resulted in a middle school that would be 109,519 square feet in size. The total cost of the project was set at $5,065,000.

Prior to beginning construction on either public school, a key issue was brought to my attention by the Metropolitan Codes Administration in the autumn of 1998. The issue involved the minimal size of the campus upon which both the Hickman Elementary School and Donelson Middle School were proposed to be situated. The 17.99-acre campus site was approximately four acres smaller than the minimum campus size required by the Metropolitan Zoning Code to house two public school facilities the size of the Hickman and Donelson schools.

Upon receiving that information, I began discussions with Codes Administration officials and representatives of the Metropolitan Nashville Public School System. It was determined during these discussions that a variance could be requested from the Board of Zoning Appeals. Further discussions with the public school officials necessitated their filing for the variance.

It was at that time that the Donelson Lion's Club sold its clubhouse and surrounding acreage located on the back of the Donelson High campus to the metropolitan government. The demolition of the clubhouse and the inclusion of its acreage onto the public school site brought the total size of the campus to twenty acres. The increased campus size made the granting of a variance much more likely.

Approximately two weeks prior to the hearing of the variance by the Board of Zoning Appeals, I was notified by resident homeowners of the Donelsonwood and Cloverbottom subdivisions regarding concerns they had over the placement of two large public school facilities on the campus situated between their two subdivisions.

In a community meeting at the Donelson Senior Citizens Center, I informed the residents of the benefits a revitalized public school site would have on their property. The renovations proposed for the old Donelson High School were long overdue, and would ultimately eliminate the health and safety issues associated with the large facility that lay vacant and in disrepair.

Also addressing the meeting were representatives of the public school system. They assured the residents of a minimal amount of disruption to their residential environment upon the opening and operation of the public schools.

The residential concerns were well addressed by the close of the meeting. It was now necessary to garner the support of the Board of Zoning Appeals for the variance to allow the dual-facility public school campus site to proceed.

When the application for the variance was heard by the Board of Zoning Appeals, I spoke in favor of it. Allowing the Hickman Elementary and Donelson Middle Schools to be situated on the same campus site would promote a positive and stable learning environment for those employed and enrolled at the public schools. In addition, the Board of Zoning Appeals was informed of the community meeting held with neighboring residents and that their concerns were addressed.

The operation of two modernized public schools at the site would promote an appreciation in the value of the homes of the neighboring subdivisions. In addition, improvements to the highway infrastructure in the form of the new Stewart's Ferry Pike intersection with Lebanon Pike allowed for a freer flow of traffic into and out of the campus site.

Upon the closing of the public hearing, the Board of Zoning Appeals granted the variance with specific conditions. Because the campus was still approximately two acres smaller than the required campus size, it was noted that there could be no additions to either the Hickman Elementary School or the Donelson Middle School, and no portable classrooms would be allowed on the campus site. It was, therefore, extremely important for the Board of Education to monitor enrollment at both schools to prevent overcrowding.

I was strongly supportive of the conditional variance granted in that it allowed a productive use of the public school campus. In addition, I did not support the use of portable classrooms on public school

The new Donelson Middle School

campuses—portables adversely impact both the learning environment of the schools and the residential environment of neighboring subdivisions. The renovation and reopening of Donelson Middle School was scheduled to proceed.

Upon its reopening as Donelson Middle School in 2000, Robert F. Sasser Jr. was appointed as administrator. The completion of the new Donelson Middle School project and its opening in October of 2000, along with the opening of the new Hickman Elementary School in August 2000, revitalized the old Donelson High School site that had played such a vital role in the history of the Donelson-Hermitage community.

The Donelson Middle School project represented a positive investment by metropolitan officials in the public school infrastructure. The project preserved a respected and historically significant educational facility of the Donelson-Hermitage community for the benefit of both current and future generations. In addition, it promoted a stable learning environment for the students enrolled at the school. Finally, the creation of this dual facility campus site was accomplished only through a cooperative interaction between officials representing several different metropolitan departments and the citizens of the community.

McGavock Cluster Capital Needs Committee

In April 2000, I organized and chaired the McGavock Cluster Capital Needs Committee. The committee objective was to be responsible for reviewing the capital needs of each educational facility in the McGavock cluster and properly prioritizing those needs

Hermitage Elementary kindergartners listen as Councilman Stanley reads a favorite book to them

for presentation to the Board of Education and the mayor. This objective was accomplished through the committee goals. These included touring each facility in the McGavock cluster and determining the capital needs of the educational facilities.

Membership on the committee included a wide variety of citizens representing both public and private interests of the community. The members included councilmembers Phil Ponder, J. B. Loring, Tony Derryberry, and Feller Brown; Board of Education member Kathy Nevill; former councilman and Board of Education member Vic Varallo; and Marc Hill, special assistant to Mayor Bill Purcell. Additional members included Larry Keeton and Betty Cannon, who represented the Donelson-Hermitage Chamber of Commerce, and former MNEA President Erick Huth who was a member of the McGavock Community Education Program.

The committee held five meetings from May 25, 2000 to April 23, 2001. The capital needs illustrated by school administrators were concentrated primarily on projects not addressed by the School Improvement Plan. These represented deferred maintenance projects that had been neglected in the twenty-seven years the Metropolitan Nashville Public School System was subjected to the federal busing mandate. They needed attention as rapidly as possible.

The open interaction between the committee and the administrators of the McGavock cluster brought to light the capital needs of area public schools as set forth by professional educators. Many of the capital needs were unique to each school. However, a large number of the capital improvements were identical throughout the cluster. The similarity in the capital needs of the elementary schools could be traced to the fact that the majority of those schools were constructed between 1950 and 1962.

Exemplifying such needed additions were indoor play areas for McGavock Elementary, Pennington Elementary, and Hermitage Elementary Schools. The more modern elementary schools within the cluster that had indoor play areas included Dodson, Tulip Grove, Andrew Jackson, and Hickman. The older elementary schools were constructed at a time when it was considered adequate to only have outdoor playgrounds. The committee whole heartedly supported a uniform installation of indoor play areas for all public elementary schools within the McGavock cluster. These areas would provide a uniform recreational environment in the elementary facilities.

At its final meeting in June 2001, the committee organized and prioritized the needed capital projects of the schools that served the community.

In July 2001, I presented the McGavock Cluster Capital Needs Committee thirty-page report to the Board of Education. I also presented a copy of the report to Mayor Bill Purcell. Both the mayor and the Board of Education openly accepted the report and its findings. The committee report acted as a tool to illustrate and obtain the needed improvements to the public school facilities that served Donelson-Hermitage-Old Hickory.

Following the acceptance of the report by the Board of Education and Mayor Bill Purcell, the adoption of the municipal budget for fiscal year 2002–2003 included a requested allocation of capital to fund the construction of indoor play areas at both Pennington and Hermitage Elementary Schools. The designation of these needed additions as top priority projects by the Board of Education clearly illustrated their

FROM THE TENNESSEAN

October 13, 2003

Getting Physical Easier Now with New Gym

Hermitage Elementary's Temperature-Controlled Facility Thrills Students

The Hermitage Elementary physical-education room echoed last week with the squeak of tennis shoes and the squeals and laughter of students playing lively games.

It wasn't always like this.

Last year, the 6,500-square-foot gym didn't exist, and kids played their games outside in the heat or squeezed into a portable classroom, sometimes 40 kids at a time.

Now they're running free, rejoicing in their brand new, brightly lighted, temperature-controlled and spacious facility, physical education teacher Nancy Ivancic said.

Students have already shown improvements in performance, including one fourth-grader who jogged for 12 minutes straight—two minutes longer than they had in the past.

"I think the cooler environment is more conducive to them having a good time, and we can do a lot more activities," Ivancic said.

The Hermitage Elementary School indoor play area as viewed from the school playground

Bowling, for example, used to be out of the question: The asphalt would tear up the ball and pins and could be rough on tender knees and elbows.

With the new, smooth tile surface, however, kids are learning to bowl, and they're playing basketball and badminton, volleyball and made-up games involving lots of running and jumping throughout the room.

The smooth surface also allows children in wheelchairs and walkers to propel themselves around and take part in the activities, Ivancic said, and kids with asthma or seasonal allergies seem to have fewer problems.

Children still play outside when the weather's nice, she said, but now they have options with their new $606,350 gym.

They also have more equipment.

Last year, the PTA donated $5,000 for new equipment, including beanbags, age-appropriate soccer balls and volleyballs and an interchangeable system of tennis, badminton and other game equipment.

Brayan Orozco, 9, said the physical-education room is a big improvement.

"When we used to not have one, it was boring," Brayan said, sweating after boisterous running and bowling games. "Now it's really fun."

His classmate, Ashli Ladd agreed.

"It's good to be inside instead of outside, being hot," she said.

After doing without for so long, the school is taking full advantage of the space and incorporating activities beyond the regular school day.

The fourth-graders had a "lock-in" last month, when all classes came together for an evening of volleyball—teachers against kids—followed by pizza, popcorn and a movie.

Each grade will be doing the same during the year, Ivancic said.

"It just gives us those kinds of opportunities that we didn't have before," she said. "I'm a happy apple, and I think the kids are really enjoying it."[1]

—Copyrighted, the *Tennessean*, October 13, 2003

endorsement of the McGavock Cluster Capital Needs Committee Report. These projects would not have been obtainable without the open interaction between the committee, professional educators, the Board of Education, and Mayor Purcell.

One of the primary capital projects for the public schools of the McGavock cluster designated in the report called for the renovation and expansion of the libraries of both Hermitage Elementary and Pennington Elementary Schools. The library of each facility was woefully inadequate. There had been a failure to upgrade either facility's library over the years. Hermitage Elementary School had been constructed in 1962.

Alice Quaintance, the Hermitage Elementary School librarian, claimed that, "State and federal guidelines regarding school library space and collections are updated regularly, and the library at Hermitage Elementary is far behind current recommendations for space. The standard amount of space for elementary school libraries is 4,000 square feet. Hermitage Elementary has 938 square feet." However, she claimed that the Hermitage Elementary School library had only "95 square feet of space for students to work and no storage." In addition, Quaintance further stated that, "they also have recommendations for (work) space and storage. The recommended work space is a minimum of 400 square feet." She said that "we also have no conference rooms, no small research rooms available away from the business of the main library. We're limited on the number of students who can check out books at one time."[2]

Hermitage Elementary School librarian, Alice Quaintance (Photo courtesy of Alice Quaintance)

Similarly, Pennington Elementary School represented an aging facility that had been constructed in 1959. "Pattye Evans, principal of Pennington Elementary, described her school's library as 'classroom size, plus a closet.' The school's library is 1,200 square feet, which includes a small conference room and librarian's work room." In addition, Evans stated that "recent changes in

The football field where the McGavock Raiders played and the bleachers where fans cheered the Raiders

the library's décor and creation of a flex schedule in the afternoons have increased circulation. But problems remain. We don't have space for computers and research technology." Furthermore, Evans claimed that "her school has one computer in its library, and that if more space were available for technology, she would like to have several set up with Internet access and more computers to enable students to take Accelerated Reader tests."[3]

In the months following the presentation of the report, I met with Mayor Bill Purcell to obtain his endorsement of the capital projects for the public schools in the McGavock cluster. The endorsement by the mayor was critical in that the "board usually focuses on health and safety matters before other school needs." However, "the Purcell administration seemed sympathetic to the need to adjust those priorities." Mayor Purcell and his administration were "open to the fact that we may need to move forward with these construction projects. It will require a reallocation of existing capital funds to address the expansions."[4]

I had voiced my hope that "the Metro school board will recommend the funding for the libraries to Purcell and the Metro Council." Furthermore, it was my belief that to achieve the necessary funding for these projects was "just a matter of cooperation between all three bodies. As we've moved into this age of information technology, it's just a necessity."[5]

Ultimately, the formal recognition by the Board of Education of the recommended capital needs included in the report was clear when it presented its recommended capital improvements budget to the Metropolitan Council in June 2003. Included among the capital improvements requested by the Board of Education was a $1.7 million allocation for fiscal year 2003–2004 for Hermitage Elementary School.

The money was to fund the expansion of both the library and the administrative offices at the public school, projects that were included in the McGavock Cluster Capital Needs Committee Report.

The budget was approved by the Metropolitan Council. I was extremely supportive of the budget due to the capital improvement projects for the public schools. Such projects would improve the learning environment for the students enrolled at the schools, the working environment for the teachers and administrators of the schools, and enhance the value of neighboring properties by creating a stable public school for the community. Whether or not these funds would be allocated depended on the position taken by the council-member elected to represent District 14 in 2003.

The Department of Public Works

The Department of Public Works was created by the Metropolitan Charter in June 1962. Public Works was responsible for a large percentage of the infrastructure serving Metropolitan Nashville. The definition of infrastructure is not unambiguous. However, one definition of infrastructure referred "to the foundation or underlying framework of basic services, facilities and institutions upon which the growth and development of an area, community or a system depend. Infrastructure, therefore, includes a broad spectrum of services, institutions and facilities that ranges from transportation systems and public utilities to finance systems, laws and law enforcement, and education and research."[6]

The Department of Public Works included several divisions responsible for administering a specific duty of the department. The divisions included personnel, staff services, streets and roads, equipment, parking, engineering, and solid waste. The assistant directors administering each division answered to the director of Public Works. The director was appointed by the mayor and approved by the Metropolitan Council.

In addition, there were three administrative bodies aligned with the Department of Public Works that were charged with regulating specific issues of the metropolitan government. These regulatory bodies included the Traffic and Parking Commission, the Solid Waste Regional Board, and the Stormwater Management Committee.

Upon my election to the Metropolitan Council in 1995, there were numerous infrastructure issues facing the citizens of Metropolitan Nashville and District 14. Finding solutions to these issues was considered a top priority as my tenure on the Metropolitan Council began. The two issues that received highest priority were highway maintenance/upgrades and stormwater drainage projects.

Ultimately, the stormwater drainage issue was addressed by the adoption of the Stormwater Management Master Plan by the Metropolitan Council in January 2002. The numerous issues that were addressed and projects that were completed clearly illustrated the benefits that open governmental interaction and cooperation had on the citizens of Metropolitan Nashville.

Municipal Highway Maintenance/Upgrades

One of the primary functions for which Public Works was responsible was maintaining and upgrading the municipal highway infrastructure serving Metropolitan Nashville and Davidson County. According to the Metropolitan Charter, Public Works was responsible for "the design, construction, maintenance, repair and cleaning of roads, highways, streets, alleys, storm sewers, other public places, bridges, viaducts, and other related structures."[7]

Without planned road upgrade projects or the allocation of capital to fund such projects, local councilmembers were required to cooperate with the appropriate metropolitan officials, impacted residents, and area businesses to regulate traffic speed and flow along the streets. Through such cooperation, I was able to obtain the installation of traffic signals at several key intersections located in District 14. In many instances, traffic signals would act to deter commuter traffic from residential arteries and promote a safer environment for the subdivisions situated in District 14.

Obtaining approval for the installation of traffic signals at public intersections required councilmembers to openly communicate and cooperate with the Department of Public Works. The process involved municipal traffic engineers studying a specific intersection and reporting on their findings. Based upon the report, the staff would then make a recommendation either supporting or opposing the installation of the traffic signal. The administration of the Department of Public Works based its position on the completed engineering report and the recommendation provided by the traffic engineers.

A recommendation opposing the installation of a traffic signal required the councilmember then appeal to the Metropolitan Traffic and Parking Commission. The councilmember was required to send a written request to appeal the staff's recommendation to the director of the Department of Public Works. Upon receipt of the request, officials at the Department of Public Works were required to schedule the requesting councilmember on an upcoming meeting of the Traffic and Parking Commission.

During the meeting, the councilmember was responsible for presenting arguments against the recommendation. The ability of the councilmember to persuade the commissioners to support the installation of the traffic signal was the final obstacle in obtaining approval for the signal installation.

Old Hickory Boulevard/Plantation Drive Intersection

I was informed by residents of both the Stones River Estates and Hermitage Hills subdivisions of the need to have a traffic signal installed at the intersection of Plantation Drive and Old Hickory Boulevard. Old Hickory Boulevard was a state thoroughfare, designated State Route 45. It was heavily traveled by commuter traffic. The large amount of commuter traffic had been the source of overcongestion along this thoroughfare.

Traffic congestion on Old Hickory Boulevard was extremely heavy at the intersection with Lebanon Pike. To avoid delays caused by the congestion, commuters accessed Plantation Drive as they approached Lebanon Pike.

Plantation Drive represented a residential artery that served the Hermitage Hills subdivision. It sliced through Hermitage Hills until it intersected Bonnacreek Drive on the western side of the subdivision.

Bonnacreek Drive then intersected Hickory Hill Lane, the primary residential artery serving Stones River Estates.

Hickory Hill Lane intersected Lebanon Pike just east of the Elmer Disspayne and Dr. Richard Herrington bridges that circumvented the Stones River.

The traffic signals serving the Old Hickory Boulevard/Plantation Drive intersection

Commuters viewed Plantation Drive and Hickory Hill Lane as acceptable alternatives during their daily travels. This alternative removed them from the congested Old Hickory Boulevard and allowed for a quick shortcut to Lebanon Pike. However, the high level of commuter traffic and its excessive speed promoted an extremely unsafe environment for the resident citizens of Hermitage Hills and Stones River Estates.

In May 1996, I requested the installation of a traffic signal at this intersection. However, the subsequent intersection study conducted by metropolitan traffic engineers recommended no traffic signal be installed. The recommendation was based primarily on the close proximity to the already signaled Old Hickory Boulevard/Lebanon Pike intersection.

A number of factors were not given appropriate consideration in making the recommendation. One factor was the heavy volume of commuter traffic accessing Plantation Drive from this intersection and the adverse impact it had on the residents.

The most important factor was the location of the Mr. Eldon Presley Fire Hall at the intersection. This fire hall housed Engine Company 32. It represented the only Metropolitan Fire Hall situated in the ever-expanding Hermitage community. The overly congested intersection could adversely affect a quick response time to fire calls.

Realizing the benefits the fire hall was to receive from the installation of this traffic signal, I met with Metropolitan Fire Chief Buck Dozier and obtained his endorsement of this traffic signal installation. In the meantime, I appealed the decision of the traffic engineers to the Traffic and Parking Commission.

On August 12, 1996, I appeared before the Traffic and Parking Commission to present my arguments in favor of traffic signal installation at the Old Hickory Boulevard/Plantation Drive intersection. Fire Chief Buck Dozier attended the meeting and openly supported the request. The basis of our argument was that the traffic signal would decrease the cut-through traffic accessing the residential arteries associated with the intersection. Also, it would thoroughly control the speed by which commuter traffic traveled along the residential arteries. Finally, it would allow freer access onto Old Hickory Boulevard by the emergency vehicles operating from the local fire hall. The Traffic and Parking Commission granted approval for the installation of a traffic signal at this intersection.

Despite its approval, the installation of the traffic signal at the Old Hickory Boulevard/Plantation Drive intersection ran into numerous obstacles. The most notable of the obstacles was the refusal of property owners along Old Hickory Boulevard opposite the Plantation Drive intersection to sell an easement to Metropolitan Nashville for the signal's installation. Faced with this obstacle, I worked with Public Works officials and representatives of the Metropolitan Department of Finance to determine the appropriate funding necessary to condemn the property in question and allow for the installation.

I had been informed by metropolitan officials of the unwillingness of the property owners to cooperate with Metro in granting the easements. Such a position forced me to file an ordinance with the Metropolitan Council authorizing that appropriate action be taken to obtain the needed easements.

On Tuesday June 17, 1997, I received final approval from the Metropolitan Council of Bill No. 097-782. The ordinance had been approved by the Planning Commission, Budget and Finance, Public Works, and Planning, Zoning, Historical and Port Authority Committees of the Metropolitan Council. The ordinance authorized "the acquisition of property by negotiation or condemnation for signal installation at Plantation Drive and State Route 45 (Old Hickory Boulevard); Project No. 97-M-5."[8]

The installation of the traffic signal at the Old Hickory Boulevard/Plantation Drive intersection was achieved due to the open communication and cooperation practiced by all interested parties.

The signal was deemed necessary by the ever-increasing levels of traffic on the local streets and the need to regulate traffic speed and flow through this intersection. The signal would serve the public good in the long term.

Stewart's Ferry Pike/McCrory Creek Road Intersection

One District 14 intersection that was overwhelmed each day by an excessive volume of traffic was McCrory Creek Road/Stewart's Ferry Pike. The intersection was situated approximately 150 yards from the I-40 off ramp and was subjected to heavy levels of exiting traffic. However, the most notable source of traffic accessing this intersection each day was the massive CNA corporate building located on the south side of McCrory Creek Road, just west of the intersection. The McCrory Creek Road corridor was no wider than two or three lanes at the intersection and narrowed to no more than two lanes as it flowed west toward CNA. The small municipal roadway was approximately twenty to thirty feet wide with little or no shoulder. Ultimately, the miniscule size of McCrory Creek Road proved unable to handle the heavy volume of traffic accessing it each day.

I was informed by residents of the Waterfalls Park and Hickory Bend subdivisions of the needed upgrades for the Stewart's Ferry Pike corridor. Specifically mentioned by local residents were the needed improvements to the Stewart's Ferry Pike/McCrory Creek Road intersection. Upon receiving this information and studying both the intersection and the local road system firsthand, I determined that the intersection upgrades should be a top priority highway project for District 14. The inability of the roadway to handle the daily traffic promoted an unhealthy driving environment for the local community as well as those residing or working in close proximity to the site.

During these meetings, I was informed by Chief Traffic Engineer John Gregor of an upgrade scheduled for the intersection. The scheduled work included the installation of a right-turn lane off McCrory Creek Road onto Stewart's Ferry Pike. Such a lane would allow for an easier merging of traffic.

However, I voiced concern over the fact that such a right-turn lane failed to address traffic turning left off McCrory Creek Road onto Stewart's Ferry Pike. Without a traffic signal, the movement of such

Aerial view of the CNA corporate complex

left-turn traffic would be subjected to traffic flow along Stewart's Ferry Pike. A failure to provide a consistent flow of traffic along Stewart's Ferry Pike would force traffic to back up on McCrory Creek Road.

I requested the installation of a traffic signal at this intersection to more thoroughly regulate traffic speed and flow. Upon receiving the request, a traffic study was conducted to determine the viability of the proposal. The study was conducted in July 1996 and designated that a traffic signal was not warranted at that time. Therefore, the staff recommended against the installation of the traffic signal.

I appealed the recommendation to the Traffic and Parking Commission on August 12, 1996. However, the commission voted to sustain the staff and not install the signal at that time. Their decision was based primarily on the corridor improvements that were scheduled to be implemented in the upcoming months.

I initiated open communications with representatives of CNA to determine their position on the topic. Michael Shisler, facility manager for the corporate offices, voiced his support for the installation of the traffic signal. The discussions with CNA officials as well as residents and business owners in close proximity to this intersection continued over the following two years. In addition, I maintained open communication with the metropolitan traffic engineers of the Public Works Department.

On September 9, 1998, Shisler expressed CNA's desire to have a traffic signal installed at McCrory Creek Road. The CNA position was based on the fact that their employee population had increased approximately 50 percent since 1996. In addition, there were expansion plans anticipated for the massive corporate center. Shisler claimed that there were long traffic backups in the evening, with delays exceeding fifteen minutes per vehicle. Finally, the CNA position centered on belief such a signal at that site would alleviate both the traffic congestion caused by their employees and any safety concerns for all parties accessing this intersection each day. That position was identical to the one that I had presented to the metropolitan traffic engineers in the summer of 1996.

In 1998, a traffic study was conducted at the Stewart's Ferry Pike/ McCrory Creek Road intersection. Similar to the study conducted in July 1996, the findings recommended against the installation of a traffic signal at this intersection. I appealed the decision to the Traffic and Parking Commission. The appeal was placed on the agenda of the November 9, 1998, Traffic and Parking Commission meeting.

In anticipation of the upcoming meeting, I began accumulating information to support the installation of the traffic signal. Ultimately, the information packet that was offered to each commission member included:

1. an outline of the developed environment of the Stewart's Ferry Pike/ McCrory Creek Road intersection;

2. the number of traffic accidents at this intersection from October 1997 to October 1998;

3. a comparison of other corporate facilities in the Donelson community with the CNA facility;

4. a letter from Michael Shisler to Public Works Director Marlin Keel outlining CNA's position favoring the installation of the traffic signal; and

5. a letter from Mr. Sam Mingledorff, attorney for Donelson-Hermitage Youth Football, Inc., stating support for the signalization of this intersection.

The developments of this area that fed onto either McCrory Creek Road or Stewart's Ferry Pike each day included:

1. approximately 547 multi-family residential units;

2. three single-family subdivisions (Waterfalls Park, Hickory Bend, Clover Hill);

3. two state institutions (Clover Bottom Developmental Center and Middle Tennessee Mental Health Institute) that employed 1,839 nonresident staff members; and

4. the massive CNA corporate facility that employed approximately fifteen hundred, generating approximately twelve hundred to thirteen hundred automobiles onto McCrory Creek Road each day. In addition, it was noted that there had been ten traffic accidents at this intersection from October 1997 to October 1998.

The comparison of other corporate facilities included:

1. the 25,000-30,000 square foot Gideons International facility that employed sixty individuals and had access onto Munn Road with a signaled intersection at Lebanon Pike;

2. the 67,434 square foot Bridgestone Park facility that employed three hundred individuals and had access onto Craigmeade Drive with a signaled intersection at Lebanon Pike; and

3. the 217,080-square-foot Thomas Nelson Publishers facility that employed 475 individuals and had access onto Royal Parkway with a signaled intersection at both the Elm Hill Pike and Donelson Pike intersections. In contrast, the 243,348 square foot, 1,500 employee CNA facility had no access to a signaled intersection. This information clearly illustrated the failure of metropolitan officials to recognize the need to properly upgrade the Stewart's Ferry Pike/McCrory Creek Road intersection.

Prior to the November 9, 1998, Traffic and Parking Commission meeting, the appeal was deferred until the December 14, 1998 meeting. The December 14 meeting witnessed a number of interested parties addressing the commission in support of the signalization. Those addressing the commission included residents Elaine and Jim Morgan, as well as George Engler and Doug Berryhill of CNA. Mr. Engler was associated with the CNA corporate real estate office headquartered in Chicago, while Mr. Berryhill was a lead executive in the CNA company from Nashville.

Finally, I addressed the commission and based my presentation on the evidence included in the information packet that supported the installation of this signal. In addition, I informed the commissioners of my continued cooperation with all parties involved in this proposal. Included among those were resident citizens, local nonprofit organizations, CNA officials, and the Department of Public Works.

The commission unanimously moved to allow the installation of a traffic signal if CNA would agree to fund the purchase of the traffic signal. Officials of CNA agreed to this condition. The cost of the traffic signal was approximately thirty thousand dollars. In addition, Public Works was to be responsible for maintaining the traffic signal following its installation.

The signal was purchased and installed by January 2000, and the intersection construction was designed by Gresham Smith & Partners. It has played a vital role in promoting an equitable flow of traffic through the intersection and along McCrory Creek Road and Stewart's Ferry Pike as well as a safer driving environment for the area.

Stewart's Ferry Pike/McCampbell Avenue Intersection

In 1995, one of the more congested intersections in District 14 was located at Stewart's Ferry Pike and McCampbell Avenue. The desperately needed upgrades to this intersection were brought to my attention by resident citizens. A large percentage of the overwhelming volume of traffic targeting this intersection each day was commuter traffic. In addition, the rapid speed of the traffic caused an unsafe driving environment and demanded a more thorough regulation of traffic speed and flow through the intersection.

A study of the intersection was initiated in 2000 at my request. A twenty-four-hour machine count was performed on McCampbell Avenue on February 29, 2000. There had been a previous count done at the intersection in September 1997. It was assumed that the proportion of left-turning vehicles and right-turning vehicles had remained constant since the 1997 count.

The study stated that the third highest hour of left-turns met only 69 percent of the required volume. Finally, the study included a recent accident history at the intersection. There had been two accidents in 1998 and two more in 1999. The study determined that such accidents could be corrected with the installation of a signal. However, the study ultimately recommended against the installation of a traffic signal at the intersection.

The recommendation proved unacceptable to me as a councilmember. A number of area residents had informed me of the need for a more even flow of traffic through the intersection. Based upon residents' concerns, I appealed the recommendation to the Traffic and Parking Commission. On April 28, I received notice that the appeal was to be heard at the May 8, 2000, commission meeting. In the meantime, I began open communications with other parties that stood to benefit from the installation of the light.

One of the more notable parties associated with this intersection was the Nashville & Eastern Railroad. There existed a railroad crossing just north of the intersection. It was necessary to have the crossing lights synchronized with the proposed traffic signal. During discussions with Craig Wade of the Nashville & Eastern Railroad on April 28, 2000, he agreed to cooperate with metropolitan officials in synchronizing the railroad crossing lights with the traffic signal.

Additionally, the sizeable Nashville Electric Service site opposite the McCampbell Avenue intersection and the heavy NES vehicles accessing the intersection each day required their open endorsement of the traffic signal installation. In discussions with Bill Beard, director of corporate affairs for NES, I was able to obtain the NES endorsement of the project.

Consideration for the installation of this traffic signal was deferred at the May 8 meeting of the Traffic and Parking Commission. On May 30, 2000, I received notice from Public Works Interim Director Randall Dunn that the appeal would be heard at the June 12, 2000, commission meeting. On June 12, I presented my arguments in favor of the installation of the traffic signal that included:

1. an outline of the developmental landscape situated along the Stewart's Ferry Pike and McCampbell Avenue corridors. Such development included (a) six single-family subdivisions, (b) five multi-family complexes totaling 514 units, (c) three state institutions totaling 1,959 nonresident employees, and (d) a number of private businesses;

2. a letter of support for the signal from Bill Beard of NES. Mr. Beard stated in his letter that the "entrance to NES' Donelson Service Center is very close to this intersection and it is believed that a traffic control light at this location would help with traffic calming and provide better egress for our vehicles into our service center. NES is in support of a traffic control light at this location;"[9] and

3. information of the support received from the Nashville & Eastern Railroad and State Representative Ben West Jr.

Finally, I voiced my position that the installation of a traffic signal at this location would give notice to drivers traveling north along Stewart's Ferry Pike of the upcoming Donelson Middle/Hickman Elementary School zone. Upon completion of the presentation, the commission voted to approve the installation of the traffic signal at the Stewart's Ferry Pike/McCampbell Avenue intersection.

Following the approval of the traffic signal, I began working with both the Department of Public Works and the Purcell administration to determine the upgrades required to relieve the traffic situation at this intersection. During my dialogue with Eddie Davidson of the Department of Public Works and the metropolitan traffic engineers, it was determined that a right-turn lane off McCampbell Avenue onto Stewart's Ferry Pike, a center-turn lane on Stewart's Ferry Pike to accommodate traffic turning left onto McCampbell Avenue, and upgrades to the railroad crossing at this intersection were required prior to installation of the traffic signal. These corridor improvements were estimated to cost $650,000.

In a meeting with Mayor Bill Purcell in October 2000, I outlined these necessary upgrades. Purcell was "strongly in favor of the installation of a right turn lane from McCampbell Avenue onto Stewart's Ferry Pike to handle the large volume of traffic occurring in peak morning and evening hours."[10] However, it was necessary to have this project included in the capital improvements budget as a priority project.

On March 19, 2001, I received a communication from NES voicing their support of both the installation of the traffic signal and the upgrades to the intersection. It was stated in the correspondence that "the Donelson Service Center's Table of Organization currently includes 117 positions. Another eight employees from Procurement, General Services, and Fleet are assigned to DSC. DSC currently operates 55 large trucks, 15 small trucks and passenger vehicles, and 29 trailers of various types. In addition, David H. Elloit, Inc., operates 20 large trucks and 21 employees out of DSC. This volume of traffic should help support the installation of a traffic light."[11]

That open endorsement by NES assisted in convincing Public Works officials and fellow members of the council to designate the Stewart's Ferry Pike/McCampbell Avenue intersection upgrades as a priority project in the capital improvements budget.

In December 2001, the Metropolitan Council approved a capital expenditure proposed by Mayor Purcell. The Stewart's Ferry Pike/McCampbell Avenue intersection project was to be funded through the approved capital expenditure. Although the project had been given priority status by metropolitan officials, it still remained only one of innumerable infrastructure upgrades that Metropolitan Nashville was required to address in the immediate future.

In addition, the project was to involve taking specific strips of residential parcels fronting the public corridors involved in the project. Taking such property was required to allow for the widening of both Stewart's Ferry Pike and McCampbell Avenue.

Upon the completion of my second term on the Metropolitan Council in September 2003, metropolitan authorities were beginning to focus their attention on this project. It was to be the responsibility of the next District 14 councilmember to bring about the successful completion of the project.

The highway improvements associated with the project would substantially improve traffic flow along both the Stewart's Ferry Pike and McCampbell Avenue corridors. In addition, the improvements would promote a much more stable environment for the area residents and the public schools located in close proximity. Finally, this highway upgrade project was decades behind schedule when it was finally recognized and addressed in 2000.

Metropolitan Police Department

The Metropolitan Police Department was created by the Metropolitan Charter upon its adoption in June 1962. Recognizing the need to have a uniform police force, the charter outlined that "there shall be a department of metropolitan police, which shall consist of the director thereof, and such other officers and employees of such ranks and grades as may be established by ordinance and which shall include such bureaus, divisions and units as may be provided by ordinance or by regulations of the director consistent therewith."[12]

Additionally, the charter outlined the responsibility and powers of the new police department. It was determined that "the department of the metropolitan police shall be responsible within the area of the metropolitan government for the preservation of the public peace, prevention and detection of crime, apprehension of criminals, protection of personal property rights and enforcement of laws of the State of Tennessee and ordinances of the metropolitan government."[13]

The Metropolitan Police Department has played a vital role in protecting individual citizens and enhancing the environment of our city through crime prevention. During my service on the Council, I was fortunate to work with officers and administrators of the police department on numerous issues brought to my attention by constituents. Such issues involved preserving the peace of the community, eliminating intrusion onto private property, and stabilizing public schools.

The most notable project, however, was the construction and opening of a police precinct in the Hermitage community. Such a precinct had been under consideration for some time. Its final completion was brought about by an open communication and cooperation between councilmembers of the Donelson-Hermitage community, state officials, private business, and local residents.

Hermitage Police Precinct of the Metropolitan Police Department

An announcement was made in November 1972 that there was a possibility of Donelson receiving a police station if a county restructuring plan was completed. However, that announcement proved false when it was announced that the south precinct station for the Metropolitan Police Department was going to be built on Harding Place in Antioch instead of Donelson.[14] Ultimately, that precinct was completed in September 1997.

The position of the resident citizens of Donelson and Hermitage about the lack of a local police station was best summarized by Councilman Randy Kennedy: "A police station is needed in the Donelson-Hermitage area of the county because of the tremendous growth in the area . . . We don't receive enough [police] coverage in this area."[15]

Beginning in 1992, government authorities discussed the need and the viability of constructing a new police precinct. From these discussions, Bill Gracy and the Summit Medical Center donated undeveloped land on January 16, 1995. The land was located at "the northeasternmost portion of the Lebanon Road site of the former Donelson Hospital" and was estimated to be worth approximately $250,000.[16]

However, questions about the adequacy of the proposed site were soon raised by the Metropolitan Police Department. These questions

District 13 Councilman David Randy Kennedy (Photo courtesy of David Randy Kennedy)

State Representative Ben West Jr. (Photo courtesy of Ben West Jr.)

centered on the size of the property to be donated. However, Columbia HCA formally removed the Donelson Hospital site from consideration when the sale of the former hospital was pending to a local Bible college in the summer of 1995.

Upon my election in 1995, one of the premier issues I faced was determining an acceptable site upon which to construct the proposed police precinct. Newly appointed Police Chief Emmett Turner and Metro Police Finance Manager Ken Sanders remained skeptical about targeting the donated acreage of the former Donelson Hospital. However, negotiations were ongoing between the police department, Columbia HCA officials, State Representative Ben West Jr., fellow councilmembers Phil Ponder, Vic Varallo, and me. These negotiations attempted to determine the most appropriate site for the new precinct as quickly as possible.

Resulting from the continual negotiations, it was noted that "Columbia Health System will purchase 25.37 acres located at the corner of Central Pike and Dodson Chapel Road for around $600,000 by September 1st, to fulfill their commitment made to the Donelson-Hermitage Community."[17] "Donelson Hospital originally pledged the use of three to four acres of the old Donelson Hospital site for a community-based police precinct," said State Representative Ben West Jr. "Through Columbia's generosity, we will now have not only a police precinct, but sufficient land for a community center."[18]

A local newspaper reported on the process involved in constructing a new police precinct:

> Metro Councilman Phil Ponder filed an ordinance on Tuesday, July 9, which will initiate three readings, in order for Metro to accept the property as a gift from Columbia.
>
> A group composed of Councilmen Stanley and Vic Varallo, Chief Emmitt Turner, Police Department Director of Fiscal Affairs Ken Sanders, Tom Ramsey of Columbia, real estate consultant John Brewer and I, after deliberation, came up with a profile of the ideal location for a police precinct. At this time Brewer suggested the Kay property at the northwest corner of Central Pike.[19]

This property had once been the home site of the James Kay family. However, it had been used as a horse farm in recent years. In July 1996, the Metropolitan Council approved the transfer of deed to the Kay property. On September 1, 1996, the acceptance of this property as a gift to Metropolitan Nashville was formally recognized in the conference room of Mayor Phil Bredesen. Paul Rutledge, of the Mid-American Division of Columbia HCA, made the presentation to city officials.

Although an adequate site had been obtained upon which to locate the proposed police station, a number of hurdles remained before the construction of the precinct could begin.

One of the most notable obstacles was the fact that metropolitan officials required the completion and implementation of a modern radio communications system prior to the construction of any new precinct. This system was to link all police, fire, and emergency services of Davidson County. Its projected cost was $40 million and the construction of the radio system, which was to take approximately eighteen months, was scheduled to begin no earlier than September 1997.

Another obstacle was that the Hermitage precinct was only one of five proposed precincts for the outlying communities of

Metropolitan Nashville. Two of those precincts were being given priority consideration from the Bredesen administration. These were scheduled to locate in the Antioch and Bordeaux communities. The Bordeaux community is located in the northern part of Davidson County and consisted of part of the downtown area of Metropolitan Nashville; it also included many areas of urban blight. These vacant and decaying areas promoted criminal activity.

Hermitage, however, represented the second fastest growing suburban community of Metropolitan Nashville. As a result, it was also subject to increased crime. Such criminal activity was realized when Donelson-Hermitage was struck by multiple homicides that stunned both the local citizens and the city of Metropolitan Nashville.

"On February 16, 1997, an intruder killed two workers, Manager Steve Hampton and co-worker Sarah Jackson, at the Captain D's restaurant located at 2633 Lebanon Pike as they prepared to open for the day."[20] Soon after:

> on March 23, 1997, serial homicides were once again committed in the Donelson-Hermitage community. The McDonald's restaurant at 3470 Lebanon Pike was the scene of another mass murder. This fast food restaurant was located at the Lebanon Pike and Bonnabrook Drive intersection and contiguous with the Hermitage Hills subdivision. In an apparent robbery, three workers at the McDonald's were shot and killed around midnight. The victims were Manager Ronald Santiago, Robert Sewell, and Andrea Brown.[21]

Another employee of the restaurant, Jose Alfredo Ramirez Gonzalez, was severely injured but managed to survive. Ultimately, his survival and testimony would play a vital role in the conviction of suspect Paul Dennis Reid in the multiple slayings at the McDonald's. Reid was also convicted of the Captain D's murders. In May 2000, Reid was sentenced to multiple death sentences following his conviction.

Indeed, these multiple homicides forced the Donelson-Hermitage community to unite and demand immediate attention and relief from metropolitan officials. In a meeting with Mayor Phil Bredesen, fellow Councilmen Phil Ponder, Roy Dale, Charles French, Vic Varallo, and I openly voiced our belief that it was necessary to designate the construction of the Hermitage precinct as the top priority project among those being considered.

We also requested that construction should occur in conjunction with the new communications system. Mayor Bredesen was strongly supportive of these arguments and initiated the requested changes in metropolitan policy. Motivating and supporting our arguments were the felonious attacks and the desire of the Donelson-Hermitage community to have the security concerns of their constituents addressed in an accelerated and acceptable manner.

I informed those at the meeting that when I took office, my predecessors Larry McWhirter and Randy Kennedy had notified me of the importance of pressing the precinct as a key capital improvement for Donelson-Hermitage and that failing to do this "the project would die." I claimed that "the perception among many other councilmembers and city hall was that Donelson-Hermitage was a peaceful, quiet community—immune from most big-city crime. However, the tragic events of the last six months have dispelled that myth, and have also led to demands from many residents for a stronger police presence in the area."[22]

Although the Bredesen administration agreed to accelerate plans for construction, there still remained the required approval of the entire Metropolitan Council to fund the new Hermitage precinct in the July budget.

In the meantime, greater police presence was provided to the community with the opening of a temporary substation in the Kroger supermarket located in the Northlake Village Shopping Center on September 29, 1997. It was to remain open until the new precinct building was completely operational.

The Kroger substation served as a roll call station for officers assigned to patrol the local area. With an average of thirty-five patrol officers reporting in three shifts to the office, it allowed for quicker police response times and better coverage. The officers reported for roll call in Hermitage instead of the South Precinct Station on Harding Place. They also completed paperwork, performed computer checks, and conducted interviews at the office. This local presence allowed them to spend greater time on the Donelson-Hermitage streets patrolling. Kroger supplied the office space free of charge and

Hermitage Police Precinct

erected a sign in the front of the store showing the location of the office. Dwayne Durham of Kroger played an instrumental role in the opening of the substation and the security it meant to the Donelson-Hermitage community.

In addition, "due to the size of the property, it was necessary to construct a new road between Central Pike and Dodson Chapel Road that would provide access to each of the different elements. The street was named James Kay Lane in honor of the family that bought the land for a home site in 1926."[23]

Groundbreaking for the police precinct occurred in September 1999. Newly elected Mayor Bill Purcell attended the groundbreaking ceremony. Throughout its construction, the Hermitage police precinct suffered several delays.

However, it was finally completed in March 2001 and the official ribbon cutting took place on April 7, 2001. Mayor Purcell, Police Chief Emmett Turner, and Precinct Commander Tommy McBride spoke at this ceremony. Several state and metropolitan officials were also in attendance.

The opening of this precinct ended the six-year project and finally provided the long-awaited increased security and protection that the Donelson-Hermitage community had demanded over the years.

The Department of Water and Sewerage Services

The Department of Water and Sewerage Services was created by the Metropolitan Charter upon its adoption in June 1962. The department was to be "responsible for: (1) The construction, operation and maintenance of all water and sanitary sewer facilities of the metropolitan government; (2) The collection of all charges for the services of such utilities; (3) Such other powers and duties as may be assigned to the department by ordinance."[24] Ultimately, the department represented one of the more vital utility services offered to the citizens of Metropolitan Nashville.

Issues that necessitated my interaction with the Department of Water and Sewerage Services were centered on the state-ordered takeover of the Cumberland Utility District (CUD) by the Department of Water and Sewerage Services.

The Takeover of the Cumberland Utility District

Since the adoption of the Metropolitan Charter, there existed a number of private utility companies located throughout the Metropolitan Nashville and Davidson County area. One such company was situated in the eastern portion of Davidson County, of which District 14 was a part. The existence of these private utility districts prevented the operation of a uniform water/sewer service throughout Metropolitan Nashville.

The rapid pace of growth forced upon the city by urban sprawl witnessed a substantial increase in both the demographic and developmental density of Metropolitan Nashville. Such an increase in growth increased the importance of providing modernized utility services for the community. It also obligated the private utility companies to provide appropriate upgrades to their infrastructure. The upgrades would accommodate the escalating population and ensure a healthier and safer urban environment.

Upon my election to the Metropolitan Council in 1995, the Cumberland Utility District provided both water and sewerage service to the citizens residing in the Hermitage portion of District 14. Mr. and Mrs. H. H. Richardson owned and operated this private utility company. It "began operation in 1959, when it supplied water to less than one hundred customers. By 1964, that number had grown to supplying water to approximately fifteen hundred residences and businesses and piping it out for approximately one thousand customers."[25]

Beginning in the late 1980s, the rapid growth of the Hermitage community witnessed the inability of private CUD to maintain appropriate services to its customers. An illustration of this inability was the failure to provide the necessary upgrades to its water/sewer infrastructure. Such infrastructure upgrades included the installation of larger water/sewer piping for the community to accommodate the ever increasing number of developments proposed for Hermitage.

CUD had also failed to provide the required upgrades to both the water filtration plant on Jacksonian Drive and a sewage treatment plant located on Old Lebanon Dirt Road. The lack of appropriate funding was the primary factor for the failure to substantially modernize the Cumberland Utility District's water/sewer infrastructure.

The source of funding for these capital upgrades was to be the water/sewer rates charged to customers of the CUD. However, their refusal to raise water/sewer rates made it impossible to obtain the appropriate funding for upgrades.

In 1995, Metropolitan Nashville initiated the takeover of a number of private utility companies located in Davidson County. Among those targeted for takeover was the Cumberland Utility District. The takeover was considered to be in the public interest by creating uniform consolidated water utilities throughout the metropolitan government's territorial jurisdiction. Such a takeover was authorized by Section 7-3-3-2(1) of the Tennessee Code Annotated.

Initially, the takeover allowed the Department of Water and Sewerage Services to assume control of sewer service from CUD. A negotiated agreement needed to be entered into between metropolitan officials and representatives of the CUD pertaining to the transfer of both water and sewer services to the Department of Water and Sewerage Services. Until the takeover was finalized, CUD continued to provide water services to the area.

Following the transfer of sewer service to Metro, Hermitage citizens were astounded when they began receiving sewer bills from Metro that were approximately three times greater than what they had been paying. I began receiving calls from concerned citizens about these increased sewer rates. In response, I contacted officials of the Metro Department of Water and Sewerage Services.

They informed me of the proposed takeover and the fact that they were still in negotiations for the complete takeover of water and sewer services in the area once serviced by CUD. In meetings with Director Lester "Buddy" Williams of the Metropolitan Department of Water and Sewerage Services, the reasons for the takeover of CUD and other private utility companies were clearly outlined.

Among the reasons supporting the increased sewer rates to be charged by Metro included the fact that Metro had "high-risk fire protection areas, like the business district, which have to have larger water mains, bigger backup facilities . . . and the old central core that has combined sewage."[26]

It was also noted that continual growth in the Hermitage community necessitated substantial upgrades to the water and sewer infrastructure. Such upgrades would include the removal of smaller, antiquated water and sewer lines and the installation of larger, modern water mains and sewer lines throughout the entire Hermitage community. These upgrades were to be extremely costly. A large percentage of the capital funds needed to complete the upgrades were to be acquired through the rates paid by customers.

A key issue associated with the takeover arose with the initiation of the Hermitage Hills Sewer Rehabilitation Project in 2000. The rehabilitation project involved the removing and replacing of water and sewer lines throughout the subdivision.

I was informed by numerous resident citizens of damage done to private property by the contracting companies employed by Metro to complete the project. Several of the residents also informed me of damage done to the residential streets serving Hermitage Hills. This damage was directly attributed to the removal of underground water and sewer lines. The patchwork paving that the contractors did to the streets was considered a temporary repair and unacceptable to the residents.

In conversations with Bob Wingo of the Department of Water and Sewerage Services, I was informed that Metro Water did not consider itself responsible for making the permanent repairs to the streets. Because public street maintenance was under the jurisdiction of the Department of Public Works, I was informed that the district councilman would be responsible for allocating the necessary capital to Public Works for them to pave the entire length of the streets. I disagreed with that position.

In early October 2000, I traveled the streets of Hermitage Hills and took many pictures of the inadequate patching by Metro Water. On October 11, 2000, in a meeting with Mayor Bill Purcell, the photographs were used to challenge the position taken by Metro Water officials. I informed the mayor that the Hermitage Hills Rehabilitation Project was only one of many such projects to be undertaken throughout Metropolitan Nashville as Metro Water took over numerous private utility companies. The refusal to repair such extensively damaged public streets as rapidly as possible would prove extremely costly to the city and its citizens. In addition, Mayor Purcell was informed of the need to have damaged private property repaired as quickly as possible.

Following the meeting, Mayor Purcell contacted the Water Services Department and notified them of its responsibility to repair in full the public streets damaged by these projects. In addition, I was informed that "any damage done to private property as a result of the replacing and upgrading of the sewerage system will be repaired by the contracting company doing the work."[27] I was extremely appreciative of the quick and positive response from both the mayor and the Department of Water and Sewerage Services pertaining to this issue.

The full and complete takeover of the Cumberland Utility District was finalized with the adoption of Ordinance No. BL2003-1425 by the Metropolitan Council on June 24, 2003, and its approval by Mayor Bill Purcell on June 25, 2003. The ordinance authorized the assumption and taking over by Metro of all public functions, rights, duties and property, assets and liabilities connected with First Suburban Water Utility District of Davidson County and assuming service jurisdiction and the metropolitan mayor to execute the agreement.

The ordinance was recommended by Director Scott Potter of the Department of Water and Sewerage Services and Director David Manning of the Department of Finance. It was also recommended by representatives of the Cumberland Utility District, illustrating the successful completion of negotiations for the takeover. Among those from CUD who signed onto the bill were President Dorothy L. Sanders, Vice President Charles C. Hudson, Secretary Hubert Wiles, and attorney Cecil D. Branstetter Sr. I co-sponsored the ordinance with fellow councilmembers Lawrence Hall Jr. and Phil Ponder.

The adoption and approval of the ordinance ended an era in the Hermitage community of private utility service. It ushered in a movement toward substantial upgrades to the water and sewer infrastructure which promoted a healthier and more efficient community environment for the citizens of Hermitage.

State Government

Numerous projects were sucessfully completed by a coordinated effort between state and metropolitan authorities. The interaction that I had with State Representative Ben West Jr., State Senator Joe Haynes, and representatives of various state departments was vital to accelerating the completion of these projects.

In addition, the source of certain adverse issues facing the community involved the refusal of state authorities to grant municipalities greater authority to control and monitor development within their boundaries. Such an issue dealt with the failure of titleholders to maintain property within established residential subdivisions.

Also, there were numerous instances where mandated state programs adversely impacted the local community. Exemplifying this issue was the placement of group homes for the mentally challenged in private, well-established subdivisions. During my tenure on the Metropolitan Council, there were numerous instances where constituents of District 14 were negatively affected by such issues.

"Actual Notice" vs. "Constructive Notice"

One of the key issues that required my close interaction with state authorities involved vacant and neglected properties situated throughout Metropolitan Nashville. Such properties had an adverse impact on neighboring properties, specifically with the emergence of urban sprawl.

I cooperated with State Representative Ben West Jr. in an attempt to address this issue. Upon my election to the Metropolitan Council, I had been informed of a number of vacant residences throughout District 14 and the devaluation they projected onto neighboring residences. These vacant residences were situated within large residential subdivisions.

The completion of a title search of the properties in question illustrated that the titleholders were either individuals who resided, or companies that were headquartered, outside of Metropolitan Nashville and Davidson County. In many instances, the titleholders were located outside the state of Tennessee.

Many of these nonresident titleholders refused to maintain their properties, which often resulted in lowered property values of surrounding homes. The unoccupied residences acted as enticements to vermin, unruly teenagers, and vagrants. Intrusions into the vacant residences promoted an extremely unhealthy and unsafe environment.

Metropolitan authorities were extremely limited in action they could take to alleviate such issues. I discovered that state authorities controlled local procedures governing the addressing of vacant sites. The primary procedure that raised concern dealt with the notification process required of metropolitan authorities. Metropolitan officials were required by state law to give "actual notice" to the titleholders of unoccupied structures prior to taking any punitive action to alleviate the situation. Actual notice had been defined as "notice expressly and actually given, and brought home directly to the party."[28]

The law stated that "inspectors must send any hearing or order notification by certified mail, which requires a signature from the property owner receiving the notice. Each notification can take three to five weeks to deliver because it requires an exact address of the property owner, which may not be on file with the Metro trustee's office." It was further illustrated that "though the notification process usually takes three to five weeks, the entire process, including inspections and hearings, could take inspectors six to 10 weeks."[29]

During numerous meetings with Representative West, legal advisor Don Jones, and officials from both the Metro Legal Department and the Codes Administration, it was agreed that the Metropolitan Council should adopt a resolution calling for the General Assembly to require only "constructive notice" be sent to titleholders of unoccupied and unkempt properties. Constructive notice was defined as "providing information or knowledge of a fact imputed by law to a person (although he may not actually have it), because he could have discovered the fact by proper diligence, and his situation was such as to cast upon him the duty of inquiring into it."[30]

Basically, it involved informing the titleholder of the issue with their property through a letter sent to the address on record at the office of the Assessor of Property. Providing such notice to the titleholder would be far less time consuming to the metropolitan authorities. "Under the amended law, the process would be cut to two to four weeks."[31]

Such a streamlining of the process was considered in the best interest of the city. "Terry Cobb, Metro Codes Administration director, said amending the law makes sense because 'any time you can take a few days or weeks out of the bureaucratic process, it benefits everyone.'"[32]

Failure to respond to the notice by the titleholder would allow local authorities to step in and maintain the property. The subsequent governmental maintenance would require a lien be placed on the property. To regain full and clear title of the property, the titleholder was then required to repay the lien.

There were several properties that exemplified such vacant and neglected sites in District 14. One example was a single-family residence on Bonnavue Drive in Hermitage Hills. Upon my election in 1995, the residence had stood uninhabited for approximately seven years and had promoted an extremely unhealthy environment on the neighboring homes. The titleholder was a resident of San Diego, California. According to Barbara McGlasson, who lived across the street, "the house directly in front of ours has become a bigger eyesore every year. The shutters are broken, the grass is never mowed, and there are about two truckloads of trash in the backyard. It looks and smells just awful, and

The vacant Bonnavue Drive residence in 1996

in recent years it has become a meeting place for some of the young kids around here. Last year, some of them broke into the house, and set a fire in the living room."[33]

In an attempt to have the site stabilized, I notified metropolitan authorities of the situation. Metropolitan Nashville was unable to take any appropriate action on the property until actual notice was provided to the titleholder as dictated by state law. However, the titleholder had proven completely unresponsive to attempts to notify him of the problems. Due to the titleholder's failure to respond, questions were raised as to whether the address applied to the notice was in fact the correct address. In the meantime, I attempted to correspond with the titleholder about his property.

His continued lack of response forced metropolitan authorities to board the residence and maintain the yard. "Finally, Metro confiscated the property and the federal Housing and Urban Development agency (HUD) purchased it from the city government. After renovating the house and property, HUD later sold it. But that sequence of events took almost three years."[34]

Additional vacant and unkempt homes were located on Lakeland Drive and Surrey Road. The Lakeland Drive residence was owned by a mortgage company headquartered in Des Moines, Iowa. Its failure to maintain the property resulted in numerous attempts by metropolitan authorities to notify the company of the situation. Finally, the property was sold to HUD, which stabilized the property and sold it to private homeowners.

The Surrey Road property was brought to my attention by several neighboring residents. After hearing their concerns, I notified both the Metropolitan Health Department and the Department of Codes Administration, requesting that they inspect the site. Following their inspection, the owner of the property was notified that the residence on the site was designated as uninhabitable. The findings of the inspection included:

- Adequate electrical outlets not provided, inadequate or defective service entrance, defective wiring creating a fire hazard
- Bath facilities, kitchen sink cold and hot water not provided as required by Section 16.24.110 of the Housing Code

***Left:** A view of the Surrey Road residence front door notifying the public of the instability of the site* ***Right:** The back door of the vacant Surrey Road residence illustrating the accumulation of unwanted debris*

- Interior of house in a very unsanitary condition creating a health and fire hazard
- Roof leaks in several places
- Dilapidated shed and fences and garage creating a fire hazard
- Yard area in a very unsanitary condition (tall grass and weeds)
- Cornices, eaves, steps, siding, foundation and underpinning in a highly deteriorating condition
- Windows and doors defective; glass and screens not provided for all openings
- Interior highly damaged and in a very unsanitary condition including walls, ceilings, floors, doors, and woodwork
- Defective electric wall heating system in violation of Section 16.24.120 of the Housing Code.[35]

Finally, it was stated in a letter to the titleholders that they were responsible for the demolition of the residential structure and the clearing of all the debris. This was based upon the fact that the cost of repairs necessary to make the dwelling fit for human habitation would exceed 50 percent of the physical value of the residence.

In an attempt to force immediate action on such a procedural amendment by state authorities, I introduced Resolution No. RS2002-949 in February 2002, and Resolution No. RS2002-1203 in October 2002 to the Metropolitan Council. The Council unanimously adopted both resolutions. However, following the adoption of the

October resolution by the Metropolitan Council, Representative West "said that before he will introduce the bill in January, he plans to take the proposal to the state attorney general to ensure that the amendment won't violate anyone's property rights."[36]

The lack of action on the part of state authorities following the passage of the resolution motivated my continual communication with Representative West. I was informed of certain legal questions associated with the state approving the use of constructive notice. Such legal questions were centered on the possible violation of the property rights of individual citizens by a governmental entity.

Would the allowance of constructive notice by government officials to inform private titleholders of their violations to local property standards represent adequate notification? If not, the failure to provide adequate notification would represent neglect on the part of government officials and violate the property rights guaranteed to citizens.

In addition, West informed me that members of the General Assembly representing semi-rural and rural communities of Tennessee had voiced severe reservations about relieving municipal officials of the actual notice requirement. Their reservations were based upon their belief that amending the notification process and requiring only constructive notice be given to nonresident titleholders would substantially increase municipal power to regulate the use of property by private citizens. Such an increase in municipal power was considered unacceptable.

In contrast, I believed that an extremely dense urban environment represented a completely unique municipal environment in Tennessee. There should have been no comparison between urban and semi-rural/rural communities. The dense development of an urban environment necessitated a strict property standards code to regulate property usage in the urban environment. The failure to enforce the code undermined its primary purpose of presenting a stable environment in the city and protecting individual property investments. The amendment would in no way violate individual property rights.

However, at the end of my tenure on the Metropolitan Council in September 2003, state authorities had taken no action to allow municipal authorities to streamline the notification process.

State-Sponsored Group Homes

In 1968, the federal government adopted the Civil Rights Act. Title VIII of that federal law was the Fair Housing Act that prohibited "discrimination in the sales, rental, and financing of dwellings, and in other housing related transactions, based on race, color, national origin, religion, sex, familial status (including children under the age of 18 living with parents of legal custodians, pregnant women, and people securing custody of children under the age of 18), and handicap (disability)." In addition, the Americans with Disabilities Act of 1990 was adopted to prevent "discrimination based on disability in programs, services, and activities provided or made available by public entities."[37]

The U.S. Department of Housing and Urban Development (HUD) was responsible for administering and enforcing these federal acts. HUD was to enforce Title II of the Americans with Disabilities Act "when it relates to state and local public housing, housing assistance and housing referrals."[38]

The federal government prompted state governments to implement public housing programs through the guarantee of sizeable federal grants that were to be used to fund such programs. One of the key housing programs implemented by the state of Tennessee and mandated by the federal government was centered on the reintegration of mentally challenged individuals into society. This reintegration was to be achieved by grouping a number of mentally challenged individuals into a single residence. Such residences were to be situated in well-established, private, single-family subdivisions. Each residence was administered by employees of either for-profit or not-for-profit companies that were under contract with the state of Tennessee. The program was under the jurisdiction of the State Department of Mental Health & Developmental Disabilities. It was specifically administered by that department's Division of Mental Retardation Services.

The failure of government to adequately fund state-sponsored mental health institutions promoted the implementation of the program. One of the key controversies surrounding the program dealt with where mentally handicapped individuals were to be housed upon their release from state institutions. The overwhelming number of group homes associated with this program were situated in well-established, single-family subdivisions.

Questions were raised by neighboring residents pertaining to the extent of the reintegration into society of mentally challenged individuals residing in such group homes. Also, homeowners had concerns pertaining to the care of such group home residents by the companies under contract with the state.

Such concerns were best illustrated by the fact that neighboring homeowners rarely, if ever, saw the residents or had any interaction with them, thereby questioning whether the residents were being forced to stay indoors to their own detriment. This failure to interact seemed to undermine the primary purpose of such group homes.

The first issue the citizens of District 14 had with this program occurred in October 1999. Involved in the issue was rental property located on Jacksonian Drive in the Hermitage Hills subdivision. In mid-October, a flyer was circulated by homeowners through the subdivision notifying the area residents of the intended use for this property. The flyer named the titleholder of the single-family residence as James T. Ivey, a resident of McDonough, Georgia. The residence was to be leased by two mentally handicapped young men in their twenties. In addition, the young men were "under the supervision of Community Options, Inc., a non-profit organization under contract with the State of Tennessee to provide care for the disabled."[39]

Questions and concerns raised by the area residents were centered on the government agency involved in this program, the source of the funding, who the residents were, the process used in placing mentally challenged residents in the group home, the manner in which they were to be supervised, and what, if any, dangers these residents presented to themselves or the neighborhood.

The flyer also said that the placement of government group homes in the subdivision could adversely affect the standard of living of the neighborhood, threaten the safety and security of the neighborhood, and open the door for further group homes in Hermitage Hills. This would devalue the private residences of the subdivision. The flyer called upon the area residents to contact Representative Ben West Jr., Mayor Bill Purcell, and me to obtain answers to the questions raised.

Upon receiving a number of telephone calls from area residents, I was made aware that the placement of group homes was a state-sponsored program. Based upon that information, I attempted to contact the state officials responsible for administering this program. However, the state officials were unresponsive to my queries. I then contacted Representative Ben West Jr. and cooperated with him to sponsor a community meeting for those affected by the placement of this home.

On October 21, 1999, the community meeting was held at Hermitage Elementary School and was attended by approximately sixty-five area residents. I informed those in attendance that the purpose of the meeting was to "address community concern over this house" and that Representative West and I "asked representatives from Community Option, Inc., and the Mental Health Department to be present to answer questions."[40]

West claimed that, "I think there is an issue of people not understanding what is going on. I also think the homes need to be scrutinized and the caregivers made more cognizant of the concerns of neighbors."[41] Since there was little understanding of the program by the general public, there was a need for government officials to be more cooperative and communicative with the affected citizens.

In the question-and-answer session of the meeting, area resident Ronald Robinson voiced that he was appreciative of "the opportunity Stanley and West gave us to meet with people involved. We have been concerned about moving mentally disabled people into a residential area. Those kind of people can have conditions that are difficult to deal with, and we have worried about how the home would be managed, staffed and controlled."[42]

In attempting to provide answers to the community, Barbera Brent, deputy commissioner for Mental Retardation Services, claimed that the houses involved in the program "have from one to three residents. Most care providers are non-profits; however, we've had more for-profits coming in in the last few years." She further "stressed that occupants of the home are subject to 24-hour supervision, though the number of caregivers present varies from case to case."[43]

The conclusion of the meeting left few residents satisfied with the answers provided by state authorities. Because this placement program represented a state program that was mandated by the federal government, there was virtually no action that could be taken to restrict the placement of group homes in private subdivisions. The closing of such homes could only be brought about by state or federal authorities who had acknowledged illegal or abusive activity from a specific home. A more cooperative relationship between federal, state, and local authorities was needed to educate the public on this placement program. This cooperation would relieve viable concerns pertaining to such homes.

Similarly, another government group home was opened in District 14 in 2001. Upon receiving notice from neighboring residents of suspicious activities occurring from a single-family residence on Downeymeade Drive, I discovered the placement of a government home in the well-established subdivision. I contacted Representative West to ask if the residence had been purchased for use in the state-sponsored group housing program for the mentally challenged. West was notified by officials of the state Mental Health Department that the residential property was being used in the program. It was at that time that we determined a community meeting was necessary to answer questions and concerns of the neighboring citizens.

A meeting was held at the Hermitage police precinct in February 2002. In addition to numerous concerned residents, representatives of the Division of Mental Retardation Services, the Office of Legal Counsel, and representatives of the Evergreen Presbyterian Ministries, Inc. (who administered this particular group home), attended the meeting. The meeting clearly evidenced tension between government authorities and the private citizens.

When questioned by residents why they had not received notice of the opening of this group home in the area, Cindy Tyler of the Office of Legal Counsel claimed, "the men's right to privacy were the same as anyone else's, ruling out any notification of the move."[44]

In addition, Norma Steadman of the Evergreen Ministries, Inc., chided the residents: "When you moved in, did you go around to every neighbor and say, 'Hi, I'm normal and I'm moving in?' They have the right to live just like we do."[45]

However, such mentally challenged residents did not live the same as others in society. They required constant monitoring by caregivers. Such monitoring, especially of those that were extremely mentally challenged, did not allow for independent living.

Although the vast majority of residents "had little objection to three mentally challenged men moving into their neighborhood, most were strongly opposed to the noise and traffic congestion that the home brought with it."[46] This was best illustrated by one neighboring resident who noted that "there is constant traffic at all hours of the night, often with raucous music playing as the cars pass by."

Another neighbor complained that the additional autos parked along the street, supposedly driven by caregivers, had blocked her drive, forcing her to call the police. In addition, resident David Schankle claimed "I don't care what [officials] say, it's constant traffic up and down the road all night long."[47] The increased traffic along the residential street raised concerns pertaining to the safety of children.

Finally, the safety issue forced one resident to ask about the history of the mentally challenged men who were to reside in the home. However, "Janet Simons, Regional Director for the Middle Tennessee region of the Division of Mental Retardation, pointed out that such information is considered confidential under state rules. It is actually against the law to notify anyone of such a move without the express permission of those involved."[48]

Obviously, the refusal of government authorities to notify neighboring citizens about the placement of a group home in private residential neighborhoods pointed to a noticeable flaw in the program. Homeowners had invested heavily in their properties and should have been notified of the placement of a government-sponsored group home. In addition, any information of the residents' past that hinted of possible dangers to the local community should have been shared with the resident citizens. However, state administrators of the program gave little or no consideration to the citizens neighboring the group homes.

During the meeting, I made reference to the fact that the federal law that mandated such group homes was "passed over 30 years ago and that decreed the integration of people with disabilities into the general population, including those with mental handicaps." Furthermore, I stressed that it was "time for the federal government to take another look at this law," adding that "the law never took into consideration cities the size of Nashville" and the heavy impact the placement of group homes would have on the resident citizens of a densely developed urban area. Finally, I observed that "until the legislature rectifies this law, there will be no change in the situation. The state needs to expand on its responsibility."[49]

Following the meeting, I corresponded with Congressman Bob Clement in an attempt to obtain his endorsement of a review of the federal Fair Housing Act. I recommended to Congressman Clement possible amendments to the law that would more thoroughly involve the general public in the placement of group homes.

However, there was no desire on the part of the congressman to review or amend the law. As a result, state authorities were allowed to continue placing group homes in neighborhoods without notifying the resident titleholders.

Federal Government

Proposed Leasing of Corps Property for Public Schools

The Donelson-Hermitage community witnessed a rapid expansion of both demographic and developmental growth with the progression of time. Additional single-family subdivisions and multi-family complexes were constructed at an ever-increasing pace. The areas specifically targeted for residential development were located in the Hermitage community, south of Interstate 40. This was directly contiguous with the J. Percy Priest Reservoir.

Infrastructure improvements were needed for this residential expansion. One notable area of infrastructure improvements involved the construction of public schools to house expanded student enrollment. The construction of these schools could not occur unless the metropolitan government obtained the appropriate acreage upon which to construct the needed schools. However, the increasing number of new developments eliminated open, undeveloped tracts of property that could be targeted for public school construction. Locating and obtaining the appropriate public school sites was proven to be an extremely tedious process.

The federal judiciary released Metropolitan Nashville from the busing mandate in 1998. A prerequisite for this release was the financing of needed public school improvements and/or additions to the public school infrastructure by the Metropolitan Council. As a result, the Council passed a twelve-cent property tax increase in July 1998. This tax increase raised approximately $206 million of revenue for capital upgrades to the public school system.

One of the projects to be funded by this capital allocation was a new Ruby Major Elementary School. This school was to be located south of Interstate 40, preferably in the Hermitage community. It was needed to relieve overcrowding at Dodson, Tulip Grove, and Hickman Elementary schools. The Ruby Major Elementary School was scheduled to be completed by the beginning of the 2002–2003 school year. In addition, a new Hermitage Middle School was included in the capital improvements budget to relieve the overcrowding at Dupont Tyler and Donelson Middle schools. Authorities from the Board of Education desired to have both the scheduled Ruby Major Elementary School and the proposed Hermitage Middle School share the same campus.

This dual facility campus concept was popularly accepted and was already represented by the existing Tulip Grove Elementary/Dupont Tyler Middle School and the Hickman Elementary/Donelson Middle School campus sites. However, such a campus required a larger parcel of land to be acquired. The requirement delayed the acquisition and ultimate construction of these schools.

In late 2000, I initiated a dialogue with Congressman Bob Clement requesting federal assistance to obtain the appropriate acreage upon which both the Ruby Major Elementary and Hermitage Middle schools could be constructed.

In a December 11, 2000, letter to Congressman Clement, I proposed that the federal government "donate approximately 30 contiguous acres of property under the jurisdiction of the U.S. Army Corps of Engineers to the Metropolitan-Nashville Board of Education for use as a campus for the proposed Ruby Major Elementary School and a new Hermitage Middle School." In the letter, I suggested that "due to their close proximity to the J. Percy Priest Reservoir both schools could be designated as 'greenway schools' to further educate the public on the Greenway Program and promote its benefits to the community."

In addition, I outlined that "federal and local authorities would cooperate to incorporate both a nature studies program and a government studies program into the curriculum." Both programs were directly linked to the location of this public school site on corps property and the cooperation given by both federal and municipal government officials to establish this site.

Congressman Bob Clement and Councilman Stanley

Finally, I noted that "similar to the recent passage by the Metropolitan Council of a resolution to locate a new middle school on an 18-acre parcel of property belonging to the Nashville Zoo, Inc., this educational campus along the J. Percy Priest Reservoir in Hermitage will play a vital role in stabilizing the public school infrastructure and improving the quality of education for the children of the community."[50]

Congressman Clement responded to my request by addressing a letter to Lieutenant Colonel Pete Taylor on February 1, 2001. Taylor was the Corps of Engineers commander for the Nashville district. In this letter, Clement outlined the requests made by me and requested, "that the Corps of Engineers donate approximately 30 acres of property south of Interstate 40 along Bell Road on J. Percy Priest Lake to the Metropolitan Government of Nashville and Davidson County."[51]

However, in response to this request, the Corps of Engineers refused to donate or lease any property to Metropolitan Nashville for use as a public school campus site. Their position was based on the fact that the J. Percy Priest Master Plan had designated that property contiguous with this site and under the jurisdiction of the corps was to be used solely for recreational purposes. This negative response from the corps motivated the calling of a meeting to discuss this issue in greater detail.

Congressman Clement scheduled a meeting for June 12, 2001. Held at the federal courthouse in downtown Nashville, the meeting was attended by representatives from the Corps of Engineers; the offices of Congressman Clement and Senators Frist and Thompson; the office of the mayor; the Board of Education; the Metropolitan Board of Parks and Recreation; and the U.S. Army Reserve. I attended the meeting with fellow councilmember Phil Ponder.

In an attempt to meet the recreational land-use provision of the J. Percy Priest Master Plan, it was proposed that, similar to the existing McGavock Comprehensive High School campus, the Board of Parks and Recreation and the Board of Education would jointly administer the proposed Ruby Major/Hermitage Middle School site. This joint administration would provide both recreational and educational opportunities for the rapidly growing Donelson-Hermitage community.

The possibility of specifically amending the J. Percy Priest Master Plan to allow for the leasing of unused corps property for educational purposes was also mentioned. Following a substantial discussion over the merits and the limitations of this proposal, the Corps of Engineers agreed to take it under consideration and provide a formal answer no later than mid July.

On July 17, 2001, the Corps of Engineers responded that existing policy prohibited them from leasing property to the government of Metropolitan Nashville and Davidson County for use as a public school campus. They believed that the development of project lands, even for a laudable purpose such as public schools, was not in the long-term interest of the J. Percy Priest project. It was contrary to the regulations that governed land use in this project.

Upon receiving this decision, I attempted to have Congressman Clement consider amending the J. Percy Priest Master Plan. In August 2001, I filed a resolution requesting that federal legislators amend the master plan to allow the leasing of corps property to Metropolitan Nashville upon which to construct the desperately needed schools. However, the Corps of Engineers was a powerful lobbying force in Washington, D.C., and its influence prohibited any members of Congress from filing or considering legislation that did not meet its criteria.

Federal authorities refused to recognize the benefits that could be obtained from leasing corps property to the metropolitan government for use as public school/recreational campus. Such long- and short-term benefits included the creation of a stable public school site for students, teachers, administrators, and the public in general. The wide variety of educational and recreational uses associated with the site would promote a constructive lifestyle for all citizens of the community. Finally, the leasing of this property would have projected a much more cooperative relationship between the federal and municipal governments as they worked in the best interest of the citizens.

Congressional Forum

In 2002, Congressman Bob Clement announced his intent not to seek reelection to the Fifth Congressional District seat of Tennessee. The announcement opened the door for several candidates to seek election to this federal legislative position. Among them were Gayle Ray, John Arriola, and Jim Cooper. The campaign to elect a new representative allowed the citizens of the Fifth Congressional District greater interaction with those attempting to be their next representative in Congress. The open attitude exuded by the candidates in this campaign promoted the scheduling of a congressional forum. The forum was designed to give the citizens of the Donelson-Hermitage community of Metropolitan Nashville a chance to openly question the candidates about issues of local importance. In addition, the forum provided the candidates an opportunity to illustrate their positions on the issues in a face-to-face environment.

Upon the announcement of the candidates seeking election as the Fifth Congressional District representative, I began to cooperate with numerous residential groups to sponsor a political forum for such candidates. The residential groups that agreed to cosponsor and organize the congressional forum included the Nashville Neighborhood Alliance, Inc., the Donelson-Hermitage Neighborhood Association, the Stanford Estates Homeowners Association, the Lake Park Homeowners Association, and the Hermitage Hills Neighborhood Watch.

It was agreed that questions for the candidates would come from both the forum organizers and the audience members. Bob Taylor, president of the Stanford Estates Homeowners Association, stated that the forum should "focus not just on national issues, but on the issues that affect us mainly here in East Davidson and Donelson and Hermitage . . . things that affect us more in our community that involve federal funding."[52]

Some of the more notable issues involving the federal government to be addressed at the forum included the "Fair Housing Act provision that allows state officials to locate homes for the mentally ill in suburban neighborhoods. Some residents believe such homes depreciate surrounding property values." In addition, there were resident homeowners who feared "the homes will function more like mental hospitals than traditional residences."[53]

Another federal policy that was to be addressed at the forum involved federal funding for the placement of public school magnet programs in suburban communities. "Current federal policy refuses to provide capital for operation grants for the establishment of magnet schools in middle-class suburban areas."[54]

It was my belief that such a policy promoted economic class discrimination. The public school system of Metropolitan Nashville uniformly served the entire Davidson County area. The refusal of federal authorities to fund public schools throughout the entire system was clearly inequitable and required a review by federal authorities.

Finally, the issue of amending the U.S. Army Corps of Engineers land lease policy was to be discussed at the forum. I hoped that the congressional forum would present a "congressman willing to step up to the plate and get the Army Corps of Engineers to take a second look at their policy of leasing property in large urban areas." Such an amended land lease policy "would reduce the burden on taxpayers by lowering property acquisition costs"[55] associated with public school sites.

The moderator for the forum was Pat Nolan, senior vice president of the Nashville public relations firm of Dye, Van Mol and Lawrence. In addition, he had a long and respected career as a political analyst for Metropolitan Nashville. It was agreed that the forum would begin with Nolan presenting "nine prepared questions to the candidates, who individually had 90 seconds to respond to each question."[56] Those questions and answers would be considered the first part of the program.

The second part of the program involved the candidates answering questions presented by the citizens in the audience. "As audience members arrived, each was given an index card. From the questions written on these cards, nine more questions were directed to the candidates."[57]

The first set of questions presented to the candidates included one that asked their position on amending the federal Fair Housing Act that allowed the placement of government group homes in private residential subdivisions.

Jim Cooper responded that he was concerned over residential property values. However, as he understood it, "this is a state licensing issue and not a matter for the federal government. I would call the commissioners and urge that homes are licensed in a particular place."[58]

Gayle Ray quickly noted that she supports Fair Housing. However, she did believe that "the devil is in the details . . . the regulations, the contracts, the supervision, the folks who are running group homes. People around the group homes are not informed, they have no idea what's happening. A lot of work needs to be done to regulate, have oversight and to make sure that the appropriate folks are placed—that you don't have any criminal backgrounds, and that the rules and regulations of being a good neighbor are followed."[59]

Finally, John Arriola designated that "we need to work with the contractors to make sure there is open communication between the folks that are in the neighborhoods and contractors for the homes. The first key is understanding what is coming into the neighborhood, what the function is."[60]

The question that asked about the placement of public magnet schools in suburban communities followed. Ray stated that "since transportation is now provided [by busing], it seems fair to have a more widely distributed system of magnet schools, so that you can have better, more even access by all kids."[61]

Arriola targeted the importance of the local school boards to make decisions on this matter. He claimed that "we do have an elected school board, the leadership in our school system that certainly could make those decisions . . . decisions based on what's good for the community." In addition, he believed that the federal government should continue to assist in funding magnet programs, "but leave placement to the local school boards."[62]

Jim Cooper believed that "the government should offer more flexibility. Local people have always determined education policy. The federal government helps out with about 5 percent of overall spending. Flexibility is best, so local people can determine their own priorities."[63]

The next question dealt with the refusal of the Corps of Engineers to lease property to metropolitan authorities for the construction of a new elementary and middle school. The question specifically asked what actions the candidates would take to amend corps leasing policy.

Arriola declared, "I cannot think of a better use for such land than for educational purposes. To be able to build a brand-new school on land you all helped to buy . . . what a perfect use."[64]

Cooper responded, "I think it's idiotic when the government already owns land and won't allow it to be transferred to another government entity to be used for a worthy purpose. And there's no more worthy purpose than education. The Army Corps of Engineers may not have gotten the message yet, but I guarantee if I go to Congress, they'll get the message."[65]

Ray answered, "This is part of government bureaucracy at its worse. These rules were made for a certain day and time with no flexibility. It's just common sense that the local entity, in this case Metro government, determines that it already has enough recreational facilities, but it needs more educational facilities. Then that agreement should be worked out very easily. I would work hard to cut through the bureaucratic rules to get what the local community needs."[66]

Additional questions asked of the candidates at the forum involved federal regulation of floodplain development, the candidates' position on a state income tax, and the illegal placement of campaign signs in the community. All three candidates were very forthright in their answers. That gave the individual citizens of the Donelson-Hermitage community the opportunity to openly meet and discuss issues with the person who would represent them in the U.S. Congress.

I was extremely appreciative of the cooperative attitude of the candidates and their staffs regarding their involvement in the forum. In addition, the forum moderator Pat Nolan presented a very professional demeanor that benefited the forum and its proceedings. Finally, cooperating with residential associations to organize the event brought the forum to the general public.

It was my belief that the forum achieved its purpose. During an opening statement at the beginning of the meeting, I stated that "I want all candidates to [be aware] that community organizations within Donelson-Hermitage are extremely strong. They (the candidates) need to understand that once they are elected, even though they will be in Washington, D.C., they still represent this community. They must not bow to lobbying groups, but must listen, first and foremost, to their constituents and the concerns they have within the community."[67]

The interaction between candidates and constituents at the forum promoted an understanding of some of the more important issues facing the community.

Chapter Five

Rezoning and Development Proposals

The emergence of sprawl into the suburban communities of metropolitan Nashville in the mid-1980s initiated a rapid increase in new development and raised substantial concerns from the resident citizens of the communities. These concerns centered primarily on the adverse impacts new development was to have on both the established community and the long-term investments made by local citizens in their property. Donelson-Hermitage represented one of the more notable suburban communities of Metropolitan Nashville that was immediately impacted by sprawl, which, in turn, necessitated a more active involvement in the local political process by the citizens of the community.

Active citizen involvement would enhance the council representation of the area by questioning candidates whose priority allegiance was to large business and development interests and not the resident citizens. Citizen political involvement supported a council candidate who promoted citizen input on rezoning and development issues. Active resident citizens created a more thorough understanding of the process involved in considering land-use proposals. Finally, thorough resident involvement benefited the local community by ensuring that citizen input on rezoning and development proposals was given key consideration by municipal officials. This would protect citizen investments and preserve the established community.

Upon my election to the Metropolitan Council in 1995, the Donelson-Hermitage community had been dealing with controversial land-use proposals for approximately eight years. Thus, the rezoning and development proposals that were brought before me represented sensitive issues for the community. The manner in which the community develops can have long-term impact on the citizens and their investments. It was my responsibility as the elected councilman to ensure that development that was to receive my endorsement would have positive consequences for the community and its citizens.

I was given the ultimate responsibility of regulating the growth of the community. The proper regulation of municipal growth included sponsoring community meetings between the citizens, the developers making the proposal, and the metropolitan officials involved in reviewing the proposed development. These meetings promoted citizen input which represented one of the more vital elements required to accomplish controlled growth within the community.

Since 1987, I have been involved in development issues facing Donelson-Hermitage. This continued involvement educated me on the metropolitan political process associated with rezoning or the review of proposed developments. The emergence of urban sprawl represented an eye-opening experience for the citizens. Among the more notable issues brought to light as a result of increased growth were the inadequacies of the existing infrastructure serving the community and the desperate need to improve and upgrade the highway, water/sewer, public schools, and stormwater drainage infrastructure. In fact, these infrastructural improvements were needed prior to approving sizeable development proposals. A failure to give needed infrastructure upgrades appropriate consideration would undermine and adversely impact the already strained facilities serving the community.

One of the more controversial arguments voiced by supporters of new development dealt with resident citizens being prohibited from standing in the way of progress. They considered any proposed development as a progressive addition to the community without question. Established citizens were criticized when they questioned or opposed such proposals. However, the overwhelming adverse impacts projected on the established community by certain development proposals ultimately brought open opposition by the citizens.

It soon became evident that progress and development were not synonymous. Ultimately, these factors undermined the argument that all new development proposals represented progress and should be supported without question.

Throughout the eight years that I served as a metropolitan councilman, there were few developmental proposals that were brought before me and the district. Many developers had labeled me a "neighborhood activist" and, therefore, unwilling to support any new development in District 14.

That labeling was extremely flawed. I was never anti-development. However, it was my experience that not all proposed development was progressive. In many instances, a developmental proposal was regressive, in that it adversely impacted large segments of society. Such developments failed to address specific infrastructure improvements needed to accommodate such a proposal.

For a development to be truly progressive, there were certain criteria that developers had to be willing to meet prior to my supporting a proposed development. Among these criteria were:

1. new development was to have a minimal impact on the existing infrastructure;

2. private developers must be willing to assist in funding the needed improvements to the public infrastructure dictated by their proposed development; and

3. developers must be willing to attend open community meetings with those resident citizens projected to be impacted.

During the community meetings, sponsored by the councilmember for the area, the developers were required to openly inform the resident citizens of their proposed development and consider citizen response before finalizing their proposed plan. The primary role of these criteria was to assist in establishing open communication and cooperation in order to eliminate the controversy associated with a proposed development. In addition, it would assist me in defending the position of my constituents.

Government Components Involved in the Planning Process

There are numerous government agencies involved in the planning process of Metropolitan Nashville. Many of these agencies provided educated insight on the impact new development would have on the existing municipal infrastructure and ultimately the established community. Included among the more notable of these agencies are the

Department of Public Works, Codes Administration, Water Services Department, and the Metropolitan Nashville Public School System. They provided recommendations as to approval or rejection of a specific land-use proposal to both the Metropolitan Planning Commission and the Metropolitan Council. The Planning Commission and the Council are the two governmental bodies that are given the ultimate authority to approve or disapprove rezoning or development proposals.

Planning Commission/Department of Planning

Planning and regulating the growth of an urban area represented an extremely sensitive task for municipal officials and necessitated the creation of a governmental department and commission to accomplish such a task. The Metropolitan Charter created the Department of Planning and the Planning Commission to act as the "official planning agency for the Metropolitan Government of Nashville and Davidson County."[1] Ultimately, the Planning Commission was empowered to make recommendations to the Metropolitan Council on such things as rezoning issues, development plans, and planned unit development proposals.

The Planning Commission was to have "ten (10) members. The mayor shall serve as a member of the commission by virtue of his public office and one (1) member of the metropolitan county council shall be elected by that body from its membership to serve as a member of the commission for a term of two (2) years. The member of the council selected to serve as a member of this commission shall be the chairman of the council committee on planning, provided such a committee is established."[2]

The Planning, Zoning, Historical and Port Authority Committee represented one of fourteen standing committees of the Metropolitan Council. These committees were appointed by the vice mayor each year. In addition, the vice mayor also appointed the chairs of each standing committee for a term of one year.

There were two exceptions to the designation of committee chairs. These exceptions were the Traffic and Parking Committee and the Planning, Zoning, Historical and Port Authority Committee. The Metropolitan Council was responsible for electing the chairs of those committees.

Finally, "eight (8) members shall be appointed by the mayor and shall be confirmed by a majority vote of the whole membership of the council. The eight (8) members appointed shall serve a term of four (4) years, respectively, or until a successor is duly appointed and qualified; except, of the members first appointed, two shall serve for a term of one (1) year, two (2) for a term of two (2) years, two (2) for a term of three (3) years, and two (2) for a term of four (4) years."[3]

In terms of organization, the Planning Commission was to elect one of its appointive members as chair. The elected chair of the Planning Commission was to serve for a period of one year. Any other officers that the Planning Commission deemed necessary were to be chosen to serve in such a role. Additionally, the Planning Commission was to "meet regularly at a public building at least once a month and its meetings shall be open to the public."[4]

It was designated that "six (6) members shall constitute a quorum for the transaction of any business, which shall be accomplished in accordance with bylaws adopted by the commission. A majority vote of the members present and constituting a quorum shall be necessary to decide any item of business requiring action by the commission."[5]

Following an analysis of land-use proposals brought before the commission, the staff of professional land-use planners employed by the commission was to make recommendations to the commission. The commission was not bound by these recommendations. However, in the vast majority of instances, the commission followed the recommendations of its staff. Many times the recommendation was in opposition to the popularly elected councilmember and the citizens to be impacted by the development.

The Metropolitan Charter also created a Department of Planning to work in coordination with the Planning Commission. This department was headed by an executive director. The director was to be appointed by the Planning Commission, with the option of entering into "an employment contract with such person for a period not exceeding five (5) years, and at a compensation to be fixed by the commission."[6]

The executive director was to "attend all meetings of the planning commission, act as its secretary, keep minutes of its proceedings, direct the staff of the commission in its work, and shall have such other authority, duties and responsibilities as the commission may

RICK BERNHARDT, FAICP, TOWN PLANNER

Rick Bernhardt is executive director of the Metropolitan Nashville-Davidson County Planning Department. A town planner for over thirty years, he has applied integrated urban design solutions to specific planning problems. Bernhardt has focused on using growth management techniques together with multi-modal transportation investments and policies to coordinate the timing and staging of development to achieve specific land use and community objectives. His practice has focused on creating sustainable communities, neighborhoods, and places through the use of traditional design principles.

Prior to joining Metro, he was director of EDAW's Town Planning Studio. Previously, he was director of the city of Orlando's Department of Planning and Development for seventeen years, and he directed the designation of the city of Orlando as a Demonstration Sustainable Community by the state of Florida.

Bernhardt grew up in Nashville, graduating from Glencliff High School before entering college. He received a bachelor of science in economics from Auburn University and a master of city planning with a concentration in housing and urban structure from the Ohio State University. Bernhardt was the recipient of the Distinguished Alumni Award from the Ohio State University in 1997.

He currently serves as the chair of the planners task force for the Congress of the New Urbanism and is coordinating the CNU codes project. Bernhardt previously served as a two-term president of the Florida chapter of the American Planning Association and chair of APA's chapter presidents council where he also served on the Board of Directors. Most recently, he was elected to the initial College of Fellows of the American Institute of Certified Planners.

He is a recipient of APA's National Distinguished Service Award as well as the Outstanding Planner Award from the Florida chapter. The Congress for the New Urbanism presented the Catherine Brown Award for his contributions to the field of new urbanism and traditional town planning.

Through his interest in housing, Bernhardt founded the Orlando Neighborhood Improvement Corporation. This represented Orlando's largest non-profit affordable housing corporation. He also served on the founding Boards of Directors for the Central Florida Coalition for the Homeless and the Orlando chapter of Habitat for Humanity.

In addition, he is currently on the program advisory committees of the graduate schools of Public Administration and Urban and Regional Planning of the University of Florida as well as the executive council of the Shimberg Center for Affordable Housing.

Bernhardt serves as a faculty associate with the Lincoln Institute of Land Policy and served on the Executive Advisory Committee of the Florida Growth Management Conflict Resolution Consortium as well as the Board of Directors of the Governor's Council for Sustainable Florida.

He has written, lectured, and participated in the formation of major planning policy issues nationwide.

Upon his selection as the new director of planning for Metropolitan Nashville in 1999, Bernhardt realized the importance of cooperation between the Planning Department and the popularly elected Metropolitan Council when addressing land use controversies. To instill such cooperation, Bernhardt toured each council district with the council member. These tours educated him on specific land use issues within each district and the position council members had on such issues. The district tours worked to establish a cooperative and communicative relationship between him and district council members.

Rick Bernhardt and his wife, Linda, have been married since 1968. They have two daughters, Shannon Baughn and Ashley, and one granddaughter, Trinity.

require and establish or as may be provided by ordinance."[7] Other authorities and duties of the executive director were the coordination of activities between the professional staff of the commission and the Metropolitan Council in developing land-use policy.

From 1999 to 2002, Director Rick Bernhardt and the land-use planners of his staff worked closely with me and other councilmembers to develop a floodplain ordinance. This represented a much more restrictive and comprehensive municipal policy for floodplain development than had ever existed in Metropolitan Nashville.

The passage of this regulatory ordinance by the Metropolitan Council in March 2002 illustrated the benefits of having representatives of the Planning Commission/Planning Department and the Metropolitan Council cooperate to develop land-use policy for an ever growing municipality. The development of land-use policy by the Planning Commission and the Metropolitan Council was guided by a general plan adopted by metropolitan authorities.

During my tenure as a councilmember, the Metropolitan Council, Planning Commission, and Department of Planning cooperated to develop and adopt a revised zoning code for Metropolitan Nashville and Davidson County. The zoning code created "a diverse range of zoning districts which establish appropriate land uses and associated standards of development needed to implement the land-use policies of the General Plan."[8]

The new zoning code also established "special overlay districts, including Planned Unit Development districts, which are intended to address specific aspects of land-use control or design not easily accomplished by conventional zoning techniques."[9]

In addition, the new code established "development standards which are designed to protect the value and integrity of neighboring properties, enhance the general character and appearance of the community, reinforce the Central Business District, and provide for a reasonable balance between efficient utilization of land, protection of this community's environmental resources and assuring the operational integrity of streets."[10]

Finally, the code established "rules and procedures deemed necessary and appropriate to administer and enforce the provisions of this code, so as to protect the public health, safety, morals, convenience, order, prosperity and general welfare of the present and future inhabitants of Metropolitan Nashville and Davidson County."[11]

The process leading to the adoption of the revised code included open public hearings whereby citizen input played a vital role in the development of the final draft of the zoning code. The revised zoning code was adopted by the Metropolitan Council and made effective on January 1, 1998.

General Plan/Subarea Planning

The general plan of Metropolitan Nashville played a key role in influencing the position the Planning Commission was to take on rezoning or development proposals. The general plan is defined as "an official public document adopted by a local government as a policy guide to decisions about the physical development of the community."[12]

Both state law and the Metropolitan Charter required the adoption of such a plan. In 1981, metropolitan officials adopted The General Plan for Nashville, 1980–2000 to regulate growth in Metropolitan Nashville during the upcoming years. However, by 1989, the plan was proven to be woefully inadequate as a regulatory document for development in the city.

One of the major flaws in the general plan involved a failure by planning officials to acknowledge the emergence of sprawl throughout the suburban communities of Metropolitan Nashville and the growth with which it was associated. This population surge significantly exceeded the expectations of the general plan and "placed considerable pressure on the community's public services."[13]

Among the more notable public services adversely impacted by this extreme growth were the highway infrastructure, water/sewer infrastructure, and public school facilities. For example, metropolitan officials refused to initiate the division of the 533-square-mile Metropolitan Nashville and Davidson County urban area into small area plans as recommended by the general plan. It was recommended that these small areas be created to allow for the adoption of a much more refined land-use policy for each area. However, antiquated politics controlled metropolitan authorities and all policy considerations at the time. This included the land-use policy that would govern the development of the city. The heavy influence of business lobbyists at that time allowed planning commissioners to refuse to acknowledge the introduction of sprawl into Metropolitan Nashville.

This lackadaisical attitude toward regulating growth forced citizens to question the adequacy of the existing land-use policy in Metropolitan Nashville and the competency of the metropolitan officials who were responsible for its adoption. In response to the pro-development stance taken by metropolitan officials during this time, residential interests throughout Metropolitan Nashville began organizing into politically oriented homeowners associations. These associations became active in opposing rezoning and development proposals that were projected to have an adverse impact on their residential environments and individual investments.

In addition, the active involvement of resident citizens in the political process began a new era in regulating growth throughout Metropolitan Nashville. The new era was most vividly demonstrated when many of the councilmembers were defeated at the polls in 1987. The new councilmembers began the process of developing a new general plan in cooperation with the Planning Commission and their staff of professional land-use planners as well as the general citizenry.

One of the first steps taken by metropolitan planners and councilmembers to address the inadequacies of the former general plan occurred when "jurisdiction of Metropolitan government was divided into fourteen subareas in order to focus on specific issues or problems in each area and develop specific responses to problems."[14] The division of Metropolitan Nashville unveiled the subarea planning process to the citizens as a key component in the planning process.

Subarea planning was defined as "an ongoing process that involves the preparation, implementation, and periodic review and updating of subarea plans. Public involvement is important in all aspects of the subarea planning process."[15] The overall goals of the subarea planning process included:

- Progress and Preservation—To create planning documents which are dynamic instruments for guiding development decisions while protecting Nashville's character;
- Public Involvement—To promote a thorough understanding of the planning and decision making process, and to insure that public participation is meaningful and informed;
- Economic Opportunities—To address the community and regional development factors influencing the planning process in Nashville;
- Predictability—To provide for a degree of certainty about the future regarding development decisions in the area; and
- Implementation—To provide guidelines for implementation of the plans.[16]

The adoption of the subarea planning process was truly representative of the acknowledgment by metropolitan officials of the need to have an appropriate land-use policy that would protect the interests of all sections of the community.

The first subarea plan to be addressed was Subarea 14, which included the Donelson, Hermitage, and Old Hickory suburban communities. Subarea 14 was "approximately 35,000 acres of land area or approximately fifty-five (55) square miles."[17]

It was the largest of the fourteen subareas, representing approximately 11 percent of the total land area of Davidson County. Developed land represented approximately 50 percent of the total land area of Subarea 14. In addition, over 60 percent of the developed land was residential. These figures illustrated that large tracts of property located throughout Subarea 14 remained undeveloped and vacant. Therefore, developers targeted this area for rezoning and development resulting in controversy within the community.

The metropolitan government adopted Resolution No. 92-135 on February 19, 1992. The resolution accepted a new general plan, entitled Concept 2010: A General Plan for Nashville-Davidson County Government. It superceded "all other previously adopted master, general or comprehensive plans. This plan is the first document in a series of studies that taken together will encompass the General Plan for Nashville-Davidson County."[18] The adoption of the Concept 2010 General Plan designated the subarea planning process as a vital feature of future land-use planning in Metropolitan Nashville.

Subarea planning was considered an ongoing process, thereby it was necessary to update each subarea plan within five years of its original adoption by the metropolitan government. In 1995, the Subarea 14 Plan was scheduled to be updated, which coincided with the election of a new Metropolitan Council. Citizen participation was still considered a necessary component of the planning process. The Planning Commission thus established three levels of citizen participation to be considered when updating a subarea plan. These levels included:

1. Level 1—Allowed for one open public workshop-style meeting for updates that were not expected to be too complex;

2. Level 2—Allowed for numerous open public workshop style meetings; and

3. Level 3—Called for the appointment of a new citizen advisory committee (CAC) and the scheduling of numerous CAC meetings to address extensive changes in the original subarea plan.

The update to the Subarea 14 Plan was designated as Level 2. The update effort included nine open public workshop style meetings that were held between June 22 and October 26, 1995. However, the adoption of an amended land-use recommendation by the Planning Commission did not ensure that proposed development would proceed unimpeded. This was because the Metropolitan Council remained an important component in the planning process.

The Metropolitan Council

The Metropolitan Council was created by Article 3 of the Metropolitan Charter in 1963. Section 3.01 specifically designated that "the legislative authority of the metropolitan government of Nashville and Davidson County, except as otherwise specifically provided in this Charter, shall be vested in the metropolitan county council."[19] The Metropolitan Council was to "exercise its legislative authority only by ordinance, except as otherwise specifically provided by this Charter or by general law."[20]

This legislative authority provided that the Council was primarily responsible for developing and adopting municipal policy for the benefit of the citizens of Metropolitan Nashville. One of the most prominent types of legislation that the Metropolitan Council was to consider involved land-use ordinances. Such ordinances included rezoning and development proposals that had been considered by the Planning Commission. The recommendation of the Planning Commission on the proposed ordinance was included in a report on the land use that was to be considered.

To progress through the legislative process, each land-use ordinance must be sponsored by a councilmember. Ultimately, the councilmember in whose district the rezoning or development was proposed was given priority consideration to be the sponsor. However, a refusal of the district councilmember to sponsor the ordinance required its sponsorship by an at-large councilmember. A refusal by a district member to sponsor an ordinance was primarily based on opposition to the bill.

However, I observed that a failure to sponsor such a bill would remove control of it from the district councilmember and give legislative control to an at-large member. This would certainly not guarantee the defeat of the ordinance. In some instances, it would promote the passage of a land-use ordinance to which the district member and the constituents were opposed. It was always my position to sponsor any ordinance that was proposed for District 14. The legislative control that was given to me as the sponsor would allow for either the approval or disapproval of such an ordinance as dictated to me by the constituents of District 14.

Each ordinance was first considered by the Metropolitan Council's Planning, Zoning, Historical and Port Authority Committee prior to its second of three readings before the Metropolitan Council. Following a review of the ordinance and giving consideration to both the recommendation of the Planning Commission and the position of the sponsoring councilmember, the Planning Committee voted to either support or oppose said ordinance. During both the second and third readings, the position of the sponsoring councilmember had great influence on what stance the Metropolitan Council was to take on a specific ordinance.

Throughout the history of the Metropolitan Council, the policy of "councilmanic courtesy" was practiced by the elected members. This longtime practice involved "giving a district council member absolute control over all zoning in his or her district."[21] This prevented any substantive questions from being raised or objections being made to a rezoning or development proposal by other councilmembers outside the district.

There was little attention given to this practice until the appearance of sprawl throughout Metropolitan Nashville and Davidson County in the mid 1980s. This sprawl promoted a rapid and unregulated growth that adversely impacted the established community. Many councilmembers at that time were heavily influenced by the development lobby and believed their decisions pertaining to rezoning and development proposals should be unquestioned by either other councilmembers or their constituents. The controversies that arose from sprawl made citizens aware of councilmanic courtesy and the refusal of many councilmembers to debate the positive and negative impacts of rezoning and development proposals.

The adoption of an open, communicative process when deliberating land-use proposals did not allow councilmembers to buckle under the demands of the developmental lobby and misrepresent their constituents.

My sponsorship of rezoning or development ordinances was based on researching the ultimate impact such a rezoning or development would have on the local community. The research involved my cooperating with the professional staff of the Planning Commission, sponsoring open community meetings to obtain citizen input about the proposal, and meeting with the attorney to the Metropolitan Council to be advised on legal aspects.

I was not dependent on councilmanic courtesy to ensure the approval or disapproval of the ordinance. My arguments both for or against such a proposal were supported by research and presented to each of the councilmembers. Based on the merits of these arguments, the ordinance was then either approved or disapproved. This position successfully regulated growth in District 14 and benefited the established community.

District 14 Rezoning and Development Proposals (1995–2003)

Since 1987, I had worked extensively with the Metropolitan Council, resident citizens, developers, and metropolitan officials from various departments to address rezoning and development proposals in our community. These experiences and interactions resulted in my understanding of the current land-use planning process. This understanding, in turn, allowed me to develop a land-use philosophy that would address the needs of all parties involved. In addition, this philosophy preserved and protected the established community from intrusive rezoning and developments.

The key component to this philosophy was open communication. It required open dialogue between officials from different metropolitan departments or agencies involved in the planning process. Finally, open communication was essential between the developer of the proposal and the resident citizens who were to be impacted. This promotion of open communication and cooperation pertaining to growth was achieved through community meetings sponsored by the district councilmember. The community meetings were to be attended by resident citizens, the developer(s), pertinent metropolitan department officials, and the district councilmember.

During these meetings, questions and concerns were addressed. The district councilmember used public opinion to determine the position to take pertaining to the land-use proposal. The more notable land-use proposals that were addressed during my eight years on the Metropolitan Council included a Ravenwood rezoning, the Cloverwood development, and land-use proposals along Millionaire Row on Lebanon Pike.

Ravenwood Rezoning and Development Proposal

In 1995, interest in developing the eleven hundred-acre bend in the Stones River was revitalized. Adopted in January of 1990, the Subarea 14 Plan recommended that the undeveloped tract was to be developed in both a residential and office concentration manner. Residential density was recommended to be no greater than two to four units per acre. The 1996 Subarea 14 Plan Update was amended to recommend that the entire tract be developed residentially. In addition, the maximum density of development should not exceed two dwelling units per acre because of the unanswered questions pertaining to needed highway infrastructure improvements.

Development of this property required a change in zoning. To achieve this rezoning, the development proposal needed to meet the recommendations set forth in the Subarea 14 Plan Update. In addition, developers and community members needed to cooperate in order to gain acceptance for specific land-use proposals. This cooperation was encouraged through the initiation of an open dialogue between the developers and the existing community.

A neighborhood steering committee was organized to work with Ravenwood officials and the proposed developers to address the issues that surrounded the proposal. The Ravenwood Steering Committee consisted of David and Mary Thoms, John Marshall, Bob Sheehan, John Wilburn, and Jerry Box.

The Ravenwood Club, Inc., was a private social organization located in the bend of the Stones River. It was situated to the northwest of the Stones River Estates and Hermitage Hills subdivisions and encompassed approximately 265 acres. Stones River Road was the sole access to the club.

In 1996, Ravenwood decided to seek the rezoning of approximately seventy acres of its property for a residential development. It was believed that the time was right from both an economic and market standpoint to propose this rezoning and development. I was notified by representatives of Ravenwood of their developmental intentions in April 1996. In addition, they informed the homeowners of Stones River Estates of their proposal.

Residents raised issues immediately upon the unveiling of the Ravenwood residential plan. The most notable of these concerned the lack of an appropriate access to the property and the likelihood of increased traffic levels on the existing highway infrastructure.

The residential proposal consisted of a request to rezone sixty-five to seventy acres of the Ravenwood property. This property abutted the north margin of Stones River Road, approximately 550 feet west of Lebanon Pike. It was requested this property be rezoned from agricultural to residential. This rezoning allowed for the development of no more than two houses per acre. The property targeted for development had been used as pasture for horses. It was contiguous with both the Binns property and the Stones River Estates residences located along Eversong and Nora Lanes. The plan called for the construction of approximately 122 single-family homes. This developmental density met the recommendations set forth by the Subarea 14 Plan Update.

The primary access to this development was to be provided along the existing Stones River Road. A secondary access was to be obtained by extending Hickory Hill Lane through the Binns property and intersecting the proposed development. This access was to be obtained by the purchase of a highway easement through the Binns property. However, both access ways to this proposal proved to be controversial.

I sponsored the first community meeting that addressed the issues raised by this proposal; it was held on May 6, 1996 at the home of David and Mary Thoms. It was at the meeting that both proponents and opponents of the proposal voiced their positions. Proponents stressed the benefits to be obtained from the proposed development of this property.

Opposition to the proposal centered on where the accesses serving this development were to be located. Questions arose regarding the ability of the narrow, rural-type Stones River Road to act as the primary access to the proposed development. In addition, this roadway was questioned regarding its ability to serve any future development once this property was rezoned. The ability to widen Stones River Road to provide appropriate access to any new development was considered extremely limited because it was located along the bank of the Stones River.

In addition, the Stones River Road intersection with Lebanon Pike was only approximately 250 feet west of the existing signaled intersection of Central Pike/Lebanon Pike. Questions were raised regarding the installation of a lighted traffic signal at either the Stones River Road or the Hickory Hill Lane intersection. Residents believed the inability to install traffic signals created more traffic problems for the area.

Another area of contention was based on the Stones River Road intersection with Lebanon Pike being only approximately forty feet east of both the Elmer Disspayne Sr. and Dr. Richard Herrington II Memorial Bridges. It was pointed out that this extremely short distance prohibited the establishment of an appropriate left-turn lane on Lebanon Pike as traffic fed into Stones River Road. The likelihood of rear end collisions was increased because of the lack of an appropriate left-turn lane.

Intersection of narrow Stones River Road with Lebanon Pike, just east of the Elmer Disspayne Sr. Memorial Bridge

Questions were raised pertaining to the advisability of using existing residential streets as access ways to the proposed development. The extension of Hickory Hill Lane through the Binns property increased its eligibility for rezoning and development. This 285-acre tract was isolated behind both Stones River Estates and Hermitage Hills subdivisions. It lacked a direct access to Lebanon Pike. The development of this property required the extension of existing streets into the Binns property to gain access to Lebanon Pike. Ultimately, this extension would result in increased traffic levels on residential streets in these subdivisions. These increased traffic levels would adversely impact the existing subdivisions and were considered unacceptable by the established residents.

The conclusion of the meeting illustrated that the residents would only support this development if an acceptable access serving the property was obtained. My position of supporting only those developments favored by the impacted residents forced Ravenwood officials to agree to additional meetings in an effort to eliminate conflicting opinions regarding the proposal and gain support for its passage.

The Ravenwood zone change proposal came before the Metropolitan Planning Commission at its May 16, 1996, meeting. The applicant requested a two-week deferral. This deferral was sought because of the numerous issues associated with the proposal. In the meantime, residents of the area organized a petition drive to illustrate their opposition to the proposal in its current form. The petitioners ultimately gathered more than two hundred signatures of those opposed to the proposal.

The Metropolitan Planning Commission heard the Ravenwood rezoning request on May 30, 1996. The Planning Commission approved the request because the property fell within residential low-medium policy. This policy permitted up to four dwelling units per acre, and the RS20 (residential) district designated for this development would implement that policy. After the Planning Commission approved the Ravenwood rezoning, it was placed on the agenda of the Metropolitan Council. The endorsement of the Council of this rezoning was necessary for this project to proceed.

During this time, I maintained an open line of communication with the traffic and parking engineers of the Metropolitan

Department of Public Works. I had meetings with Chief Traffic Engineer John Gregor and Senior Traffic Engineer Ali Afis on June 12–13, 1996. I received a letter from Gregor evaluating the traffic situation on June 14, 1996. In the letter it was made clear that the only access to the property would be via Stones River Road. Further, the letter stated, "Stones River Road is a narrow, winding rural-type roadway currently providing access to the country club and a few estate properties. It intersects Lebanon Road about 250 feet west of the signaled intersection of Lebanon Road and Central Pike. The intersection is hampered by continuous heavy traffic from either inbound Lebanon Road or Central Pike, limited sight distance, lack of a turn lane from the west, and an unconventional crossover design that would not work well if traffic were increased significantly."

Based upon this information they felt in this case it would be "premature" to allow any development in this specific area that would increase the density prior to adequate arrangements being "made to bring the infrastructure up to an appropriate urban standard or to develop alternate access routes."[22]

Conversations with the metropolitan land-use planners dealt with the influence the rezoning and development of the Ravenwood seventy-acre tract would have on the approximately 1,030 remaining acres. The land-use planners informed me that the rezoning of only a small portion of the Stones River site would initiate rezoning requests for the remainder of the acreage and accelerate its development. Because of the lay of the land, there were no natural buffers within which to limit development. The development of the remaining acreage would result in approximately 2,060 residential dwelling units being constructed in accordance with the recommendations set forth in the Subarea 14 Plan Update. This development would adversely impact the existing Donelson-Hermitage community by increasing traffic levels on the established highway system. This system had operated above capacity for a number of years. In addition, there were no immediate plans to upgrade the highway infrastructure.

I sponsored a community meeting on June 20, 1996, at the Donelson Senior Citizens Center to discuss the proposed development and the impact it would have on the existing residential subdivisions. Access to the property remained the key issue associated with this development.

Referring to the access issue as an infrastructure problem, I informed those in attendance of the conversations that I had with officials from the Planning Commission and the traffic and parking engineers of the Department of Public Works. The traffic engineers had advised me that the Ravenwood proposal was going to place too much stress on the existing road system. In addition, a secondary access through the Binns property would increase traffic levels on Hickory Hill Lane and was not advisable. Finally, the engineers stated that the primary access along Stones River Road was questionable because of its physical condition, and that there was to be no installation of a traffic signal at the Stones River Road intersection. This was due to its close proximity to the signaled Central Pike intersection.

Ravenwood requested a deferral of its rezoning proposal from the Metropolitan Council to the September 3, 1996 council meeting. The deferral was requested in an attempt to address the issues raised by the residents to the development. In addition, it was necessary to obtain the approval of the residents to ensure the passage of the proposal through the Council. Meetings were scheduled to determine if acceptable solutions to the issues could be obtained during this two-month deferral. The focal points of these meetings included the establishment of a proper access to the property and ways to minimize the impact the additional traffic was scheduled to have on the existing subdivisions.

The Hickory Hill Lane extension was removed from the Ravenwood proposal in September 1996. The withdrawal of the Hickory Hill Lane access established Stones River Road as the sole access to the property. All parties now considered improvements to the Stones River Road corridor and its intersection with Lebanon Pike as the issue of primary importance. Widening the Stones River Road corridor was limited due to its location along the banks of the Stones River.

In addition, Metro refused to install a traffic signal at this intersection because of its close proximity to the signaled Central Pike intersection. Discussions were begun regarding the possibility of aligning Stones River Road with Central Pike. The alignment would create one large intersection with Lebanon Pike and allow both Central Pike and Stones River Road to be serviced by a single traffic signal.

To realign Stones River Road eastward with Central Pike, the Ravenwood developers needed to obtain a portion of the Stone Hall

Estate. However, the titleholders of the Stone Hall property were not interested in selling any part of the historical property. Therefore, the Stones River Road realignment propsal was removed from further consideration.

Another possible solution involved extending Stones River Road across the Stones River and intersecting it with the north side of Lebanon Pike. This intersection would be directly opposite the recently installed signaled intersection serving the Jackson Downs commercial development. The extension of Stones River Road would make it necessary to construct a bridge to circumvent the Stones River. In addition, the purchase of a highway easement through the south-eastern corner of the fifty-four-acre agricultural tract was required. However, this was a private project and all infrastructure improvements were to be funded by the company involved in the endeavor.

The estimated $3 million required for both the construction of this bridge and the purchase of the highway easement was considered much too expensive to be financed solely by Landmark Realty Services Corporation. As a result, this proposal was no longer considered an option.

I sponsored a community meeting on August 13, 1996, at the Hermitage Elementary School to inform the residents of both Stones River Estates and Hermitage Hills of the status of the Ravenwood rezoning request. Developer Brock Rust, representatives of the Ravenwood Club, and the neighborhood Steering Committee attended the meeting to present their positions on the proposal. The community was notified that no changes worth mention had been made in the development plans and that highway infrastructure improvements were minimal. The lack of appropriate highway improvements would force the existing residential streets to accommodate the increased traffic. I relayed the belief of the Planning Commission that rezoning any part of this eleven-hundred-acre tract enhanced the possibility that the remaining acres would be rezoned and developed. The conclusion of the meeting witnessed the community's opposition to the proposal. I was therefore asked to defeat the proposal on the Council floor.

On August 14, 1996, I received a copy of a letter from Chief Traffic Engineer John Gregor that reviewed the traffic study for the Ravenwood residential development proposal. David H. Moss of the engineering firm Barge, Waggoner, Sumner, and Cannon submitted the study to the Department of Public Works on August 5, 1996. Gregor stated that the "estimates of trip generation and future traffic conditions appear to be technically sound."[23] Metro's engineers were:

> concerned, however, that these improvements are not enough to overcome Level of Service F (excessive delay) conditions for exiting traffic at Stones River Road and Lebanon Pike during the peak evening hour. With the roadway widened only to 24 feet, left-turning vehicles will inhibit any vehicles behind them that might otherwise be able to turn right with little delay. At a minimum, this roadway should be widened to provide two exit lanes, but we understand that right-of-way is not available and the property is not under the applicant's control.[24]

In addition, Gregor expressed that the engineers did:

> not agree with the finding that the left-turn storage lane on Lebanon Pike can be extended adequately to accommodate traffic entering the area. Field inspection indicates that this turn lane is already squeezed against the departure end of the Stones River bridge, and there is no effective transition. Additional traffic generation will increase the risk of rear end collisions caused by vehicles in the left through lane slowing down to enter the turn lane. This intersection was clearly designed to serve a low volume, rural-type road and cannot readily be made suitable for urban-level traffic volumes.[25]

Gregor also noted that residents of both the proposed Ravenwood subdivision and the existing subdivisions and any subsequent development, "will experience poor traffic service until substantial access improvements can be made."[26]

The improvements recommended by Gregor to relieve the traffic situation included one or more of the following:

1. northward extension of Donelson Pike and a new river crossing at this location;
2. diversion of existing Stones River Road across a new river crossing, to intersect Lebanon Pike at Jackson Downs East;

3. major realignment and reconstruction of the Central Pike/Stones River Road intersection with Lebanon Pike which would also include the widening of the eastbound river bridge to develop a proper left-turn lane; and

4. logical extension of the existing street stubs in the Hermitage Hills neighborhood.

All of these recommendations were identical to the improvements considered during the negotiations between the neighborhood Steering Committee and Brock Rust. However, these proposed improvements proved to be either unobtainable or unacceptable.

The Ravenwood proposal came before the Metropolitan Council at its September 3, 1996, public hearing meeting. More than fifty residents of the Stones River Estates and Hermitage Hills subdivisions attended to voice their opposition to the proposal. Following the presentation made by Brock Rust to the Council in support of this proposal, resident opponents presented their position.

The opposition of the residents centered on the inadequate infrastructure serving the area. In addition, there was an inability to secure the appropriate infrastructure improvements in the foreseeable future. Finally, the adverse impact that this, and subsequent developments, was projected to have on their property forced their opposition to the proposed development. Their petition with over two hundred signatures opposing this rezoning was submitted to the Council.

A statement prepared by historic preservationist Sarah Fessler Peveler was also made part of the record. The statement outlined the historical significance of the area by designating the historic properties situated in close proximity to the Ravenwood property. The historic Stone Hall mansion and Eversong cabin were both located on either side of Stones River Road at its intersection with Lebanon Pike, while the Binns' farmhouse was situated at the end of Hickory Hill Lane. The Metropolitan Historical Commission had deemed both Stone Hall and the Binns' farmhouse eligible for listing in the National Register of Historic Places. Peveler believed that these historic properties "could be adversely impacted by future development" and that "their preservation must be integral to this and future decisions made about the inevitable development of this section of Davidson County."[27] At the conclusion of the public hearing, I requested and obtained disapproval from the Council regarding the Ravenwood rezoning proposal.

The defeat of the Ravenwood proposal illustrated the desire of Hermitage residents to have their elected officials subscribe to an open-door policy to address development of this property. The policy dictated that the proper infrastructure improvements were needed to serve additional developments in this bend of the Stones River. Until these improvements were made, the property was to remain agricultural.

Cloverwood Development Proposal

In late autumn 2001 an undeveloped tract of property was targeted by Landmark Realty Services Corporation to construct a residential development. The tract of property was directly contiguous with the Hickory Bend subdivision. In addition, due to the fact that it was only 16.81 acres in size the development of this acreage was not considered a threat to the established community by the developers. However, a close review of the proposed development proved otherwise. The most obvious issue associated with the development of this tract was inadequate drainage and subsequent flooding.

The entire tract of property was situated within the McCrory Creek one-hundred-year floodplain. Lakeland Drive, Hickory Bend Drive, and Cloverwood Drive were all recorded as stub streets into this property; in essence, the property was to be accessed by these existing residential streets. The proposed single-family residential development "would comprise two cul-de-sacs, one for 15 homes on an extension of Hickory Bend Drive and the other for five homes at the very end of Cloverwood Drive."[28] There were to be no more than nineteen single-family homes constructed in the proposed development. There were issues associated with the proposed development from its beginning.

The property had been rezoned from agricultural to residential in January 1988. However, following the rezoning it had lain dormant for over fourteen years before Landmark Realty announced its intentions to develop the property. The rezoning was approved over seven years prior to my election to the Metropolitan Council.

I was extremely critical of the lengthy dormancy of this property. The lack of interest in developing the property had promoted complacency among the neighboring residents pertaining to its development. However, there still remained issues about the developmental stability of the site and the adverse impacts it could have on both the natural environment and the established community.

Landmark Realty filed a request for preliminary plat approval with the Planning Commission in November 2001. The filing requested the Planning Commission approve the nineteen lots included in the proposed Cloverwood subdivision. The subdivision was to abut the southwest corner of Stewart's Ferry Pike and the south margin of McCrory Creek Road.

The request was placed on the agenda for the December 6, 2001 Planning Commission meeting. After being informed of the proposed development, I notified the neighboring residents of the proposal. Citizens residing on Cloverwood Drive, Lakeland Drive, Waxhaw Drive, Hickory Bend Drive, and Truxton Court were all notified due to the immediate impact they would feel from such a development.

During my conversations with the residents, I informed them that it was necessary for them to organize into a cohesive group with designated leaders. The residents in the group included Jerry and Jennifer Fraley, Sally Oru, Jeff and Roberta Walter, William G. Wilkes, Wilson P. Collins, Sue Cunliffe, Joseph Villa, Jim Dolan, and Joe Turley.

I began conversations with Landmark Realty and Dale and Associates regarding sponsored community meetings on land-use proposals. During these conversations, it was agreed to defer the request at the December 6 Planning Commission meeting in order for me to hold a community meeting on the proposed development. The meeting allowed for the developers to unveil plans for the proposal. In addition, it gave the impacted residents the opportunity to ask questions and voice concerns over the proposed Cloverwood development.

The community meeting was scheduled for December 17 at the Clover Bottom Developmental Center auditorium. Attending the meeting were Ernie Lehning of Landmark Realty Services, engineer Kevin Estes of Dale and Associates, and numerous residents from Hickory Bend Subdivision. I informed the residents that the proposed development would require only the approval of the Planning Commission because the proper zoning of the site had been obtained years earlier.

The main issue voiced at the meeting involved development in the floodplain and the adverse impacts it could have on the homes located on the periphery of the proposed site. The most notable concern from residents dealt with stormwater runoff caused by the new homes.

During their presentation, Lehning and Estes attempted to explain how the project would skirt the floodplain issues if approved. "Estes explained that developers would have to fill in the lots for the new homes to raise their levels at least five feet above the floodplain. He noted that dirt from open areas of the development would be used as fill."[29] The explanation represented the "cut-and-fill" method of developing in floodplains.

However, questions had been raised in recent years pertaining to the long-term stability of such a method. Many developments that had been constructed in floodplains throughout Metropolitan Nashville over the years had begun to show signs of instability, including the sinking of structures into the ground upon which they were constructed. Sinking caused cracking in the foundation of these structures, resulting in internal damage such as plumbing and electrical wiring problems. In addition, Estes claimed that "holding ponds would be excavated to handle runoff from the new homes during the rainy season."[30]

The maintenance of these ponds was considered vital by the neighboring residents and involved "fencing, security to keep children out, and keeping down mosquitoes that could breed in the standing water." When asked who would be held responsible for the maintenance of the ponds, Estes responded "that the homeowners association would be responsible for such upkeep."[31] However, that brought severe criticism from the residents as many noted that there were other instances where maintenance responsibilities were simply ignored.

The main area of contention from the residents pertained to the flooding and drainage issues, in particular the annual flooding associated with the McCrory Creek waterway. The natural waterway continually overflowed its banks and flooded the residential parcels situated on Cloverwood Drive, Waxhaw Drive, and Truxton Court. The damage done to their homes by the flood waters was extreme.

Information was provided that the construction of nineteen homes and subdivision streets onto the acreage that was situated entirely within the floodplain would increase the impervious surface ratio.

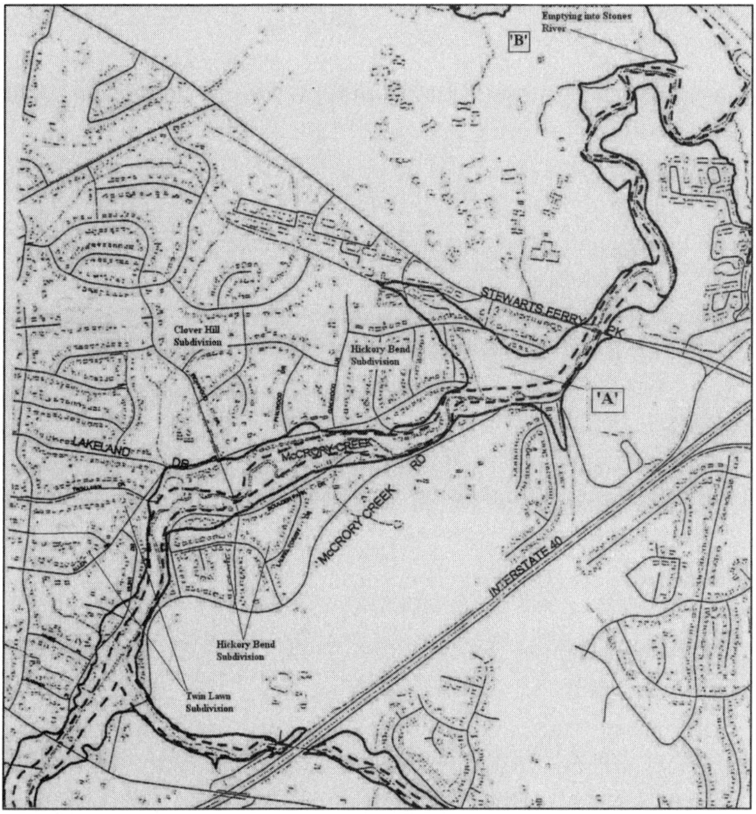

Map 5-1: The McCrory Creek floodplain as it winds through the Hickory Bend, Clover Hill, and Twin Lawn subdivisions. "A"—The 16.81-acre floodplain tract upon which was proposed the Cloverwood residential development; "B"—McCrory Creek intersection with the Stones River. (Source: Metropolitan Planning Department of Nashville and Davidson County—Mapping Division.)

This would make the flood waters incapable of penetrating or saturating the ground and would substantially increase the volume of floodwater displacement on the residences of Hickory Bend.

The developers were further probed by the residents about the amount of work it would take to raise the area out of the floodplain. Estes claimed that "just the area of the lots where homes would be constructed would be raised." However, residents voiced concern over this response, believing that the elevating of these lots would act to channel rising water from the creek through the new subdivision and into the yards of Hickory Bend. Estes also claimed that approximately 50 percent of the proposed development "would be left in the open flood plain area. This open area would include the storage ponds."[32]

In addition, questions were raised by the residents pertaining to the value of the houses to be included in the development. The fact that the homes were to be constructed by using the cluster lot option allowed the parcels of the subdivision to be much smaller than a straight subdivision. This was due to the need "to work around such things as sink holes and rock shelves."[33]

Estes claimed the homes would be very small in square footage and avoided giving the group of residents any type of dollar figure pertaining to the value of the homes. This brought sharp criticism from the residents. Pamela Shaffer opined that the refusal of Estes to give any specific dollar value for the homes and claim that they were to be small structures designated that "they're starter homes, which means . . . they are lower-cost housing. Those things have to be discussed. Money is not the only issue here. There are property value issues . . . the transiency of the neighborhood."[34]

Another issue raised at the meeting dealt with traffic congestion on the local streets and the adverse impact that the development would have on the highway system. "One resident pointed out that Stewart's Ferry Pike has been over capacity for years, adding that 19 lots would mean a minimum of 38 more cars added to the traffic jam—if not more." The resident "recalled that, at times, she cannot get out of her driveway for the traffic."[35] It was also noted the numerous traffic accidents that continually occur on the narrow, two-lane Stewart's Ferry Pike.

One of the most important factors used to determine the viability of the Cloverwood proposal was the adoption of a comprehensive floodplain development ordinance. Such an ordinance would thoroughly regulate development in the one-hundred-year floodplains located throughout Metropolitan Nashville. By the time consideration was being given to the Cloverwood proposal, I was prepared to introduce a new floodplain ordinance into the legislative process. Upon its passage this ordinance effected the procession of floodplain developments throughout Metropolitan Nashville, including the Cloverwood proposal.

The Planning Commission heard arguments both for and against the Cloverwood proposal on January 10, 2002. A number of residents voiced their opposition to the proposed development. Included among those speaking in opposition were Granville Bailey, David Bryce, Don Shepard, Bill Hailey, Ellen Collins, and Roberta Walter. Their opposition was based primarily on stormwater drainage, traffic, and safety issues. Residents Jim Dolan and Joseph Villa both presented photographs of recent flooding from McCrory Creek. They expressed concerns about the increased adverse impact the development of the natural floodplain would have on their property and the neighbors in general.

During my presentation, the Planning Commission was informed of the overdevelopment associated with this area off Stewart's Ferry Pike. I notified the commission of the numerous drainage projects that were located in the area and the costs associated with them. In addition, it was explained that the source of the capital used to fund these drainage projects was from a general allocation by the Metropolitan Council. This was due to the fact that Metropolitan Nashville had never adopted a comprehensive stormwater drainage program. From 1996 to 1999, there had been allocated approximately $450,000 to each of the thirty-five council districts in Metropolitan Nashville. I had designated that approximately $405,000, or 90 percent of the funds, be used to provide flooding and stormwater drainage relief for the citizens.

Approximately 24 percent of funds for flooding and stormwater drainage relief was used for properties situated along the McCrory Creek natural waterway. The McCrory Creek projects illustrated the instability associated with residential parcels contiguous with the McCrory Creek natural waterway and its floodplain.

I informed the Planning Commission that the approval of proposed developments within the one-hundred-year McCrory Creek floodplain would only act to increase the impervious surface ratio along the natural drainage basin. This would, in effect, eliminate uncovered acreage needed for stormwater saturation, thus increasing stormwater overflow along McCrory Creek. Such stormwater overflow would adversely impact the existing residences contiguous with the floodplain.

Until a comprehensive stormwater drainage program was adopted, I believed there should be a moratorium on floodplain development. Finally, I updated the Planning Commission of the floodplain ordinance that was to be introduced into the planning process within the next few weeks. Ultimately, I requested the Planning Commission disapprove the Cloverwood preliminary plan.

However, the Planning Commission approved the development. The resolution adopted by the Planning Commission addressing their approval of this project included a request that "the Department of Public Works make a presentation prior to approval of the final plat identifying how the final plat satisfies Section 2.3 of the Subdivision Regulations."[36]

The approval of the Planning Commission did not allow for the immediate construction of the Cloverwood subdivision. The Department of Public Works was responsible for reviewing the plat of the proposed subdivision to ensure its compliance with existing floodplain development laws.

However, I had introduced the newly proposed floodplain ordinance to the Metropolitan Council in January 2002. The ordinance

Figure 5-1

Chart Presented to the Metropolitan Planning Commission Illustrating Drainage Projects Funded and Completed Along McCrory Creek

McCrory Creek Stormwater Drainage Projects (Completed as of June 2001)

	Project	Location	Amount
1.	Boulder Park (Phase I)	3017 Boulder Park Drive	$ 8,482.79
2.	Boulder Park (Phase II)	3017 Boulder Park Drive	$16,930.01
3.	Lakeland Drive	3124 Lakeland Drive	$32,395.90
4.	Boulder Park	3054 Boulder Park Drive	$ 6,371.36
5.	Cloverwood Drive	3220-3222 Cloverwood Drive	$20,109.60
6.	Truxton Court	644 Truxton Court	$11,479.68
		Total:	$95,769.34

passed first reading on April 2, 2002. Thus, the Cloverwood proposal was deferred by Public Works while negotiations on my floodplain ordinance were ongoing.

The ultimate passage of the ordinance on March 18, 2003, removed the Cloverwood proposal from further consideration. The new regulatory law directed that a full 50 percent or eight acres of the targeted McCrory Creek site was to remain undisturbed. This prohibited using the property as the acreage upon which storage ponds were to be situated. These ponds were a key method used to deal with stormwater overflow and prevent flooding from floodplain developments. In addition, the reduction in the number of acres eligible for development noticeably reduced the projected profits of the proposed development.

Ultimately, the removal of noticeable profit for the Landmark Realty Services brought about its decision to withdraw the proposed Cloverwood development. Finally, if the Cloverwood acreage was to be targeted in the future for development, Metropolitan Nashville's floodplain law would substantially restrict the number of structures to be constructed on this floodplain acreage, eliminate a substantial percentage of the impervious surface ratio associated with such development, and substantially protect the established community from increased flooding and drainage problems.

Land-Use Proposals for Millionaire Row

Millionaire Row of Donelson was one of the more notable areas targeted for intensified redevelopment. This area included twenty-two parcels of residentially zoned property fronting the north side of Lebanon Pike from Guill Court east to Danyacrest Drive. The parcels ranged in size from 1.26-acres to 14.18-acres. The subdivision had been constructed from 1899–1935. The large brick and stone single-family homes were each situated on large parcels of property and represented a unique, historical, well-established residential development in the Donelson community.

In addition, the residential character of this stretch of Lebanon Pike was viewed by many as an open, uncongested length of the highway that served Donelson-Hermitage and communities further east. The architectural style of the homes of Millionaire Row illustrated historically unique residential structures and acted to stabilize the entire residential district of this area of Lebanon Pike.

A redevelopment proposed for Millionaire Row was unveiled in 1995. The Subarea 14 Plan was scheduled to be updated and coincided with my election to the Metropolitan Council. However, debates would arise regarding how the plan should be updated. Developer William Cooper had purchased the vacant residence situated on a 1.88-acre parcel at 3008 Lebanon Pike in 1995. Cooper stated that he had "bought the property from the heirs of Ruby Elizabeth Peek, for the price of the land alone. The dwelling was in very poor condition, with a fallen ceiling and other structural damage. On the kitchen door was a red letter sign stating it could not be inhabited, so I contacted to have it demolished."[37]

Following the demolition and clearing of the parcel of the single-family home, Cooper planned to develop a condominium complex of approximately sixteen units. However, such a development required an amendment to the recommended land-use policy for this section of Lebanon Pike. The original Subarea 14 Plan had designated that the residential parcels along this stretch of Lebanon Pike be classified RLM (Residential Low/Medium). Such a classification allowed for the construction of no more than two to four units per acre.

That recommended policy was unacceptable for Cooper. It allowed for the construction of no more than three to seven condominium units on his 1.88-acre parcel, thereby preventing the construction of the proposed sixteen-unit complex. Cooper began lobbying the professional staff of the Planning Department to amend the recommended land-use policy of the area to RM (Residential Medium) which would allow four to nine units per acre.

In the Subarea 14 Plan update public hearing held before the Planning Commission in December 1995, the proposal to recommend an increased developmental density for this area was debated. Resident citizens of the area addressed the Planning Commission on the proposed amendment. There were approximately thirty-five to forty residents in the immediate vicinity of the Cooper property that would be adversely affected by any such change in the recommended developmental density. They resided on Lebanon Pike, Disspayne Drive, and Jenry Drive. During the public hearing, the residents "lined up to oppose Brentwood developer William Cooper."[38]

The basic argument raised by the existing resident homeowners in opposition to the change in land-use policy was based on the impact developmental density would have on the existing homes. There existed numerous historically significant single-family residences in the area and the developmental density was sparse, promoting a quiet residential environment for the citizens who had invested and lived there. The adoption of a more intense developmental policy promoted the construction of numerous multi-family complexes alongside the well-established single-family residences. In the overwhelming number of instances, multi-family developments were incompatible with single-family subdivisions due to the increased traffic and noise levels generated from such complexes.

Following the presentations by resident citizens, I addressed the Planning Commission as the elected councilmember of the area. During my presentation, the Planning Commission was informed of the historical significance of this area of Lebanon Pike. It was once part of Clover Bottom Plantation, and the historical structures remaining included the Clover Bottom Mansion and the Millionaire Row subdivision.

I requested the Planning Commission give priority consideration to both the short- and long-term adverse impacts such intense multi-family development was to have on the already overcrowded Lebanon Pike when determining their position on the amendment. Maintaining the recommended RLM policy would restrict both the number of residential units to be constructed and the number of additional automobiles accessing Lebanon Pike on a daily basis. This would assist in managing traffic flow through the area.

The Planning Commission failed to agree with the arguments opposing the amendment. I felt that the commission's failure illustrated a desire to adopt land-use policy based on agreements with nonresident developers and a refusal to accept the position of the resident citizens that would be ultimately impacted by the change in policy. In addition, the adoption of the amendment exemplified an irresponsible position taken by the Planning Commission given that they also refused to acknowledge needed infrastructure upgrades that were required prior to allowing the construction of dense multi-family developments.

Finally, the position taken by the Planning Commission approving the amendment undermined the purpose of the subarea planning process. Following their approval of the amendment, I stated that "the Commission needs to realize that one of the key factors involved in the Subarea Planning Process is public opinion. The Commission's staff reported that the overwhelming majority of the homeowners in Area 3 have indicated that they want to retain the present residential status. If they ignore these citizens, and change the plans for Area 3, the entire Subarea Planning Process may need to be reviewed."[39]

The adoption of a more intense recommended land-use for the Millionaire Row section of Lebanon Pike by the Planning Commission did not provide ultimate approval of the proposed condominium complex. For construction of that proposed complex to proceed, the rezoning of the parcel from R10 to RM9 was required. Although the updated Subarea 14 Plan recommended such a rezoning, the Metropolitan Council would be responsible for its approval. The endorsement of the proposed rezoning from the district councilmember was a necessity for its approval to be obtained. However, I could not endorse the proposal because of the overwhelming residential opposition.

The failure of Cooper to obtain the support of the community and their elected councilmember for his proposed rezoning and development forced him to shelve the project until after the 1999 council elections. Within a few months, the parcel had been sold to a neighboring resident, thus ending the controversial proposal.

In 1996, local developers Frank Batson and David Parker approached me to inquire about the possibility of rezoning a 14.18-acre Millionaire Row parcel. The proposed rezoning was from R10 to an RS10 Planned Unit Development (PUD). The existing zoning allowed the construction of residential homes on lots that were a minimum of ten thousand square feet. Due to the size of the parcel, as many as fifty-two residences could be constructed on the site. In addition, the zoning allowed for approximately 25 percent, or thirteen, to be duplexes. Finally, there was no guarantee that a reputable development company would obtain the rights to develop the site, thus raising questions about the material consistency, size, and value of the homes that could be constructed under the existing zoning.

B&P Development, Inc., was the development company owned by Frank Batson and David Parker. The numerous residential developments they had completed over the years had established them as reliable and dedicated developers. In addition, Frank Batson was raised in the community and his uncle Carl Batson had developed residential subdivisions in Donelson in the 1950s and 1960s.

My endorsement was sought for their rezoning and development proposal. The proposal called for the demolition of the vacant and dilapidated single-family home on the site. The rezoning allowed for the construction of only single-family residences, thereby eliminating the inclusion of any duplexes in the development. The PUD overlay that was included in the rezoning proposal allowed for a minimum lot size of eighty-five hundred square feet. However, this smaller lot size was offset through the designation of approximately four acres of undeveloped open space within the development. The open space was targeted for the part of the parcel that was contiguous with the Stones River at the rear of the lot. The open space along the natural waterway was to be dedicated as a part of the Stones River Greenway. There would be forty-two single-family homes constructed in the proposed development. The residences were to range in price from $200,000 to $300,000.

In July 1996, I held a meeting between Batson and Parker and the neighboring residents. The proposal was outlined, questions were asked and answered, and the residents were supportive of the proposal at the end of the meeting. With that information in hand, I sponsored the rezoning and development proposal before the Planning Commission and the Metropolitan Council. The proposal was approved by both the Planning Commission and the Metropolitan Council. The approval resulted in the construction of the Rivercrest subdivision from 1996 to 2000. Upon its completion, Rivercrest represented a stable residential addition to the Donelson community.

In 1997–98, a proposal for a twenty-six-unit condominium complex was unveiled for the rear 2.5 acres of a Millionaire Row parcel located at 3040 Lebanon Pike. The long-time homeowners of the property were relocating their residence. A development company had purchased an option to buy the property and develop the back 66 percent of the property in a manner that fit within the recommended developmental density of the area adopted by the Planning Commission. However, even this proved controversial as the majority of resident citizens were opposed to the recommended increased developmental density.

I sponsored a number of community meetings to promote interaction between the resident citizens, the developer, and me. The first such meeting was held on June 23, 1997, at the Donelson Senior Citizens Center. During these community meetings, "concerns were raised pertaining to increased storm water runoff which would be created by the construction of this complex and the possible flooding it would unleash on adjacent properties."[40]

These concerns were well founded in that the back 2.5 acres of the parcel targeted for the development were situated at a much lower level than Lebanon Pike, which it fronted. There already existed a substantial volume of stormwater runoff from Lebanon Pike through the property as it made its way through Stanford Estates and toward the Stones River behind it. The development of a multi-family complex involved an increased impervious surface ratio on the property that resulted from the construction of multi-family buildings and the paving of a noticeable percentage of the property for driveways and parking.

The elimination of this open ground would displace a substantial volume of stormwater onto neighboring properties and result in flooding. There existed no metropolitan program for stormwater flooding relief at that time. One of the key ways developers attempted to address the stormwater overflow issue was to construct detention ponds on the property targeted for development.

However, questions were raised regarding these ponds. The questions centered on the ability of the developers or the subsequent residents of the development to maintain the ponds. In addition, health issues were raised regarding such detention ponds allowing pools of water to stagnate and become infested with mosquitoes that carried certain viruses which caused harm to the general public.

Another issue raised during these meetings was the effect this multi-family complex was to have on the developmental potential of the remaining properties. Allowing this complex to develop would act as an endorsement of the controversial recommended developmental density by the resident citizens. In addition, it would promote additional multi-family complexes along this stretch of Lebanon Pike.

Many homeowners in Millionaire Row were uncomfortable with that policy. In response to this issue, a petition was circulated among the homeowners of Millionaire Row. The "petition requested that properties fronting this entire length of Lebanon Pike be rezoned to permit only single-family residences."[41]

Approximately nine years earlier, the neighboring Stanford Estates had been rezoned to permit only single-family residences in the subdivision. Millionaire Row now wanted the same protection of their residential environment. The community meetings thoroughly illustrated the position of the resident citizens toward the multi-family condominium complex and their desire to maintain this area of Donelson as a single-family residential district.

Upon being presented with this petition, I initiated the legislative process that ultimately witnessed the rezoning of all the Millionaire Row properties to residential single-family. The rezoning prohibited the development of any further multi-family complexes along this stretch of Lebanon Pike. It worked to preserve the historic and single-family residential environment of the area.

In addition, the rezoning of Millionaire Row ultimately brought about the construction of Wellington Square on the same 2.5-acre parcel that had previously been considered for the twenty-six-unit condominium complex. Wellington Square is a single-family subdivision with eight residences. It promoted a much more stable environment for the area in that there remained substantial open ground for stormwater saturation and the single-family structures in Wellington Square were much more compatible with the existing residences of the area.

In 2001, the status of the Millionaire Row property located at 3052 Lebanon Pike was questioned. The property had recently been purchased by attorney David Randy Kennedy. The residence at this address was a twenty-seven-hundred-square-foot, two-story, Tudor-style brick home. The parcel was approximately 1.5 acres. When considering this purchase, Kennedy had contacted me to determine whether I could support a rezoning of this property to allow the operation of his law office from this site. The rezoning of this property to office neighborhood (ON) would require the rezoning of the remaining residential parcels fronting the north side of Lebanon Pike in a similar manner. During our conversation, I determined that I could support a rezoning only if it were favored by the residents.

In January 2001, Kennedy met with the board of directors of the Stanford Estates Homeowners Association to outline his objectives for the property. During this meeting, Kennedy announced that he had been working with Rick Bernhardt, director of the Department of Planning, to determine what actions could be taken to allow for the use of this residence as a professional office.

Following a review of the property, Bernhardt understood the historical character of the property as part of Millionaire Row. The residence was constructed in 1932. It was thus eligible for placement on the National Register of Historic Places. He recommended the implementation of a Neighborhood Landmark Overlay District on the property.

The neighborhood landmark district provisions were established to preserve and protect neighborhood features that are important to maintain and enhance neighborhood character. Neighborhood features were defined as buildings, structures, objects, sites, and areas of historic, cultural, civic, neighborhood, or architectural value or importance to Metropolitan Nashville and Davidson County.

A Neighborhood Landmark Overlay was to be established following approval of an ordinance by the Metropolitan Council as recommended by the Planning Commission. Upon obtaining approval of the Neighborhood Landmark Overlay, the owner of the property was required to submit a development plan for any feature included in the overlay. The development plan was required to be approved by the Planning Commission at a public hearing. No zoning permits, building permits, or other land-use development permit would be issued prior to obtaining approval of the development plan.

Both Bernhardt and Kennedy believed this overlay would retain the historic structure and preserve the existing residential character along Lebanon Pike. The overlay allowed for the operation of a professional office from the residence, while maintaining the base residential zoning of the property. In a printed statement to the local residents of the area, Kennedy announced that the Neighborhood Landmark Overlay:

> guaranteed to the residents of Stanford Estates and to the other residents along Lebanon Pike that no other property will be negatively impacted. Nor will the 3052 Lebanon Road property be rezoned to some objectionable commercial zoning. To the contrary, while Randy (who grew up on Jenry Drive) will be allowed to maintain his law practice (which he has served the Donelson-Hermitage community for 24 years) on the property; should he or son David R. Kennedy Jr. (an attorney in his office for the last 4 years) discontinue their law practice and fail to provide a successor attorney to serve our community at this location, the property will revert to its underlying zoning designation of Residential (RS10) only.[42]

The proposed Neighborhood Landmark Overlay District for 3052 Lebanon Pike was presented to the Planning Commission on February 1, 2001. The professional staff of the Planning Department recommended approval. Following a brief discussion over the proposal, the Planning Commission unanimously approved the Neighborhood Landmark Overlay District. It was noted in the Planning Commission resolution of approval that the overlay was "appropriate for the properties on either side of this property which also contain architecturally unique residential structures which add value to the surrounding residential neighborhood."[43]

Following the approval from the Planning Commission, Ordinance No. BL2001-622 was filed with the Metropolitan Council on the placement of the Neighborhood Landmark Overlay District at the site. It passed through the Metropolitan Council without delay, being approved on third and final reading by a vote of 32-0. The approval by the Council allowed Kennedy to proceed with the redevelopment of the property.

A development plan for the property was established over the next few weeks. Ultimately the plan identified the location, orientation, and size of the existing site and proposed specific improvemets. It included details of the home's use and a time frame for the proposed improvements. The plan called for the addition of an eight-car parking area to the rear corner of the lot to accommodate

Sign of the Law Offices of Kennedy and Brown allowed by a Neighborhood Landmark Overlay

employee and client parking. There would be a three-foot-high row of shrubs planted around the new parking area to act as a buffer between the parking area and the surrounding homes. All existing trees and landscaping would remain undisturbed. In addition, a five-foot-wide walkway was to be constructed from the parking area leading to the home's entrance. Finally, the plan proposed the installation of a four-foot tall by six-foot wide sign. The sign would be set back thirty feet from the front property line facing Lebanon Pike. The proposed development plan was to be completed 90 to 120 days from the day the first permit was issued by the Codes Department.

The development plan was presented to the Planning Commission on April 26, 2001. Attorney Randy Kennedy addressed the commission in support of the plan. When considering the proposed plan, Bernhardt stated that the Neighborhood Landmark Overlay District would establish this residence as a professional office use. Following their discussion, the Planning Commission unanimously approved the plan.

True to Kennedy's word and intent, the development plan was completed within the allotted time and the Law Offices of Kennedy and Brown were opened to those citizens of the community needing legal assistance. This type of use preserved the historic character of the area and protected the residential integrity of the area as well.

Conclusion

The rapid pace of rezoning and development associated with sprawl necessitated the election of councilmembers that would consider all aspects of a proposed development prior to offering unquestionable support. This open consideration was necessary because of the projected impacts, both positive and negative, that new development might have on the established community. In addition, this consideration promoted confidence in both the local legislative process and the elected councilmember from all sections of the city. It also represented the most prudent way of regulating growth in a major urban municipality.

One of the most vital methods used to consider all aspects of a proposed development was open communication and cooperation. This was accomplished through community meetings and active participation of the residents. The meetings promoted an open interaction between all parties affected by a proposed rezoning or development and provided individual citizens with information to make informed decisions. They gave the developers the opportunity to openly address the impacted community and answer questions pertaining to their proposal. In turn, the impacted citizens were given the opportunity to voice their position.

Rezoning and development proposals play an important role in an ever growing municipality. Such proposals can have either a positive or a negative impact on the established community. It is essential that councilmembers determine the effects such proposals are to have on the community they were elected to represent. The determination can be made through open communication and cooperation between the councilmember, developer, resident citizens, and the various city departments or agencies that are responsible for reviewing the rezoning and development proposals. The determination will direct the councilmember to either support or oppose the proposal. It will also allow for growth to be more thoroughly regulated and thereby eliminate or substantially reduce any adverse impact a rezoning and development proposal may have on the established community.

Chapter Six

Corporate Incentive Deals

The adoption of the Metropolitan Charter in June 1962 established a uniform urban environment that, in turn, promoted the installation of a modern infrastructure to serve the larger community. Among the more notable infrastructural projects that received priority attention from the metropolitan government were public highway upgrades, water/sewer installation, and the extension of public transportation throughout Davidson County. These improvements served to attract regional and national businesses to locate their operations in Metropolitan Nashville and Davidson County.

The city of Metropolitan Nashville experienced a steady growth throughout the years. In April 1963, the population of Metropolitan Nashville was 170,874.[1] The 1970 census by the U.S. Bureau of the Census showed the population had grown to 447,877.[2] By 1981, the population of Metropolitan Nashville had expanded to 455,651, making it the twenty-fifth largest city in the United States.[3] According to the 1990 census, Metropolitan Nashville had grown further and surpassed one half million in population, totaling 510,784 resident citizens. In addition, Metropolitan Nashville was now the twenty-third largest city in the United States.[4] Finally, the opening of the twenty-first century witnessed the population of Metropolitan Nashville being 576,502, making it the twenty-first largest city in the United States. The population of the Metropolitan Statistical Area (MSA), which included Metropolitan Nashville and Davidson County and the surrounding counties, had reached 1,262,094.[5]

Metropolitan Nashville's continual growth acted as an enticement for regional or national businesses to locate their operations there. In general, businesses were welcomed by the city. In addition, residents benefitted from the influx of new businesses, most notably by increased employment opportunities. A projected increase in property tax revenues would assist in funding upgrades to the local infrastructure.

However, as Metropolitan Nashville continued to grow and receive attention from large corporations, certain practices were instituted by metropolitan officials in an attempt to attract and guarantee the placement of reputable businesses within the city. The most notable of these practices involved Metropolitan Nashville entering into incentive deals with large corporations. Incentives were offerings by metropolitan authorities to private businesses in order to encourage their move to Metropolitan Nashville.

Public incentives are a double-edged sword. When used in moderation, incentives can play a positive role for all areas of the community in that they create an environment conducive to economic growth through the creation of jobs. Moderate incentives can entice reputable and well-established commercial interests to locate to the city. They ensure that both the public entity and the private commercial interest benefit from the deal as they act as a stimulus to the local economy.

In contrast, heavily laden incentive deals represent an inequitable division of benefits generated from the public/private agreement. In these deals, the public entity agrees to fund infrastructure upgrades, construction costs, grants property tax exemptions to the commercial interest, and allows the commercial interest to control the overwhelming percentage of revenue generated from the commercial site. Additionally, the agreement that the public entity be responsible for continual maintenance of a newly constructed or renovated facility from which the private interest is to operate proves to be extremely costly to local taxpaying citizens. Finally, holding private commercial interests responsible for the damaging impact that their operations have on the established community and its infrastructure has prompted the relocation of certain businesses.

Extreme incentives place a heavy burden on the local municipality while allowing the private interest to be enriched at the expense of the local citizens. A noticeable percentage of the public funds needed to meet the city's fiscal responsibility in these deals come from redirecting funds from municipal departments. Such public funds are needed to pay for required municipal services as well as infrastructure upgrades for the city as it continues to grow, not to enrich a private business.

Beginning in the mid-1980s, the resident citizens of Metropolitan Nashville had to pay inordinate amounts of money to fund the construction of new corporate sites to house relocated private companies. The city was required to fund and proceed with infrastructure improvements to stabilize and enhance the sites on which the companies were to locate.

In addition, many of the benefits the community was promised to receive from these deals never reached fruition. Among the more notable benefits projected to emanate from these deals was the role of the corporation as a stimulant to the local economy. The role of the private company as an economic stimulant was used to garner the support of the resident citizens as the deal was debated. Certain deals promised expanded services that were to be made available to the local citizens, including travel and entertainment. However, the progression of time witnessed the failure of many of these promised returns, thereby removing certain deals from consideration as a true benefit for the community. Instead, a few of these deals were considered a liability rather than an asset to the city and its citizens. Exemplifying such projects were the Nashville Arena and the Coliseum.

Throughout its history, incentive deals brought before the Metropolitan Council for their review and support had been hammered out between corporations and metropolitan administrative officials. The negotiating teams appointed by the mayor worked tirelessly with corporate representatives to develop agreements that were projected to benefit all areas of the city. These negotiations were held in private and involved the granting of overwhelming incentives to the corporations by the city. The failure to include representatives of the popularly elected Metropolitan Council in the negotiations removed a powerful regulatory voice from the process. This allowed for substantial incentives to be included, without question, in the finalized deal that was forced on the Metropolitan Council and the city.

A refusal to allow the heavily laden incentive deals to be amended by the Council motivated noticeable conflict between the legislative and administrative branches of our city. In many minds, these deals were illustrative of politics of old that were based on the belief that decisions made by elected officials should remain unquestioned. It involved strong alliances between influential special interest groups and elected officials. It was characterized by decisions being made behind closed doors with little or no input from impacted citizens.

Due to the immense size of these corporate incentive deals, the overall community of Metropolitan Nashville would be affected.

Among the more notable incentives offered to private corporations by Metropolitan Nashville included long-term property tax exemptions, publicly financed payments to corporations for meeting contractual obligations, and granting private corporations unquestioned control over publicly funded sports venues. In addition, designating large sums of unreserved capital from specific metropolitan departments to assist in funding the construction of large athletic projects generated noticeable criticism from the Metropolitan Council and the citizens. The Council believed that such capital should have been designated to fund required infrastructure upgrades or provide a reduction in utility rates for the citizens.

Finally, over the years the effects of hidden benefits for corporations became evident as resident taxpaying citizens were responsible for funding improvements to the infrastructure specifically serving the corporate sites. The improvements occurred prior to the completion of more desperately needed infrastructure upgrades throughout the city. Among the more notable of these needed infrastructure improvements were public highway construction and upgrades, water/sewer upgrades, and public school construction and renovations.

Nashville Arena and the NHL

The budget proposed by Mayor Phil Bredesen in 1993 included a property tax increase. The vast majority of the tax revenue was scheduled to be used to fund the construction of a new state-of-the-art arena in downtown Nashville. The arena was to replace the Municipal Auditorium, then considered to be outdated, as the key facility to accommodate large gatherings. The ultimate cost of construction for the facility came to $144 million. The Nashville Arena opened in December 1996. Upon its opening, the arena could seat approximately eighteen thousand fans for a hockey game and twenty thousand for a basketball game. It had 1,850 club seats and 70 luxury suites. It also had 350 on-site parking spaces.

During its construction, the Bredesen administration attempted to persuade numerous professional sports franchises to relocate to the newly constructed Nashville Arena. Bredesen had even "offered $20 million to any NBA or NHL team wanting to relocate"[6] to Nashville. Among the more notable hockey franchises courted by the Bredesen administration were the New Jersey Devils, Florida Panthers, Winnipeg Jets, and the Hartford Whalers. However, none were willing to accept the generous offer for relocation.

In June 1997, the possibility of having an empty arena was eliminated when it was made public that the expansion committee of the National Hockey League was recommending to the Board of Governors to expand to Nashville, along with Columbus, Atlanta, and Minneapolis-St. Paul. "Nashville was the only city among six finalists with a brand-new arena open and operating. That swayed the committee along with an ownership group featuring Racine, Wis., businessman Craig Leipold and the S. C. Johnson family as majority owners, with Nashville's Gaylord Entertainment Co. a minority partner."[7]

Mayor Bredesen requested that the Metropolitan Council authorize spending of approximately $34 million to locate the professional hockey franchise in the arena. The allocation included a $20 million franchise fee for the team, a $6.5 million practice rink for the team, and $7.5 million to complete locker rooms, offices, and a VIP club at the arena. Although the costs associated with locating the Nashville Predators in the arena was a difficult sale to the Metropolitan Council, the most controversial aspect of the deal was the arena lease agreement negotiated between the Bredesen administration and the hockey franchise administrators.

The arena lease agreement offered substantial incentives to the Predators. Among the more notable of these incentives included the extreme control of arena revenues and scheduling given to the hockey franchise by metropolitan officials. Specifically, giving the naming rights and any revenue associated with the naming to the Predators represented a questionable clause of the lease agreement.

The arena was a publicly subsidized facility with the cost of construction being obtained by raising property taxes on the citizens of Metropolitan Nashville. Therefore, it was my belief that the public should share in the revenues generated from the site. The questioning of these incentives was brought to full debate when, in 1999, the

GOVERNOR PHILIP BREDESEN

Philip Norman Bredesen, Metropolitan Nashville's fourth mayor, was born on November 21, 1943. He grew up in Shortsville, New York, a rural farming community, and he earned a bachelor's degree in physics from Harvard University.

Bredesen and his wife, Andrea Conte, moved to Nashville in 1975. Doing research at the public library, he drafted a business plan in the couple's small apartment that led to the creation of HealthAmerica Corp., a health-care management company that eventually grew to more than six thousand employees and traded on the New York Stock Exchange. He sold the company in 1986.

As mayor of Nashville from 1991 to 1999, Bredesen restored confidence in city government and charted a course that made Music City one of the best places in America to live, work, and raise a family. Among numerous accomplishments, he brought the Tennessee Titans to the state, built a new local library system, and drove down the city's crime rate.

Bredesen's proudest accomplishment as mayor was to infuse nearly one-half billion dollars into the local education system—adding more than 440 new teachers, building thirty-two new schools, and renovating forty-three others. He also implemented a back-to-basics curriculum to teach students what they need to know.

Two of the most noteworthy education projects included funding the new Hickman Elementary School and the renovated Donelson Middle School. His willingness to cooperate with the Metro Council in obtaining these as top priority projects with the Board of Education illustrated an understanding of the importance of stabilizing public school infrastructure for the enhancement of the community.

Nashville saw record economic growth during Bredesen's tenure and recruited high-quality jobs with major corporations such as Dell Computer Corporation and HCA, Inc. He oversaw the renewal of Nashville's downtown entertainment district and spearheaded public and private partnerships that led to development of the new Country Music Hall of Fame and Museum and also the Frist Center for the Visual Arts.

Community involvement has been a central part of Bredesen's life. He is a founding member of Nashville's Table, a nonprofit group that collects overstocked and discarded food from local restaurants for the city's homeless population. He founded the Land Trust for Tennessee, a nonprofit organization that works to preserve open space and traditional family farms. He also served on the Frist Center's board.

In 2002, Phil Bredesen was elected the forty-eighth governor of Tennessee. He has built a reputation for effective leadership in business and government. He campaigned for governor on a platform to better manage state government, improve Tennessee's schools, and fix TennCare. The Bredesens have one son, Ben.

Gaylord Entertainment Company entered into a twenty-year contract to have the name of the company placed on the arena at a cost of $80 million. The $2 million annual fee for the naming went exclusively to the Nashville Predators as designated in the lease agreement. Metropolitan Nashville did not receive any revenue from the naming of this publicly funded facility.

Questions were also raised regarding the popularity of an NHL team in Metropolitan Nashville. Baseball, basketball, and football represented popular athletic programs that Metropolitan Nashville students were introduced to from an early age. Organized hockey programs were lacking and had never established a firm footing in the sports landscape of the city. Questions were raised regarding the level of support the team could expect from those unfamiliar with the game.

In addition, the fact that the Nashville Predators represented an expansion franchise meant that there was no tradition associated with the team. Also, expansion teams were typically one of the weaker franchises in the league. These arguments seemed to indicate that the Predators would represent a less-than-profitable presence at the arena.

The Gaylord Entertainment Center (Photo courtesy of Metro Government of Nashville and Davidson County/Gary Layda)

The repayment of the $34 million funding for this hockey team was to be achieved by borrowing on long-term municipal bonds, a ticket tax, and sales taxes generated by the team. If hockey sales fell short, Metropolitan Nashville would be faced with a large bill. When I left office in 2003, the lack of success by the Nashville Predators, and conflicts over scheduling of other events in the arena that could generate some revenue for the city, led to the arena operating approximately $5 million to $10 million in the red.

In addition, questions were raised within the community about the credibility of Powers Management, the firm responsible for operating the arena that was owned by Predators owner Craig Leipold. The questions were based on the October 2001 firing of Powers employee John Day and Predators employee James Corn who were accused of using secret surveillance in the dressing room of the cheerleaders for the Nashville Kats, an Arena Football League team. The operation involved the scandalous taping of the cheerleaders as they undressed.

The cheerleaders filed a $13-million civil suit against both the Predators and Powers Management in 2003. The allegations in the suit illustrated the need to more thoroughly debate both short- and long-term impacts on the city of a publicly subsidized athletic venue prior to endorsing such a project. The actions taken by employees of Powers Management cast severe doubt on the ability of private franchises to administer public facilities in good faith.

Ultimately, the questions raised by the shortfall in ticket sales and the credibility of the private management group caused the arena to be considered more of a liability to Metropolitan Nashville than a profitable venture. It motivated further questions of the acceptability of entering into heavily laden incentive deals with private corporations and both the short- and long-term benefits to be received by the citizens from these deals. By 2004, the Gaylord Entertainment Center carried its largest deficit to date, "a projected bill of $6.1 million for Metro taxpayers to cover."[8]

In addition, there was an "operating deficit of $5.19 million and $900,000 in debt service for the building."[9] Due to the approximately $100 million shortfall in the Metro budget in 2004, Powers Management was called upon to substantially cut the operating budget of the arena. The request was similar to that made to other metro departments and agencies serving the community. However, Powers Management was somewhat reluctant to make the necessary budget cuts. In fact, it was projected that the operating budget would be greater than the previous year.

Hugh Lombardi, general manager of the arena and employee of Powers Management, claimed that "the budget increase was due, in part, to changes in the way the capital budget is managed." Lombardi further stated that Powers was "continuing to look at making cuts."[10]

In response to this issue, Metro Finance Director David Manning stated that if the budget did not "come down, though, there is little Metro and its taxpayers can do but continue to foot the bill."[11] This issue clearly illustrated major shortcomings in funding massive incentives to private corporations at the public's expense.

Dell Computer Agreement

In May 1999, Mayor Bredesen unveiled an incentive deal with the Dell Computer Corporation. The incentives represented an enticement to the computer giant to relocate its operations to Metropolitan Nashville. The free land, tax breaks, and other incentives offered by both state and metropolitan officials were estimated to be worth approximately $200 million over the next thirty years. The agreement reached by the Bredesen administration and Dell included:

1. offering of a 149.8-acre tract of property on Murfreesboro Pike that once housed the Middle Tennessee Mental Health Institute (This tract of property was appraised at $6.5 million, and Dell was assured by Bredesen that Metropolitan Nashville would pay for the demolition of the existing buildings on the site at an estimated cost of $1.5 million.);

2. a commitment from the city that it would pay a minimum of $8 million for infrastructure upgrades serving the industrial site;

3. a forty-year property tax exemption for property upon which the Dell Computer Corporation was to locate its manufacturing site (The cost of the exemption was estimated to exceed $100 million for the city.); and

4. a maximum five-hundred-dollar-per-employee tax credit paid to Dell by Metropolitan Nashville as part of an Economic and Community Development Incentive Program. In order to be eligible for the credit, Dell was to be responsible for creating a minimum number of two thousand new jobs within the boundaries of Metropolitan Nashville.

Following heated debate among councilmembers (including motions to table the legislation), the Council approved the Dell deal. This was in spite of the fact that "a number of local groups protested the decision."[12]

My opposition to the Dell deal was primarily based on the overwhelming incentives associated with the agreement and the fact that these substantial public funds were to be used for infrastructure upgrades in a concentrated area of Metropolitan Nashville. There remained infrastructure issues located throughout the county that demanded immediate attention. The public capital designated for this deal alone could have been expended more equitably allowing for its allotment throughout the county to address infrastructure issues facing the citizens of Metropolitan Nashville.

Although the deal did include certain community enhancements (i.e., the Central State Redevelopment Plan), there would be no guarantee that the economy of Metropolitan Nashville would be stimulated by the Dell Computer Corporation locating its operations to our city. Questions remained unanswered as to the stability of the relationship between Dell and the city of Metropolitan Nashville. These questions centered on how effective metropolitan officials could monitor the obligations of Dell to the city, and how long the Dell Computer Corporation would maintain its factory operations in Nashville before possibly relocating to another urban area. After the Metropolitan Council approved the deal, only time would bring answers to the questions surrounding this publicly subsidized, heavily laden incentive deal.

Supporters of this type of public/private agreement thought that incentive deals would stimulate the local economy and have long-term benefits for both the city and private businesses. However, as a metropolitan councilman, I was responsible for supporting only those agreements that were truly beneficial for the community I was elected to represent.

The main area of contention I had with these agreements dealt with the substantial tax reduction or exemption offered to private businesses by metropolitan authorities. The refusal to provide some property tax relief to individual residents, specifically senior citizens, illustrated an inequity that needed to be addressed.

In addition, a failure to provide concrete evidence that these deals would, indeed, stimulate the local economy raised questions regarding the appropriateness of such large public expenditures.

Finally, the fact that the vast majority of such deals were created behind closed doors with little or no representation or input from the popularly elected Metropolitan Council was a reason for my not supporting these deals.

From 1995 to 1999, the Metropolitan Council questioned and debated the projected benefits corporate incentive deals would bring to the city. Many of these debates became heated, with one resulting in councilmembers giving final voice to the citizens in the form of a referendum. The actions taken by the Metropolitan Council at that time truly represented a responsible legislative body that considered the long-term effects of these deals on the city itself. These actions also acted as notice to the business community of Metropolitan Nashville, and the private corporations that had entered into deals with the city, that the council was not prepared to accept any heavily laden incentive deals without debate.

The incentive deal offered to the Houston Oilers best exemplified the adversity these deals promoted in the metropolitan government. The failure of this deal to deliver on its promise to act as a prominent stimulus to the economy of the Metropolitan Nashville and Davidson County illustrated noticeable shortcomings in heavily laden incentive deals. As a result of the failings, further deliberation of the incentive deal concept was held in subsequent years.

Houston Oilers Relocation/Stadium Deal

The National Football League represented the most popular professional athletic entertainment in the United States in 1995. It consisted of thirty franchises located in major municipalities throughout the United States. Throughout its history, the NFL had provided fast paced, physical entertainment for the public. Beginning in the 1960s, the NFL began to supplant baseball as the national pastime. Over the next two decades, professional football had replaced baseball as the most popular form of athletic entertainment.

In January 1978, "a Louis Harris Sports survey found that 70 percent of the nation's sports fans said they followed football, compared to 54 percent who followed baseball."[13] In addition, by 1996 the NFL was "the dominant sports league in this country. Though it's trendy to talk about the flash and savvy of those who run the NBA, the fact remains that the NFL could buy and sell the NBA several times and still have change left over. . . ."[14]

However, the continued growth in popularity of professional football and the overwhelming profits obtained by franchise owners and players from this popularity led to conflicts within the National Football League and also between specific team owners and the cities that housed them. The most notable action taken by franchise owners that altered public perception of the league and challenged its credibility was the relocation of numerous well-established teams from their home cities to new sites.

These relocations were motivated by extremely lucrative incentive deals offered to franchise owners by cities desiring to become a part of the exclusive NFL club. The moves illustrated that professional sports was a for-profit venture. The numerous relocations that occurred during this time motivated even the most ardent professional football fans to question the long-term stability of agreements between private NFL franchises and state/local governments. In addition, it was openly evident that the franchises would reap the greatest benefit from relocation agreements.

The mass migration of football franchises raised questions pertaining to the loyalty of these teams to their fans and the stability of relocation deals. This was best illustrated in an article by Larry Woody, a *Tennessean* sports writer.

By 1995, the Metropolitan statistical area (consisting of Davidson, Cheatham, Dickson, Robertson, Rutherford, Sumner, Williamson, and Wilson counties) represented the fastest growing area in Tennessee. The population of the area at that time was approximately 1.1 million.

FROM THE TENNESSEAN

November 9, 1995

No Room for Loyalty in the NFL

News flash! NFL owners are greedy!

Yeah, and water has been discovered in the Atlantic Ocean.

Any day now I expect Dallas Cowboys owner Jerry Jones to announce he's moving his team to a $400 million gilt-domed stadium in Starkville, Miss.

The Starkville Cowboys.

That's got as much natural ring to it as the Baltimore Browns.

Art Modell is determined to yank his team out of Cleveland. What's 45 years of tradition and fan loyalty compared to a fatter wallet?

Modell is driven by the same motivation that appears to be steering Bud Adams and his Oilers to Nashville; that sent the Rams to St. Louis, the Raiders (back) to Oakland, and before that the Colts to Indy and the Cardinals to Phoenix.

Juicier deals and more money.

Does anyone think Art suddenly discovered a craving for crab cakes? Or that Bud decided he wanted to be closer to the Grand Ole Opry?

The once-stable old league has turned into a U-Haul race.

NFL should stand for No Fan Loyalty.

The nomadic owners say they're merely exerting their rights as free enterprise capitalists.

If they can sell more hot dogs—or higher-priced hot dogs—on Corner A than on Corner B, they should be free to move.

Instead of hot dogs, they're selling professional football—to the highest bidder.

The owners claim spiraling costs, especially in the area of players' salaries, are forcing them to seek new sources of revenue.

That's why Jones defied league policy and cut his own corporate endorsements. Jones threatens to drive a wedge between the league's Haves and Have-Nots.

His response: Tough.

Question: Who paid Deion Sanders a $12 million bonus?

Answer: Jerry Jones.

Question: Who gave Andre Rison the key to the safe?

Answer: Art Modell.

If the owners are looking for the root of the problem they should glance in the closest mirror.

Instead of exercising a little payroll restraint, the big spenders are looking for ways to pass the costs along to someone else, or to make an extra quick buck.

That's why Jones signed deals with Pepsi and American Express. Without them Jones couldn't afford the $35 million for Sanders.

How much is enough? There's something unseeming about a multi-millionaire on his knees, trying to fish loose change out of the gutter.

Former Cowboys coach Jimmy Johnson said during a visit here last week, "Jerry can be greedy, and not just about money."

Cities such as Nashville can capitalize on the NFL's shifting landscape, seizing the opportunity to grab one of the NFL's yard sale franchises.

But what happens if a city gets one of these vagabond teams and the owner, after a few years, stumbles on a sweeter deal elsewhere?

That's why a city had better make sure it has an iron-clad, no-loopholes contract binding an incoming team to its new home for a specific number of years.

Seems there's no place in modern sports for an old-fashioned concept like loyalty.[15]

—Copyrighted, the *Tennessean*, November 9, 1995

The population surge witnessed specifically by Metropolitan Nashville at this time created a new image of the city as being one of the largest urban areas in the nation and capable of playing a major role in professional sports. In order to take advantage of this new image, the Nashville Sports Council was established. "The Nashville Sports Council was created in 1992 out of a partnership between the

Mayor's Office, Nashville Convention & Visitors Bureau, and the Nashville Area Chamber of Commerce."[16] It represented "a private, 501c-6 not-for-profit, membership based organization that was established in 1992 to serve as the driver behind developing Nashville's sports landscape."[17]

It was believed that ultimately sports would be capable of unifying the different interests of the community. The ultimate objective of the Nashville Sports Council was to "attract quality-sporting events to the area that produce economic benefit through tourism activity, improve the quality of life, and showcase Nashville and its world-class community to an international audience."[18] It played a vital role in influencing the public and certain elected officials to believe that the expenditure of large amounts of public capital to construct massive sports facilities would be in the best interest of Metropolitan Nashville. These facilities would house private professional sports franchises and act as the venue for numerous entertaining events.

In 1995, the Houston Oilers franchise was looking to other cities in which to relocate their operations. This was based primarily on a cooling relationship between Oilers owner K. S. "Bud" Adams Jr. and officials from the city of Houston. The Oilers franchise had called Houston its home since its inaugural season of 1960. Demands made by Adams for an improved stadium led to Houston taxpayers spending "$70 million to improve the Astrodome, only to hear Adams say he's leaving eight years later."[19] Among the cities that Adams targeted Jacksonville, Florida, and Nashville, Tennessee. The designation of an expansion franchise for Jacksonville to begin play in 1995 removed that city from consideration.

In July 1995, the Houston Oilers expressed an interest in a possible move to Nashville. On July 7, 1995, a meeting was held in Chicago between Tennessee businessmen and Oilers Vice President Mike McClure. The positive attitude generated from that meeting led to Mayor Phil Bredesen meeting in Nashville with McClure on July 25, 1995, to discuss the possible move and to tour potential stadium sites. Over the following four months, the Bredesen administration and the Oilers franchise hammered out a relocation deal that was to bring the Oilers to Nashville by 1998.

The overwhelming incentives offered by Metropolitan Nashville to Adams in this deal became one of the most controversial issues associated with the proposed relocation. This deal included offering massive public incentives to a private franchise, thereby guaranteeing it overwhelming revenues.

However, these incentives seemed to directly contradict the issues the Metropolitan Council was responsible for addressing. Infrastructure upgrades represented the most prominent issues needing to be funded and completed to stabilize and enhance the urban environment of Metropolitan Nashville. None of the representatives of the Metropolitan Council were involved in the negotiations; therefore, the Oilers organization met little resistance in obtaining incentives.

One of the more controversial aspects of the Oilers move was the fact that the negotiations that led to the subsequent relocation agreement were held during the 1995 council campaigns. Responsible government necessitated informing the newly elected councilmembers of these negotiations. The update should include those incentives being offered to the Oilers organization. However, the administration and influential downtown businesses considered the new councilmembers highly inexperienced legislators and were believed by the key initiators of the Oilers relocation as being easily swayed to support the deal.

The belief was based on the erroneous belief that the elected Council governing Metropolitan Nashville was still controlled by influential business interests and political heavyweights. However, as debate over the deal continued, the new councilmembers reviewed the large amount of material associated with the relocation agreement, understood its intricacies, and informed their constituents of all aspects of the deal. Finally, the new council was prepared to take a position either supporting or opposing this deal based upon those factors, not simply because the mayoral administration or certain business interests requested their support.

On November 16, 1995, Mayor Phil Bredesen and Bud Adams signed the relocation agreement that would relocate the Oilers to Nashville. This deal was signed approximately one month after my election to the Metropolitan Council. It was the first massive project forced upon the newly elected Metropolitan Council and represented one of the largest publicly financed projects in the history of Metropolitan Nashville.

On Saturday, November 18, the Metropolitan Council was briefed by attorney Byron Trauger, chief negotiator for Nashville in the Oilers deal, and Don Jones, legal advisor to the Metropolitan Council. In reviewing the fifty-four-page document, councilmembers voiced numerous concerns pertaining to the deal. These concerns centered primarily on risks taken by the city, such as whether the $42 million projected by the council as acquisition costs for east bank properties to be relocated to make room for the stadium was appropriate.

Jones stated that the "risk that we have in this deal by fast-tracking is that we have budgeted $42 million and if the court says that is not enough, then we have to pay it." It was also noted that when acquiring properties for the downtown arena, "land purchases ended up costing $20 million more than was budgeted."[20]

Finally, it was asked whether the stadium could generate a profit for the city. "Jones explained that because the stadium is financed with tax-exempt bonds, it is illegal for it to make a profit for the city." The Oilers were "to operate the stadium at an annual cost of $6 million, and pay the city $1 million in rent each year."[21] The annual budget of Metropolitan Nashville was approximately $1 billion at that time. The cost to be paid by the Oilers to the city for use of the stadium was viewed as negligible by certain councilmembers.

Over the next three months, discussion of the possible relocation of the Oilers to Metropolitan Nashville and the overall effects this could have on the city continued in the council and throughout the community. It was at that time that I began distributing survey sheets to the citizens of council District 14 while attending community meetings. I considered the opinions of those citizens participating in the survey.

The vast majority of those surveyed commented that excess public funds should be used for infrastructure upgrades and improvements, specifically the public schools, public roads, and stormwater drainage. Additional input from citizens came from telephone conversations and e-mail in determining the overall opinion of those in District 14.

On February 15, 1996, the stadium package was presented to the Metropolitan Council. The package was an overview of all aspects of the agreement, including the East Bank Redevelopment Plan, the Stadium Development Agreement, the Memorandum of Understanding with the State, the Intergovernmental Project Agreement, Payment-in-Lieu-of-Taxes, G. O. Bond Package, Execution of Indenture, and the Sports Authority Bond Package.

The estimated construction cost of the stadium project was $292.1 million. The sources of funds for the stadium project included the city of Metropolitan Nashville spending approximately $154 million, the state of Tennessee investing approximately $67 million, and the sale of permanent seat licenses (PSL) by TENNFL, an organization formed to sell both PSLs and luxury suites, contributing approximately $71 million.

The city would reap certain benefits from the agreement. One of the most notable benefits prompted by the agreement was the 115-acre East Bank Redevelopment Plan. The redevelopment plan included $25 million to purchase and relocate the antiquated industrial sites along the Cumberland River and facing the lower Broadway commercial district across the river. The redevelopment plan also promoted the removal of vacant structures and the clearing of blighted areas along this stretch of the Cumberland River. It would serve to enhance the urban environment of this part of downtown Nashville. "Where there are now warehouses, there will be street-lights, green, manicured walkways, bike trails, restaurants and stores."[22]

Furthermore, the plan included money to save and renovate the historically significant Shelby Avenue Bridge. These renovations ultimately brought about the reopening of the bridge as a pedestrian crossing and preserved this historical monument of the downtown area as a supplement to the planned recreational environment that was established along this stretch of the Cumberland River.

In addition, a new Juvenile Justice Center was constructed contiguous with the stadium site. However, the improvements associated with the redevelopment plan were to be financed with general public funds and not revenues from the operation of the new state-of-the-art stadium. The Oilers franchise and Tennessee State University (whose football team would also use the stadium) were to be the benefactors of the stadium and reap substantial profits from its opening.

In contrast to the East Bank Redevelopment Plan, there were numerous parts of the agreement that brought questions and controversy during the subsequent deliberations by the Metropolitan Council. One of the main areas of controversy dealt with targeting public funds to assist in paying for the construction of the stadium. An example of this controversial aspect of the agreement was the resolution that required the Department of Water and Sewerage Services to make an annual in-lieu-of-tax payment in the amount of $4 million to assist in paying construction costs for the stadium.

This proposal brought noticeable criticism from members of the Metropolitan Council. Bredesen had found surplus funds in this public utility and, in cooperation with Water Department Director Buddy Williams, had designated that the surplus was sizeable enough to allow for a $4 million payment each year for the next thirty years for the stadium. However, Councilman Lawrence Hart openly voiced his opposition to using this surplus capital in such a manner. Hart argued "that if Water Services acknowledges a surplus it must refund the money to the customers."[23]

Since the takeover of the water and sewer service of Cumberland Utility District by the Metropolitan Department of Water and Sewerage Services, a sizeable percentage of the citizens had already been billed by Metro Water. Those citizens saw their monthly payments increase nearly three times what they had been under the Cumberland Utility District. Concerns were voiced to the district councilmembers serving this area of Davidson County.

Upon receiving notice of the substantial surplus, I believed that it should be used to provide rate relief for citizens or to fund the scheduled upgrades to the water and sewer infrastructure serving portions of Donelson, Hermitage, and Old Hickory. "When I asked Mayor Bredesen if Metro Water would turn around and request a 12 percent hike in water rates in the near future, he said he could not guarantee that it wouldn't happen."[24]

Perhaps the most controversial part of the agreement dealt with the ordinance that would approve the stadium lease between the Sports Authority of Metropolitan Nashville and Davidson County and Cumberland Stadium, L. P., which was another designation for the Oilers organization. The term of this lease was thirty years. The

Oilers were to pay a base annual rent of $3 million. This could be reduced by up to $2 million per year in annual operating expenses. The total amount of revenue guaranteed to the Oilers from their use of this publicly financed stadium surpassed any benefits to be received by Metropolitan Nashville.

The creation of the Sports Authority of Metropolitan Nashville had been authorized by the General Assembly in 1993 through Tennessee Code Annotated, Section 7-67-108. This state law designated that all:

> counties have a metropolitan form of government, there shall be no more than thirteen (13) directors. Nine (9) of such members of the board of directors shall be appointed based on residency with at least one (1) director being appointed from each metropolitan public school district. Of the remaining four (4) members, one (1) director shall be a resident of each of the four (4) state senatorial districts. This subdivision shall not affect the terms of the current members of the sports authority board of directors, but appointments shall be made for the new positions created by this subdivision and as terms expire and vacancies occur so as to meet the residency requirements established in this subdivision.[25]

The authority had been created to "be a public nonprofit corporation and a public instrumentality of the municipality with respect to which the authority is organized."[26] Among the wide ranging powers granted to the authority was the ability to "acquire, whether by purchase, construction, exchange, gift, lease, or otherwise, and to improve, repair, extend, equip, furnish, operate and maintain one (1) or more projects. . . ."[27]

After reviewing the lease agreement, one of the more notable areas of the document that caught my attention was Article 10 that gave overwhelming control to the Oilers over revenue generated from the stadium. Section 10.1 dealt specifically with the rights of the lessee to the revenues. It stated that:

> Except for the Excluded Revenues (such as the Civic Event Revenues, the TSU Revenues, and the PSL Revenues), Lessee shall be entitled to contract for, collect, receive and retain all gross income and revenues and other consideration of whatever kind or nature realized by, from or in connection

> with the Facilities, including, without limitation, all gross revenues, royalties, license fees, concession fees and income and receipts of any nature, including, without limitation, those arising from (a) the sale or distribution of tickets or passes (including tickets to club seats, luxury seats and general admission seats) and PSLs or any other fee with respect to any seat, (b) the sale, lease, licensing of, or granting concession with respect to, advertising and other promotional rights of every nature, including those Signage (interior or exterior) and printed material (including publications, tickets, programs, photographs, scorecards, media guides, yearbooks or flyers), (c) all Broadcast Rights, (d) parking, (e) promotion of events at the Facilities, (f) the sale of food, beverages, merchandise, programs and other goods and wares of any nature whatsoever at the facilities and (g) the naming of, or the sale, lease or license of the right to name, the Facilities or any portion thereof.[28]

The Oilers franchise acknowledged the massive amount of revenue when they presented their case for relocation to the NFL executives on March 11, 1996. A one-hundred-page booklet that was given privately to the other owners of the NFL illustrated:

> stark differences between the team's current Astrodome lease and the lease that has been written for the proposed downtown stadium. The Oilers say that under their current lease in the Astrodome, the team receives 10 percent of concessions revenues, 30 percent of parking revenues and 50 percent of scoreboard advertising. All are well below the current league averages. According to the Oilers presentation, NFL teams get an average of 54 percent of concessions revenues, 51 percent of in-stadium advertising revenues, 47 percent of parking and 61 percent of scoreboard advertising. In the proposed Nashville stadium, the team would keep 100 percent of concessions revenues and 100 percent of advertising within the stadium—including scoreboards. Since some of those revenues go into a pool that is shared—like network television money—by all teams in the league, more revenue for the Oilers means more revenue for the league.[29]

In addition, in compliance with the lease negotiated with Nashville officials, "the Oilers will also keep revenues generated from naming rights to the stadium, which is projected by many in the league to be about $3 million per year. Suite revenues and club seat

Figure 6-1

How the Metropolitan Council Voted on the Oilers Deal on February 27, 1996

Supported

- Tom Alexander	- Jerry Graves	- Phil Ponder
- George Armistead	- Morris Haddox	- Julius Sloss
- Eileen Beehan	- Leroy Hollis	- Janis Sontany
- Melvin Black	- Saletta Holloway	- Ronnie Steine
- James Dillard	- Aaron Holt	- Ron Turner
- Mansfield Douglas	- Horace Johns	- Vic Varallo
- Charles Fentress	- Vic Lineweaver	- Leo Waters
- Charles French	- Willis McCallister	- Mike Wooden
- Tim Garrett	- Regina Patton	

Opposed

- Michelle Arriola	- Chris Ferrell	- David Kleinfelter
- Earl Campbell	- Durward Hall	- Don Majors
- Stewart Clifton	- Frank Harrison	- James Bruce Stanley
- Eric Crafton	- Lawrence Hart	
- Roy Dale	- Craig Jenkins	

revenues in the new stadium are also each projected by league executives to bring between $7 million and $10 million to the team."[30]

An additional expenditure that Metropolitan Nashville had agreed to pay to the private football franchise was designated in a summary of the Stadium Development Agreement. That agreement designated that the Sports Authority was to "pay the team a $28 million transfer fee to cover the business costs of moving to Tennessee, including the cost of legal consulting fees, the cost of changing logo and uniform design, lost profits and business opportunities, as well as relocation and moving allowances for 'front office' team employees, coaches and players."[31] This transfer fee was to be paid in five installments.

Although concerns by councilmembers over certain aspects of the Houston Oilers relocation agreement and stadium deal were still being voiced, the required bills were passed through the first two readings of the municipal legislative process. On February 27, 1996, it passed second reading with several councilmembers voicing their position on the deal.

Those in support of the deal included Councilman Ron Turner who stated, "The first time they take the field, the first time they win a game—I don't care if you know a touchdown from a touchback—there will be more excitement throughout the whole state than you can imagine."[32]

Councilman Julius Sloss informed the audience that, "There's a certain electricity there that does not exist in a town that doesn't have professional sports."[33]

Councilman Horace Johns stated that, "It's not necessarily a good deal. It's not necessarily a bad deal. But it's the only deal."[34]

However, there were also numerous councilmembers that could not support the deal. Councilman Vic Varallo was in general support of the deal. And yet, he could not vote in favor when he stated that, "I'm for the Oilers coming here, but we are not going to use that water money—period."[35]

Councilman Ron Nollner abstained from all votes, claiming that "I am still for the stadium. I'm just not for this funding package."[36]

One of the more disturbing arguments voiced by supporters of this deal was that, similar to the Tennessee Volunteers, the Oilers would be Tennessee's team. It was claimed that in that role, the Oilers would generate great interest and enthusiasm from the citizens of the mid state. This would lead to a large increase in tourism to Metropolitan Nashville and bring tourist dollars to the area. However, that argument was extremely weak.

When addressing the council, I informed them of the numerous relocations of NFL teams in recent years and that this deal with the Oilers simply represented the most recent. The relocations were motivated by a desire for increased profits on the part of the owners of the private sports franchises.

Ultimately, these relocations represented the abandonment of well-established municipal homes. The recent relocations clearly distinguished the professional football franchises from university teams. The University of Tennessee represented only one of many public institutions of higher education in our state that were both publicly funded and administered, unlike the Oilers franchise that was a privately owned and administered professional football franchise.

I informed fellow councilmembers that, "This is never going to be Nashville's team. This is never going to be Tennessee's team. This is always going to be Bud Adams' team."[37]

Questions were raised pertaining to possible future demands to be made by the Oilers franchise on Metropolitan Nashville regarding desired expansion and improvements to the stadium, the cost of such alterations to the stadium, and the action to be taken by the professional football franchise if their demands were not met.

Following heated debate over the deal, the council vote resulted in its passage by a margin of twenty-six to thirteen. Due to the overwhelming number of constituents that voiced their opposition and the large amount of public money to be used for the benefit of a private sports franchise, I refused to support the deal.

The main area of contention by the citizens of Metropolitan Nashville centered on the use of public funds to construct a new stadium for a wealthy professional franchise owner and businessman. In response to concerns voiced by citizens throughout Metropolitan Nashville, Councilmen Eric Crafton and David Kleinfelter cooperated with retired banker Wallace "Red" McClary to organize a petition drive and have the question of the relocation and stadium deal placed on a referendum. This referendum would allow the individual citizens of Metropolitan Nashville to vote on the proposal in a special election. Crafton wanted "a vote on the stadium financing, regardless of whether it passes or fails."[38] Kleinfelter claimed that he "joined the Oilers fray after seeing opposition in different neighborhoods, but no organized effort to fight the deal."[39]

McClary's involvement centered on his belief that "Bredesen put too much emphasis on paying big business by tax concessions and trying to develop glitzy programs such as the arena." He also believed that, after going door-to-door with the petition, "many stadium supporters would change their mind if they realized the full financial scope of the project."[40]

The Metropolitan Council met in a special session on Thursday, February 29, 1996, to consider all legislation associated with the

Oilers deal on final reading. Mayor Bredesen addressed the Council at the opening of the session. In his address, Bredesen "pleaded with members to pass the most controversial part of the stadium funding—a $4 million annual assessment on Metro Water Services. The money is to be collected from city water customers, the utility's only source of revenue, for thirty years."[41]

In this request, Bredesen was successful, as the Council voted 23 to 17 in favor of using water revenue to assist in construction of the stadium. The Council also voted 27 to 12 to accept the negotiated terms for the construction and use of the stadium. I refused to support the legislation of this deal, however, due to the opposition voiced to me by constituents of District 14 as well as the questioned stability of the deal due to a possible relocation of the team in subsequent years.

The Election Commission designated the minimum number of names required on the petition to place the deal on a referendum to be 28,084. On Wednesday, February 28, 1996, the opponents of the stadium deal delivered 43,640 signatures to the Metropolitan Courthouse. The success of the petition drive necessitated the setting of a voting date for the referendum. The date was eventually set for May 7, 1996.

Supporters and opponents of the stadium deal used the next two months to campaign for their position. The campaigning proved costly for both sides of the stadium issue. Some of the more noticeable contributors for the "NFL Yes" campaign that supported the stadium deal included Gaylord Entertainment, NationsBank, and Nissan. "Gaylord, owner of Opryland U.S.A., contributed $25,000 to the 'NFL Yes' campaign. Eight banks put up a total of $108,000. The largest single campaign contribution was $26,500 from NationsBank. Among Middle Tennessee manufacturers, Nissan and Bridgestone-Firestone each contributed $10,000."[42]

In contrast to the supporters, the amount of funds raised by those in opposition, known as "Concerned Citizens for Metro Nashville," were extremely limited. Most donations came from individuals and averaged less than one hundred dollars per contribution. Both sides used extensive advertising and face-to-face meetings with voters to press their positions on the deal.

The key issue of this referendum centered around the use of public funds in the deal. The main question of the referendum asked voters whether they supported the issuance of bonds to build the stadium. The source of this revenue to pay off the bonds was to come from "sales tax generated by stadium events, existing real estate taxes and money collected from Metro Water Services."[43]

The most controversial source of public funds was the Department of Water Services funding, based on the fact that "rates paid by city water customers are the utility's only source of revenue. A 3 percent increase in sewer rates that was scheduled for January was questioned and repealed by the Metro Council in December; however, increases of 3 percent for 1997 and 1998—approved long before a stadium plan emerged—remain on the books. Opponents say any surplus water money should go back to rate payers directly, or water rates should be reduced, rather than using the money for the stadium."[44]

The referendum was brought before the public on May 7, 1996. The closing of the polls witnessed 74,047 voting in favor of the stadium deal with 51,850 voting against it. The vote clearly opened the door for the Oilers move to Metropolitan Nashville and into a newly constructed stadium.

The groundbreaking for the stadium occurred on May 3, 1997. Completed in time for the 1999 season, the stadium was approximately 1.5 million square feet in size and stood 190 feet high. It was a 67,000 seat stadium that included 156 luxury suites that were leased at $50,000 to $125,000 per year, and 11,800 club seats that cost $995 to $2,495 per year.

Following approval of the Oilers deal by metropolitan officials and the general populace, Bud Adams obtained a premature release from

Team owner Bud Adams signs autographs for fans beside Mayor Bredesen at the Coliseum groundbreaking on May 3, 1997

Mayor Phil Bredesen at the site of the Coliseum ground-breaking on May 3, 1997

his contract with the city of Houston and the Astrodome. The original timeline of the agreement set 1998 as the first season the Oilers would play in Tennessee. However, the early release allowed the Oilers to begin play in Tennessee in 1997. Because the Nashville stadium was not yet complete, the newly designated Tennessee Oilers played their home games at the Liberty Bowl in Memphis.

In February 1999, the Oilers changed their name to the Tennessee Titans. By 1999, the new football stadium in Nashville was completed, and the Titans played their inaugural season in the new stadium. However, over the next few years controversy would be associated with the stadium and the professional football franchise that called it home.

Upon completion of the stadium, the Titans organization exercised its right to contract with another party in the naming of the stadium as guaranteed by Article 10.2 of the stadium lease agreement. In July 1999, "Adelphia Business Solutions was awarded a 15-year, $30 million naming rights contract"[45] with the Titans organization. The contract allowed for the stadium to be named Adelphia Coliseum.

Adelphia Business Solutions was a subsidiary of Adelphia Communications Corporation, a national company that was headquartered in Pennsylvania. It offered "cable television and other high technology services to its more than 5 million customers across the country."[46] It had been operating in Tennessee since 1991 through the Hyperion Communications subsidiary. It was soon announced that Hyperion would begin operating as Adelphia Business Solutions.

During the announcement of this naming, Titans owner Bud Adams "alluded to parallels between Adelphia and the Titans, saying that both organizations have made changes that signal the charting of new courses for the future."[47] However, this comparison of the Titans and Adelphia proved to be somewhat unsettling for area citizens, when on March 27, 2002, Adelphia Business Solutions filed for bankruptcy protection after hitting hard times. The unexpected bankruptcy of Adelphia Business Solutions raised questions pertaining to the stability of the Titans organization and the plans of the football franchise to remain in Metropolitan Nashville for the entire thirty-year length of the stadium lease. The bankruptcy filing by Adelphia resulted in the Titans bringing suit against the communications company and having the name Adelphia removed from the stadium in July 2002.

The removal of the Adelphia name from the stadium raised questions among numerous councilmembers pertaining to the possibility of naming it after the city which had financed its construction. The question was brought before the Metropolitan Council on August 6, 2002, in the form of a resolution by downtown councilman Ludye Wallace. Resolution No. RS2002-1102 requested "the Mayor, the Nashville Sports Authority, and the Tennessee Titans to name the football stadium the 'Nashville Coliseum,' or other similar name until a new contract for naming of the football stadium has been executed."[48]

The resolution, approved by the Parks, Library, Recreation and Auditorium Committee, was passed by the Metropolitan Council by a vote of twenty-six in favor, four against, and one abstaining. I openly supported the resolution so that citizens who funded the stadium would receive recognition from the Titans and national audiences during televised games. However, the resolution was discarded by the Sports Authority and the Titans, which illustrated that the primary purpose of the stadium was a promotional tool that generated profit for their organization.

The public attitude toward the Titans organization included suspicions over its interactions with metropolitan officials. These suspicions primarily resulted from the establishment of the Titans as an influential lobby to the Metropolitan Council. This resulted in conflicting incidents within the community immediately following their relocation to Nashville.

For instance, complaints of alleged unethical conduct by councilmembers were filed with the Metropolitan Board of Ethical Conduct in January 2000. The complaints were based on a number of Metropolitan Councilmembers accepting an invitation from Tennessee

Titans owner Bud Adams to attend a Titans game in his luxury suite.

Mark Lambert claimed that accepting these invitations "would be just like accepting gifts from anyone that Metro is doing business with. It's a conflict of interest."[49]

Questions were raised as to whether accepting this invitation would constitute an ethical violation under the Metropolitan Code of Laws. "Board members Megan Barry, Worrick Robinson IV and Nanci Pugh Adkins voted that material in complaints against the members, if true, would constitute a violation of the code of ethical conduct the council adopted in 1995."[50]

Concerns raised by citizens were based primarily on the increased influence Adams could gain over the popularly elected municipal legislature through giving such gifts. It was noted that the "Metro Council, including some current members, voted in 1995 to bring Adams' National Football League team to Nashville by providing some public funding for the $292 million Adelphia Coliseum."[51]

The Ethics Board belief that the "council might at some point have to consider aspects of the 30-year contract between the city and the team owner"[52] motivated an investigation of the issue. In my position as a Metropolitan councilmember, I received a letter from Karl Dean, director of law, as part of the investigation. The letter requested that I answer numerous questions pertaining to the invitation. The first question was: "Did you receive an invitation to attend a Tennessee Titans game as the guest of the Titans, its owner, or anyone you associated with the team? If yes, please answer the remaining questions. If no, please return this letter with the information that you were not invited or that you did not accept the invitation."[53]

I had received the invitation in question, but I did not accept it. I notified Mr. Dean by letter of that fact. The length of the investigation was approximately six weeks. It was made known that thirty-two of forty councilmembers did accept the invitation and attended a game.

On March 14, 2000, a report was released by the Department of Law at the conclusion of the investigation. The report established that "all members of council, including some who had voted against public financing of the stadium, and Mayor Bill Purcell received invitations." The investigation also designated that the "per person value of the invitation was $300–$700 per person." In addition, it was noted that

The Coliseum, home of the Tennessee Titans (Photo courtesy of Metro Government of Nashville and Davidson County/Gary Layda)

"several council members mentioned that the Titans could not invite everyone in the city and felt they were attending as representatives of the community as a whole." In conclusion, the report "found that no legislative matters affecting the Titans are before Metro Council, and therefore cleared the Titans organization of extending the invitation with any improper motive."[54]

The overwhelming revenue guaranteed to the Titans organization through its control of the stadium established that the source of any fiscal benefits the city were to derive from the deal was to be indirect and long term. The existence of the stadium and a redeveloped east bank of the Cumberland River were designated as good for the local economy. The primary source of profit for the city from the deal was projected to be a substantial increase in sales tax revenue. The sales tax increase was to come from a noticeable rise in the levels of tourism in downtown Nashville as people attended Titans games and began to eat and shop in downtown businesses. In addition, it was projected that new businesses would move into the vacant stores located along lower Broadway. Ultimately, the economic stimulus projected for

Metropolitan Nashville from the deal was to result from:

> revenue from sale of properties, revenue from sale of construction materials, retail sales from new businesses, retail sales from new restaurants, insurance policies for homes and businesses, landscape sales, additional revenues for the Nashville Electric Service, telephone and gas companies, and the water/sewer department, increased ridership and contract use of transit buses, benefits from marketing of Nashville and Tennessee on network television, other marketing of Nashville and Tennessee in national newspapers and publications.[55]

However, by 2003, approximately four years after the opening of the new stadium, the economy had not yet prospered to the level projected in 1996. The east bank of the Cumberland River of downtown Nashville was the only area of the Nashville community that witnessed any noticeable improvements. Citizens of the suburban communities of Metropolitan Nashville were still required to pay heavy water and sewer rates. Finally, the funding for needed upgrades to the infrastructure of Metropolitan Nashville and the balancing of the ever-growing Metropolitan budget required property tax increases on the citizens of Metropolitan Nashville in 1997, 1998, and 2001.

Throughout my eight years on the Metropolitan Council, I was continually notified by representatives of the downtown business partnership of the failings of many businesses located along lower Broadway. These businesses represented well-established commercial entities as well as numerous new businesses that had located their operations to lower Broadway since the opening of the stadium. Among the more notable of these businesses were Planet Hollywood, Nascar Café, Seanachie Irish Pub, and the Harley Holt Co. The presence of the new stadium and football team was not enough to keep many of these businesses afloat. Ultimately, the failure of these downtown businesses also meant less money for the city of Nashville.

The heavily laden incentive deal hammered out between the Houston Oilers and the administration of Metropolitan Nashville illustrated the desire of certain government officials to support a policy of enticing private business interests to relocate their operations to Metropolitan Nashville. The policy promised to grant national exposure to the city and act as an economic stimulus for the local economy. However, the benefits received by the city from the deal proved to be minimal compared to the massive amounts of revenue guaranteed to Bud Adams and the Oilers/Titans organization. This clearly evidenced the inequities associated with such heavily laden corporate incentive deals.

A study by Stanford University economics professor Roger G. Noll and Smith College economics professor Andrew Zimbalist outlined the impacts the stadium construction boom was to have on the local economies funding these stadiums throughout the nation. It was stated that "new sports facilities costing at least $200 million each have been completed or are under way in Baltimore, Charlotte, Chicago, Cincinnati, Cleveland, Milwaukee, Nashville, San Francisco, St. Louis, Seattle, Tampa, and Washington D.C., and are in the planning stages in Boston, Dallas, Minneapolis, New York, and Pittsburgh. Industry experts estimate that more than $7 billion will be spent on new facilities for professional sports teams before 2006. Most of this $7 billion will come from public sources." In addition, it was noted that these "sports facilities now typically cost the host city more than $10 million a year."[56]

One issue addressed in this study dealt with the flawed economic reasoning used by supporters of these projects to obtain public support for subsidizing such facilities.

> Proponents claim that sports facilities improve the local economy four ways. First, building the facility creates construction jobs. Second, people who attend games or work for the team generate new spending in the community, expanding local employment. Third, a team attracts tourists and companies to the host city, further increasing local spending and jobs. Finally, all this new spending has a "multiplier effect" as increased local income causes still more new spending and job creation. Advocates argue that new stadiums spur so much economic growth that they are self-financing: subsidies are offset by revenues from ticket taxes, sales taxes on concessions and other spending outside the stadium, and property tax increases arising from the stadium's economic impact.[57]

However, "these arguments contain bad economic reasoning that leads to overstatement of the benefits of stadiums. Economic growth takes place when a community's resources—people, capital investments, and natural resources like land—become more productive. . . . Building a stadium is good for the local economy only if a stadium is the most productive way to make capital investment and use its workers." In addition, it was noted that "a stadium can spur economic growth if sports is a significant export industry—that is, if it attracts outsiders to buy the local product and if it results in the sale of certain rights (broadcasting, product licensing) to national firms. But, in reality, sports has little effect on regional net exports."[58]

Professional sports had never played a major role in the economy of Metropolitan Nashville. Nashville had always been known as Music City for its close relationship to the country music industry. In addition, it had been given the nickname "Athens of the South" because of the Parthenon replica in Centennial Park and the numerous colleges and universities located throughout the area. The printing industry, exemplified best by the Methodist and Baptist Publishing Houses, also played a prominent role in the local economy.

Another issue associated with publicly subsidized stadiums involved promotional studies conducted by supporters of professional sports franchises. The studies had proven to be flawed in a number of ways. "Such promotional studies overstate the economic impact of a facility because they confuse gross and net economic effects. Most spending inside a stadium is a substitute for other local recreational spending, such as movies and restaurants. Similarly, most tax collections inside a stadium are substitutes: as other entertainment businesses decline, tax collections from them fall." These "studies also fail to take into account differences between sports and other industries in income distribution. Most sports revenue goes to a relatively few players, managers, coaches, and executives who earn extremely high salaries—all well above the earnings of people who work in the industries that are substitutes for sports. Most stadium employees work part time at very low wages and earn a small fraction of team revenues."[59]

Finally, this economic study stated that "despite greater citizen awareness, voters still must cope with a scarcity of teams. Fans may realize that subsidized stadiums regressively redistribute income and do not promote growth, but they want local teams. Alas, it is usually better to pay a monopoly an exorbitant price than to give up its product."[60]

The continual growth of Metropolitan Nashville over the years made it one of the more prominent cities in the United States when the Houston Oilers wanted to relocate to another city. However, obtaining this franchise did not come without sacrifices by the citizens and questions about the long-term benefits to be received by Metropolitan Nashville and the citizens that call it home. Although the newly named Tennessee Titans played well on the field, the impact the team would have on the local economy would truly determine the worth of the franchise to the city.

The economic impact had still not been determined by 2003. The east bank of the Cumberland River in downtown Nashville was revitalized, bringing with it a much more aesthetically pleasing atmosphere for citizens of the area. And yet this represented only a small section of Metropolitan Nashville. Other sections of the city that desperately needed revitalization through infrastructure upgrades failed to receive any noticeable benefits. Granting large incentives to private corporations raised questions as to how they would stimulate the local economy and what benefits would be reaped by the citizens who were the source of funding for these deals.

Finally, statements made by NFL executives at the league meetings in Amelia Island, Florida, in May 2004, were a cause for concern for any city that was home to a professional football franchise. The cities that represented the smaller markets, including Metropolitan Nashville, were specifically targeted by the statements.

Commissioner Paul Tagliabue had voiced his desire to have an NFL franchise operating out of a newly constructed stadium in Los Angeles by 2008. Los Angeles represented the second largest televised market in the nation. One of the most prominent owners who hinted at possibly moving his franchise to this larger market was Indianapolis Colts owner Jim Irsay.

In 1984, the Irsay family had moved the Colts from their home in Baltimore to Indianapolis. The move came because the city of Indianapolis offered to build a domed stadium for the Colts to call home. By 2004, the RCA Dome in Indianapolis was the smallest stadium in the NFL. This was unacceptable to Irsay and the Colts franchise. Irsay stated that he was "falling a little more behind each day in the league's financial race because he plays in the NFL's smallest stadium—the 55,306 seat RCA Dome." In addition, Irsay was "trying to determine if there is enough long-term interest in his team in Indiana to even begin what will be a decidedly uphill fight for a new stadium."[61] The RCA Dome lease that Irsay had with the city was to run through 2013. However, there was an escape clause in the lease that would enable the team to locate elsewhere in 2007, coinciding with the time that Tagliabue wanted the Los Angeles NFL operations to be up and running.

The statements made at the league meetings illustrated that professional football was first and foremost a profit making venture by the owners of each franchise. The refusal of cities to meet an owner's demands for stadium renovation or replacement would result in the relocation of that franchise to another city.

Because the Tennessee Titans were operating from an NFL stadium that was only slightly larger than the RCA Dome, future demands by Titans owner Bud Adams for the expansion of the Coliseum were not beyond reality. In fact, such stadium renovations were to be publicly funded and the overwhelming benefits obtained by Adams and the Titans. This clearly illustrated the long-term instabilities associated with professional sports deals.

Conclusion

The negotiations involving municipal administration officials and private corporate representatives failed to include the popularly elected Metropolitan Council in the development of large corporate incentive deals. The Council was ultimately given the opportunity to consider only the finalized agreements. Such agreements were not subject to change, further hindering the development of a more equitable agreement between the public entity and the private corporations.

The failure to involve the Metropolitan Council in the development of such agreements substantially removed the public from voicing their concerns. That school of political thought had proven to be unacceptable to the citizens of Metropolitan Nashville.

Upon the completion of my eight years of service on the Metropolitan Council in 2003, it was clearly evident that the private business lobby was still promoting large incentive-based deals as an economic stimulus to the local economy. This was best illustrated by two large publicly subsidized proposals that were to be considered by the newly elected council. The proposals included a new convention center and a new stadium for the Nashville Sounds baseball franchise. Both were to be located in the downtown area of Metropolitan Nashville. The convention center was estimated to cost approximately $350 million and the stadium approximately $35 million.

However, questions pertaining to the effectiveness of previous incentive deals, specifically the Oilers relocation and stadium deal and the Nashville Predators lease agreement, cast serious doubts about funding these proposals. Mayor Bill Purcell was planning a feasibility study on the new convention center, and he had "made it clear that any Metro contribution toward a stadium would be 'modest'."[62]

Approximately two months after my leaving office, an announcement was made in the local press that stated "a formal proposal for a ballpark along the west bank of the Cumberland River is expected in the next two weeks. It would be built on the 12-acre site that now contains the Nashville Thermal Transfer Plant on First Avenue South." To ensure the approval of such a facility in the downtown area, "Mayor Bill Purcell's office has told the Nashville Sounds that they must have a third party to guarantee that taxpayers won't be on the hook for any shortfalls."[63]

Basically, the required condition called for the Nashville Sounds to contract with a financially affluent third party. This would ensure that municipal bonds issued by Metropolitan Nashville to assist in paying for the development of the project would not be lost. This would prevent the citizens from dipping into their pockets to pay off the debt. It was made known that "First Tennessee bank is slated to play a key role in the proposed project and that the bank's involvement could include naming rights." However, Glenn Yeager, general manager of the Nashville Sounds, claimed that the "Memphis-based bank is acting as a 'financial partner' in the project but would not be the sole guarantor."[64]

Metropolitan contributions to the project included the public acreage upon which the stadium was to be constructed. After spending approximately $2.5 million to demolish the thermal plant, the value of the site would be approximately $4.5 million to $5 million. In addition, Metro Finance Director David Manning announced that the city "would contribute any local sales tax revenue from the park that is above the amount generated at the team's current home, Greer Stadium."[65] Finally, the city would be responsible for paying approximately $350,000 of the $1.1 million annual stadium maintenance costs. The Nashville Sounds would be responsible for the $750,000 balance of the annual maintenance costs.

This was a notable difference in position by the current mayoral administration toward corporate incentive deals. The Purcell administration refused to be manipulated by the Nashville Sounds business franchise during negotiations. Instead, this administration "played hardball at times with the Sounds, saying that the city could easily find other suitors for the team's preferred river-front site. Metro has bristled at the notion that the appeal of the downtown stadium gives the team a negotiating advantage and an anchor hold on the site and future development."[66]

In a September 1, 2003, communication with Glenn Yaeger, David Manning stated, "I believe you are badly mistaken if you believe the growth of the area surrounding the thermal site and Rolling Mill Hill are dependent on the Sounds proposal. The city is considering contributing the hottest piece of real estate in the region to your project. It is not because of your project the site is hot."[67]

These statements clearly illustrated the maturation of metropolitan officials in negotiating with private businesses over incentive deals. The new attitude represented a much more responsible policy. It also protected the established community and the taxpaying citizens from future failings of such deals.

Finally, the position taken by metropolitan officials that the city would only be willing "to play ball on a new park, provided a third party guarantees payment on city-issued bonds" firmly established a new municipal policy involving Metropolitan Nashville in corporate incentive deals. "The Purcell administration has made it clear it does not want taxpayers liable for the construction of another sports venue."[68]

One of the key factors considered by metropolitan officials when developing this position was that "the current Sounds ownership has not always been reliable in paying what it owes the city. That's why the guaranteed payment seems prudent." In addition, it was noted that the debate over the downtown baseball park "could conjure up in some quarters ill will that was sparked when Nashville entered into arrangements on sports facilities with the Titans and Predators."[69]

Although those agreements did motivate an aesthetic enhancement of the downtown area, taxpayers throughout Metropolitan Nashville had witnessed sizeable shortcomings of those agreements and felt "the city paid too much and received too little on those deals."[70]

Obviously, the policy adopted by the Purcell administration addressing corporate incentive deals reasserted the responsibility of elected officials to the general citizens. It was extremely important for the popularly elected Metropolitan Council to adopt the same policy. Only time would tell if the downtown business lobby would succeed in reasserting private dealings between metropolitan officials and independent business interests. Such dealings excluded general public input during their consideration. Public input was a necessity to such multi-million dollar publicly subsidized deals, and "the public's voice should be an integral part of the process."[71]

It was important to base the support of such deals not simply on projected improvements to the local economy, but also the negative effects of revenue shortfalls such deals would have on the local community. The role of the previous deals in the local economy had not proven to be the economic stimulus they were projected to be for Metropolitan Nashville. Councilman-at-large David Briley said, "Metro hasn't paid off the bonds on the current convention center yet and many questions remain about building a new one."[72]

It is hoped Briley's statement signifies the attitude of the majority of councilmembers elected to represent the citizens of Metropolitan Nashville. Such an attitude would carefully regulate the inclusion of public funds for corporate incentive deals until the projected economic benefits these deals were to have on the community had been unequivocally proven.

EPILOGUE

The intrusion of urban sprawl into the suburban communities of Metropolitan Nashville promoted a new era of government for the citizens of our city. The threats posed by urban sprawl and its unregulated growth were so adverse that it motivated resident citizens to review the machine controlling Metropolitan Nashville politics in the mid-1980s. The citizens found that the old-school political machine was in power. The closed-door strategy used clearly illustrated a failing of this school of political thought. This kind of politics did not promote citizen input.

In response to this, the resident citizens of Metropolitan Nashville organized into political associations. These associations promoted an active involvement in local politics that had been previously unseen. In addition, the active involvement promoted a more inclusive strategy in local politics.

My involvement in local politics was directly linked to urban sprawl. Similar to the vast majority of resident citizens of Metropolitan Nashville, I was appalled at the perceived control exercised by developmental and commercial interests over elected councilmembers. The refusal of these councilmembers to consider citizen input when determining a position to take on a controversial land-use issue proved unacceptable to the resident citizens.

Instead, the open-door political strategy promoted open communication between councilmembers and their constituents. The achievement of open communication required the councilmembers to sponsor community meetings to address issues affecting the constituents. It was also necessary that input from diverse community interests be considered by councilmembers prior to taking a position on certain issues. The variety of input proved invaluable for all in that it included the possiblity of a compromise to a controversial proposal.

In addition, the position the community wanted the councilmember to take on a certain issue was clearly outlined at open community meetings. The benefits the community obtained from open-door politics were overwhelming. Such benefits were needed to battle the adverse effects of unregulated growth and provide a stable environment in which the citizens of Metropolitan Nashville could reside and invest. My personal political experiences educated me on the importance of the use of open-door politics in local government.

I promised to follow this strategy when running for the Metropolitan Council in 1995 and 1999. In 1999, my political philosophy was that I believed "the most important factor associated with successful political representation is cooperation. This cooperation can be accomplished by maintaining an open line of communication between the elected representative, the constituents, and the government authorities through whom certain issues or concerns must be addressed."[1]

During the eight years on the Council, I continually sponsored community meetings to address issues faced by constituents. In addition to area residents, I invited professional staff members of numerous metropolitan departments to attend these meetings. Their attendance guaranteed an acceptable answer be given to specific questions posed by resident citizens. Additionally, close cooperation with state and federal officials brought to their attention certain issues that could only be alleviated with their assistance.

It was my belief that our city had reached that point in its history where open communication and cooperation were required to regulate growth and promote a more stable and healthy environment in which to live. The events covered in this text illustrate my desire to successfully include the community's concerns in order to benefit the Nashville area as a whole.

The direction Metropolitan Nashville will now take with regard to its growth is in question. There have been attempts to revert to the former closed-door political days. Although older style politics was never completely extinct, the activism of resident citizens will prohibit a complete reversion to old-school politics. In the meantime, open communication and cooperation are required in order to be a true representative. My use of an open-door political strategy while serving on the Metropolitan Council benefited the citizens of our city. It was ***A Promise Kept.***

Appendix

Ninth Metropolitan Council (1995–99)

Vice Mayor—Jay West
District at-large—Vic Varallo
District at-large—George H. Armistead III
District at-large—Ronnie Steine
District at-large—Leo Waters
District at-large—Chris Ferrell
District 1—Regina Patton
District 2—Melvin Black
District 3—Ron Nollner
District 4—Don Majors
District 5—Frank R. Harrison Jr.
District 6—Eileen Beehan
District 7—Howard Earl Campbell Sr.
District 8—Lawrence H. Hart
District 9—James Dillard
District 10—Tim Garrett
District 11—Mike Wooden
District 12—Phil Ponder
District 13—Charles O. French
District 14—James Bruce Stanley
District 15—Roy Dale
District 16—Jerry Graves
District 17—Mansfield Douglas
District 18—Stewart Clifton
District 19—Julius A. Sloss
District 20—Morris B. Haddox
District 21—Willis McCallister
District 22—John Aaron Holt
Norma Hand*
District 23—Eric Crafton
District 24—Horace Johns
District 25—David L. Kleinfelter
District 26—Michelle Arriola
District 27—Janis Baird Sontany
District 28—Durward Hall
District 29—Saletta A. Holloway
District 30—Leroy Hollis
District 31—Tom Alexander
District 32—Craig Jenkins
District 33—Ron Turner
District 34—Charles W. Fentress
District 35—Vic Lineweaver

*John Aaron Holt resigned his position following his election as General Sessions judge. Norma Hand was elected to fill this vacated legislative seat.

Tenth Metropolitan Council (1999–2003)

Vice Mayor—Ronnie Steine
Howard C. Gentry Jr.*
District at-large—Chris Ferrell
District at-large—Leo Waters
District at-large—David Briley
District at-large—Howard C. Gentry Jr./
Adam Dread**
District at-large—Carolyn Baldwin Tucker
District 1—Brenda Gilmore
District 2—Melvin Black
District 3—Ron Nollner
District 4—Don Majors
District 5—Lawrence E. Hall Jr.
District 6—Eileen Beehan
District 7—Howard Earl Campbell Sr.
District 8—Lawrence H. Hart
District 9—James Dillard

District 10—Bettye Balthrop
District 11—Myers "Feller" Brown
District 12—Phil Ponder
District 13—Tony Derryberry
District 14—James Bruce Stanley
District 15—J. B. Loring
District 16—Amanda McClendon
District 17—Ronnie Greer
District 18—Ginger Hausser
District 19—Ludye N. Wallace
District 20—Morris B. Haddox
District 21—Edward L. (Whit) Whitmore Sr.
District 22—Norma Hand
District 23—Bob Bogen
District 24—John Summers
District 25—Jim Shulman
District 26—Michelle Arriola***
District 27—Janis Baird Sontany
District 28—Jason Alexander
District 29—Saletta Holloway
District 30—Michael Kerstetter
District 31—Don Knoch
District 32—Craig Jenkins
District 33—Ron Turner
District 34—Lynn Stinnett Williams
District 35—Vic Lineweaver
Charles Tygard****

*Ronnie Steine resigned as vice mayor in 2002. Howard Gentry was elected as vice mayor in a special election.

**Howard Gentry resigned his at-large position upon his election as vice mayor. Adam Dread was elected to fill the vacant at-large seat in a special election.

***Michelle Arriola resigned her position as district council member in 2003 when she relocated her residence outside the district she was elected to represent. Because this resignation occurred within the same year as the metropolitan general election, there was no special election held to fill this vacated legislative seat.

****Vic Lineweaver resigned his position as district council member following his election as circuit court clerk. Charles Tygard was elected to fill this vacated legislative seat.

NOTES

Acknowledgments

1. Scott Daniel Aiken and James Bruce Stanley. *Donelson & Hermitage, Tennessee: A Suburban History* (Franklin, Tenn.: Hillsboro Press, 2004), 365–66.

Chapter 1

1. The Metropolitan Charter, Article 1; Section 1.01.
2. Aiken and Stanley. *Donelson & Hermitage,* 219.
3. Ibid., ix.
4 *Nashville Banner*, July 17, 1990.
5. Aiken and Stanley, *Donelson & Hermitage,* 365–66.
6. *Nashville Banner*, July 17, 1990.

Chapter 2

1. Metropolitan Charter, Article 19; Section 19.01.
2. Ibid.
3. Ibid., Article 5; Section 5.05.
4. Nashville *Tennessean*, October 29, 1998.
5. *Metro Nashville and Davidson County Stormwater Program Assessment, Executive Summary*, November 2, 1999.
6. Ibid.
7. Ibid.
8. Mayoral Memorandum, *Purcell announces stormwater management plan*, January 30, 2002.
9. Ibid.
10. Nashville *Tennessean*, November 1, 1994.
11. Metropolitan Charter, Article 3; Section 3.01.
12. Ibid., Article 8; Section 18.06.
13. "Metropolitan Legal Opinion," November 30, 2001.
14. Metropolitan Charter, Article 3; Section 3.02.
15. *News Herald*, June 28, 1995.
16. Nashville *Tennessean*, August 25, 1995.
17. *Nashville Banner*, September 8, 1995.
18. *News Herald*, June 28, 1995.
19. Nashville *Tennessean*, July 17, 1995.
20. Ibid., August 25, 1995.
21. *Nashville Scene*, September 7, 1995.
22. Nashville *Tennessean*, June 15, 1999.
23. Ibid.
24. Ibid.
25. Ibid.
26. Ibid., July 29, 2003.
27. District 14 Candidate Search Committee handout, August 2002.
28. Ibid.
29. Ibid.
30. Ibid., March 24, 2003.
31. Ibid.
32. Nashville *Tennessean*, July 21, 2003.
33. *Nashville Scene*, July 24, 2003.
34. Nashville *Tennessean*, July 1, 2004.

Chapter 3

1. Henry Campbell Black, M. A. *Black's Law Dictionary, Fifth Edition* (St. Paul, Minn.: West Publishing Company, 1979), 811.
2. Ibid., 809.
3. Ibid., 918.
4. Ibid., 1178.
5. *Rules of Procedure of the Council of the Metropolitan Government of Nashville and Davidson County* (1999), Rule 10.
6. Ibid., Rule 11.
7. Ibid., Rule 12.
8. Ibid., Rule 13.
9. Ibid., Rule 14.
10. Ibid., Rule 19.
11. Ibid., Rule 20.
12. Black, *Black's Law Dictionary*, 379.
13. *Rules of Procedure*, Rule 22.
14. Ibid.
15. Ibid., Rule 27.
16. Ibid., Rule 28.
17. Ibid., Rule 29.
18. Ibid., Rule 31.
19. Ibid., Rule 34.
20. Metropolitan Government of Nashville and Davidson County; Department of Public Works, Engineering Division, *Stormwater Management Manual, Volume 1: Regulations* (Nashville: Camp Dresser & McKee, PBS&J, 1999), Appendix B-4.
21. http://www.amrivers.org/floodplains toolkit/value.htm, (11/23/2003).
22. http://www.amrivers.org/ templates/friendly.asp?ACTCONURL=/flood-plainstoolkit/value . . ., (12/15/2003).
23. Metropolitan Government, *Stormwater Management Manual*, Appendix B-5.
24. Nashville *Tennessean*, November 27, 2002.
25. Ibid.
26. Ibid., March 21, 2000.
27. Ibid.
28. *News Herald*, April 11, 2002.
29. Ordinance No. BL2002-1021, April 2, 2002.
30. Nashville *Tennessean*, December 18, 2002.
31. Ibid.
32. www.cumberlandrivercompact. org/about.htm
33. Planning Commission staff analysis, November 14, 2002.
34.Tennessee Environmental Council letter, December 3, 2002.
35. *News Herald*, December 19, 2002.
36. Nashville *Tennessean*, January 9, 2003.
37. Nashville *Tennessean*, February 6, 2003.
38. http://www.nashville.gov/mc/ ordinances/prev/sbl2002_1021.htm (11/17/2003)
39. Honey Brook Homeowners Association letter, 10 February 2003.
40. Lion's Head Homeowners Association letter, 18 March 2003.
41. *City Paper*, March 19, 2003.
42. Nashville *Tennessean*, March 27, 2003.
43. *Music City Planning Notes: A Publication of the Metropolitan Planning Department of Nashville-Davison County*, Spring 2003.
44. Ibid.
45. Ibid.
46. Ibid.
47. Ibid.
48. Nashville *Tennessean*, February 20, 2003.
49. http://www.nashville.gov/mc/ council/legislative_process.htm (12/15/2003).
50. http://www.nashville.gov/mc/ resolutions/prev/rs2001_643.htm (12/15/2003).
51. Ibid., /rs2001_688.htm (12/15/2003).
52. Ibid., /rs2002_950.htm (12/15/2003).
53. Ibid., /rs2002_943.htm (12/15/2003).
54. Ibid., /rs2003_1477.htm (12/15/2003).
55. Ibid., /rs2002_1202.htm (12/15/2003).
56. Ibid., /rs2003_1376.htm (12/15/2003).
57. Ibid., /rs2002_949.htm (12/15/2003).
58. Ibid., /rs2001_704.htm (12/15/2003).
59. Ibid., /rs2002_1004.htm (12/15/2003).
60. Ibid., /rs2002_1003.htm (12/15/2003).
61. Ibid., /rs2002_1203.htm (12/15/2003).

Chapter 4

1. Nashville *Tennessean*, October 13, 2003.
2. Ibid., July 31, 2002.
3. Ibid.
4. Ibid.
5. Ibid.
6. http://www.infrasturctures.tudelft.nl /infradef.html (10/22/2003).
7. Metropolitan Charter, Section 8.402 (a).
8. Ordinance No. BL097-782, June 17, 1997.
9. NES letter, June 12, 2000.
10. *News Herald*, December 14, 2000.
11. NES letter, March 19, 2001.
12. Metropolitan Charter, Section 8.201.
13. Ibid.
14. *Donelson News Diary*, November 9, 1972; January 18, 1973.
15. Nashville *Tennessean*, September 9, 1992.
16. *News Herald*, January 18, 1995.
17. Aiken and Stanley, *Donelson & Hermitage,* 23.
18. *News Herald*, July 10, 1996.
19. Ibid.
20. Aiken and Stanley, *Donelson & Hermitage,* 25.
21. Ibid.
22. *News Herald*, April 2, 1997.
23. *Councilman Ponder Memoirs*, March 29, 2002.
24. Metropolitan Charter, Section 8.502.
25. Aiken and Stanley, *Donelson & Hermitage,* 58.
26. Nashville *Tennessean*, January 17, 1996.

27. *News Herald*, December 14, 2000.
28. Black, *Black's Law Dictionary*, 957.
29. Nashville *Tennessean*, October 23, 2002.
30. Black, *Black's Law Dictionary*, 958.
31. Nashville *Tennessean*, October 23, 2002.
32. Ibid.
33. *News Herald*, June 4, 1998.
34. Ibid., May 2, 2002.
35. *H-6 Code Demolition*, 2917 Surrey Road (#096-09-124), Findings of Fact, July 25, 2000.
36. Nashville *Tennessean*, October 23, 2002.
37. http://www.hud.gov:80/offices/fheo/FHLaws/index.cfm (2/18/2004).
38. Ibid.
39. *News Herald*, October 28, 1999.
40. Ibid.
41. Ibid.
42. Ibid.
43. Ibid.
44. *News Herald*, February 28, 2002.
45. Ibid.
46. Ibid.
47. Ibid.
48. Ibid.
49. Ibid.
50. Councilman Stanley letter, 11 December 2000.
51. Congressman Clement letter, 1 February 2001.
52. Nashville *Tennessean*, July 11, 2002.
53. Ibid.
54. Ibid.
55. Ibid.
56. *News Herald*, July 18, 2002.
57. Ibid.
58. Ibid.
59. Ibid.
60. Ibid.
61. Ibid.
62. Ibid.
63. Ibid.
64. Ibid.
65. Ibid.
66. Ibid.
67. Ibid.

Chapter 5

1. Metropolitan Charter, Section 11.501.
2. Ibid., 11.502.
3. Ibid.
4. Ibid., 11.503.
5. Ibid.
6. Ibid., 11.506.
7. Ibid.
8. *Zoning Regulations* of the Metropolitan Goverment of Nashville and Davidson County, page 1-1, January 1, 1998.
9. Ibid.
10. Ibid.
11. Ibid.
12. *Concept 2010: a General Plan for Nashville and Davidson County*, page i.
13. Ibid., 4.
14. *Subarea 14 Plan*, January 12, 1990.
15. *Subarea 14 Plan: 1995 Update,* March 7, 1996.
16. *Subarea 14 Plan,* January 12, 1990.
17. Ibid.
18. Resolution No. RS92-135, February 19, 1992.
19. Metropolitan Charter, Section 3.01.
20. Ibid., 3.05.
21. Nashville *Tennessean*, June 23, 1999.
22. John Gregor letter, 14 June 1996.
23. Ibid., 14 August 1996.
24. Ibid.
25. Ibid.
26. Ibid.
27. Sarah Fessler Peveler letter, 3 September 1996.
28. *News Herald*, December 20, 2001.
29. Ibid.
30. Ibid.
31. Ibid.
32. Ibid.
33. Ibid.
34. Ibid.
35. Ibid.
36. Resolution No. RS2002-57, January 24, 2002.
37. *News Herald*, December 20, 1995.
38. Ibid.
39. Ibid.
40. *News Herald*, September 6, 2001.
41. Ibid.
42. Kennedy Statement to Residents, "3052 Lebanon Road Property."
43. Resolution No. RS2001-72, February 1, 2001.

Chapter 6

1. Crowell-Collier Publishing Company, *Collier's 1964 Year Book: Covering the Year 1963* (United States: 1964), 631.
2. Crowell-Collier Educational Corporation, *1972 Year Book: Covering the Year 1971* (United States: 1971), 544.
3. World Book, Incl., *The World Book Year Book* (Chicago: 1982), 246.
4. Ibid., (1992), 144.
5. Ibid., (2002), 141.
6. http://www.sfo.com/~csuppes/NHL/NashvillePredators/articles.htm (10/2/2003).
7. Ibid.
8. Nashville *Tennessean*, February 21, 2004.
9. Ibid.
10. Ibid.
11. Ibid.
12. http://austin.bizjournals.com/austin/stories/1999/07/19/daily22.html (10/10/2003).
13. David S. Neft, Richard M. Cohen, Rick Korch, *The Sports Encyclopedia: Pro Football, 10th Edition The Modern Era 1960–1991* (New York: St. Martin's Press, 1992), 188.
14. Steve Lowery, "Sick & Tired," *Athlon Sports Pro Football Edition*, vol. 15 (Nashville: Athlon Sports Communications, Inc., 1996).
15. Nashville *Tennessean*, November 9, 1995.
16. http://www.nashvillesports.com/nsc/foundation.html (9/9/2003).
17. http://www.nashvillesports.com/nsc/welcome.html (9/9/2003).
18. Ibid.
19. Nashville *Tennessean*, November 13, 1995.
20. Ibid., November 19, 1995.
21. Ibid.
22. Nashville *Tennessean*, May 8, 1996.
23. Ibid., November 3, 1995.
24. *News Herald,* November 22, 1995.
25. Tennessee Code Annotated, Section 7-67-108(a) (4) (A), 1993.
26. Ibid., Section 7-67-109, 1999.
27. Ibid., Section 7-67-109 (4), 1999.
28. *Stadium Lease*, February 10, 1996.
29. Nashville *Tennessean*, March 18, 1996.
30. Ibid.
31. Summary of *Stadium Development Agreement*, February 15, 1996.
32. Nashville *Tennessean*, February 28, 1996.
33. Ibid.
34. Ibid.
35. Ibid.
36. Ibid.
37. Ibid.
38. Ibid., February 18, 1996.
39. Ibid.
40. Ibid.
41. Ibid., March 1, 1996.
42. Ibid., May 1, 1996.
43. Ibid., March 17, 1996.
44. Ibid.
45. http://www.bjournal.com/news/060402c.html (9/27/2003).
46. *Stadium Place*; Vol. 3, No. 7, July 1999.
47. Ibid.
48. Minutes; Metropolitan Council Meeting, Tuesday, August 6, 2002.
49. Nashville *Tennessean*, March 15, 2000.
50. Ibid., January 28, 2000.
51. Ibid.
52. Ibid.
53. Letter, Department of Law, February 16, 2000.
54. Nashville *Tennessean*, March 15, 2000.
55. Nashville *Tennessean*, November 12, 1995.
56. http://www.breadnotcircuses.org/brooking.html (10/2/2003).
57. Ibid.
58. Ibid.
59. Ibid.
60. Ibid.
61. Nashville *Tennessean*, May 29, 2004.
62. Ibid., September 7, 2003.
63. Ibid., October 27, 2003.
64. Ibid.
65. Ibid.
66. Ibid.
67. Ibid.
68. Ibid., November 3, 2003.
69. Ibid.
70. Ibid.
71. Ibid.
72. Ibid., September 7, 2003.

Epilogue

1. http://www.smartvoter.org/1999aug/tn/dv/vote/stanley_j/philosphy.html (8/7/2004).

Selected Bibliography

Books

Aiken, Scott Daniel and James Bruce Stanley. *Donelson & Hermitage, Tennessee: A Suburban History*. Franklin, Tenn.: Hillsboro Press, 2004.

Black, Henry Campbell. *Black's Law Dictionary, Fifth Edition*. St. Paul, Minn.: West Publishing Company, 1979.

Neft, David S., Richard M. Cohen, Rick Korch. *The Sports Encyclopedia: Pro Football, 10th Edition The Modern Era 1960–1991*. New York: St. Martin's Press, 1992.

Encyclopedia Yearbooks

Crowell-Collier Publishing Company, *Collier's 1964 Year Book: Covering the Year 1963*. United States, 1964.

Crowell-Collier Educational Corporation, *1972 Year Book: Covering the Year 1971*. United States, 1971.

World Book, Inc., *The World Book Year Book*. Chicago, 1982/1992/2002.

Government Documents

The Charter of the Metropolitan Government of Nashville and Davidson County, Tennessee

Concept 2010: A General Plan for Nashville and Davidson County

H-6 Code Demolition, 2917 Surrey Road

Letter, Department of Law, February 16, 2000

Mayoral Memorandum, January 20, 2002

Metro Nashville and Davidson County Stormwater Program Assessment, Executive Summary

Metropolitan Legal Opinion, November 30, 2001

Minutes; Metropolitan Council Meeting, August 6, 2002

Music City Planning Notes; A Publication of the Metropolitan Planning Department of Nashville-Davidson County

Ordinance No. BL2002-1021, April 2, 2002

Planning Commission Staff Analysis, November 14, 2002

Resolution No. RS92-135, February 19, 1992

Resolution No.RS2001-72, February 1, 2001

Resolution No. RS2002-57, January 24, 2002

Rules of Procedure of the Council of the Metropolitan Government of Nashville and Davidson County

Stadium Lease, February 10, 1996

Stadium Package, February 15, 1996

Stadium Place; Vol. 3, No. 7

Stormwater Management Manual, Volume I: Regulations (Metropolitan Nashville)

Subarea 14 Plan, January 12, 1990

Subarea 14 Plan: 1995 Update, March 7, 1996

Summary of Stadium Development Agreement, February 15, 1996

Tennessee Code Annotated

Zoning Regulations of the Metropolitan Government of Nashville and Davidson County

Newspapers

City Paper

Donelson News Diary

Nashville Banner

News Herald

Nashville Scene

Nashville *Tennessean*

Web sites

American Rivers, www.amrivers.org

Austin Business Journal, www.austin.bizjournals.com

Ballparks, www.sfo.com

Bread Not Circuses, www.breadnotcircuses.org

The Business Journal of Tri-Cities TN/VA, www.bjournal.com

Fair Housing Laws and Presidential Executive Orders—HUD, www.hud.gov

Infrastructure definition, www.infrastructures.tudelft.nl

Metropolitan Government of Nashville and Davidson County, www.nashville.gov

The Nashville Sports Council, www.nashvillesports.com

Pro Player Stadium, www.pro-player-stadium.com

INDEX

Index